Orwell Re ✔ KU-743-997

Audrey Coppard & Bernard Crick

Audrey Coppard is a research assistant at Birkbeck College, University of London. She has had six books published by William Heinemann Ltd and worked closely with Bernard Crick on the writing of *George Orwell: A Life*.

Bernard Crick is Professor of Politics at Birkbeck College, London's evening college for mature students, at the University of London. He was born in 1929 and educated at Whitgift School, University College, London, the London School of Economics and Harvard. He lived for four years in North America before teaching at the London School of Economics and, later, at Sheffield University.

He is author of *In Defence of Politics, Crime, Rape and Gin, Political Theory and Practice* and the prizewinning *George Orwell: A Life*. He was chairman of the Hansard Society's report, *Political Education and Political Literacy*, was joint editor of the *Political Quarterly* from 1965 to 1980 and is active in the Adult Education movement.

ORWELL
Remembered

Audrey Coppard & Bernard Crick

ARIEL BOOKS
BRITISH BROADCASTING CORPORATION

© Audrey Coppard & Bernard Crick 1984

First published 1984

Published by the British Broadcasting Corporation
35 Marylebone High Street, London W1M 4AA

Typeset by Phoenix Photosetting, Chatham
Printed in England
by Mackays of Chatham Ltd

Set in 10 on 11pt Ehrhardt Linotron

ISBN 0 563 20200 9

Contents

Preface

This book arose from the BBC's *Arena* programme, *Orwell Remembered*, which was televised in three parts early in 1984. Nigel Williams, the producer of the programme, interviewed many people who had known Orwell. Bernard Crick acted as consultant to the programme.

It became clear that in addition to these interviews, much material was available on Orwell, some in print, or in transcripts of interviews, some from people who were no longer alive. And much of this material happens to originate from the BBC's archives, notably from a Third Programme feature of 2 November 1960 which Rayner Heppenstall, a close friend of Orwell's, produced.

Audrey Coppard of Birkbeck College, London, worked with Bernard Crick on his *George Orwell: A Life*. When writing the book he was granted unrestricted permission to quote from Orwell's papers and publications. Audrey Coppard's view of Orwell is different from Crick's and partly for this reason, partly so that this book does not simply restate the views of the biography, she has taken sole responsibility for choosing what should appear in *Orwell Remembered*. Bernard Crick has written the explanatory headnotes and Introduction.

Orwell Remembered has been compiled for the general reader. Scholars will find much of this material and more in the Orwell Archive at University College, London.

Orwell's character was in many ways contradictory, and that is one reason why memories of him can be conflicting. We hope that the variety of these memories will stimulate readers to make their own judgements.

We are grateful to Nigel Williams for originating the project and his generous co-operation with us, but above all we are grateful to all those whose entertaining and individual words and insights have contributed to what we hope is an illuminating book.

References to the four volumes of *The Collected Essays, Journalism and Letters of George Orwell* (Secker & Warburg, 1968), edited by Sonia Orwell and Ian Angus, are rendered as *Collected Essays*. References to *George Orwell: A Life* by Bernard Crick are taken from the revised 1982 Penguin paperback edition rather than the 1980 Secker & Warburg hardback edition.

Audrey Coppard
Bernard Crick

Birkbeck College, University of London
July 1983

Introduction

Reminiscences must be read as stories: they are not a superior form of truth, because memory can expand, if worked too hard, as well as contract, if not exercised. The memories of the old are particularly, and often peculiarly, selective: recent events can become forgotten and jumbled, the time-scales of middle life conflated, but some events of a youthful summer afternoon long ago are recalled in vivid detail. Middle-aged people can vary remarkably in their ability to recall places, faces and names: I have an appalling memory for names but, or rather so, am constantly haunted by faces. And always, of course, our memories of the interesting people we have met are *our* memories, not theirs; every memory is affected by the rememberer's view of his or her own life. I can hardly distinguish my memories of some of the great teachers I had when a student from what I have subsequently read and heard about them.

In Anthony Burgess's *Earthly Powers* an old writer, the main character of the novel, remarks: 'There is a sense in which all reminiscence is fiction.' Biographers must treat reminiscences as extraordinarily important evidence, without affording them any special privileges in the court of truth – just as, in reading any historical document, one has to ask why was it written and what was the perspective and motive of the writer. Several times in my interviewing I encountered the 'Navajo Indian and the anthropologist' phenomenon – the Indian makes the lucid responses he does because he has read the works of the anthropologist. And there is a variant of that story: the anthropologist asks the pertinent questions he does because he has read the Navajo chief's Ph.D thesis.

Encountering this latter phenomenon makes me especially sceptical of the memories of famous literary men. Again Anthony Burgess makes the point in *Earthly Powers*. The writer, Kenneth Toomey, explains his dilemma to a Prince of the Church: '"It happened a long time ago," I said. "And I don't know whether you, your Grace, would understand this, but writers of fiction often have difficulty in deciding between what really happened and what they imagine as having happened."' And later he worries about the impossibility of his whole last enterprise, writing an autobiography and confession: 'There were records. There had been witnesses. They could be found, consulted, though with trouble. But the real question for me was: how far could I claim a true knowledge of the factuality of my own past, as opposed to pointing to an artistic enhancing of it, meaning a crafty falsification? In two ways my memory was not to be trusted: I was an old man, I was a writer.'

In fact, I have more faith than that in the reminiscences published here. If all memories are stories, yet some stories are wholly true, even if shaped and pointed: they would be intolerably formless and boring if not. As a biographer, I found that the evidence of ordinary respondents, by which I mean those people who were not professional writers, was often the more rewarding, in the sense that they would come out with unexpected things and make judgements for which there was no obvious motive. Professional writers were much more self-conscious, aware of the effect they were trying to make, and were usually repeating (defending, indeed) something already in print. I hope the reader will share this view and will see why we have not repeated at length a great deal of material already to be found in printed memoirs, why we have sometimes preferred earlier versions to later ones, and have rather favoured the ordinary remembrancer compared to the professional one. For the subject matter is Orwell's life. What he was like as a person rather than his achievement. And we have not included any of Orwell's own autobiographical passages – which in any case need treating with great care: they too are perhaps written to create a particular effect for artistic purposes in a particular book or essay at a particular time.

Could one give an account of his life purely in terms of memories? Only (as the *Arena* programme has shown) with a good deal of linking commentary.

George Orwell, whose real name was Eric Blair, was born in India on 25 June 1903, the son of Richard Blair, an official in the Opium Service, and Ida Limouzin, whose French mother came from a family of teak merchants in Burma. He was brought to England when still a baby. His younger sister later told journalists and writers that they returned to England when he was four, that is, for her birth, presumably misremembering her mother's tales; so that one friend of Orwell's wrote a memoir in which he set down the 'early memories of India' which, he said, Orwell had recounted to him. The family were of what Orwell called 'the lower-upper middle class', precisely explained by him as the 'upper-middle class without money'; but for literary and polemical purposes he exaggerated. The Blairs were not 'shabby genteel': if not 'well off', they were certainly 'comfortable'.

He gained a scholarship to St Cyprian's, a fashionable preparatory school where Cyril Connolly and Henry Longhurst were among his contemporaries: so genuine reminiscences begin. In an essay called 'Such, Such Were the Joys', published only after his death, Orwell wrote a dark and bitter account of the oppression and suffering he experienced at school: St Cyprian's was awful by any humane standard, but not *as awful* as he suggests. 'Such, Such Were the Joys' is a mixture of polemical short-story and genuine recollection. One of his contemporaries told me, for instance, perhaps seeking less to defend the school than to discredit Orwell, that it was somebody else, not Blair himself, as Orwell related, who was flogged for bed-wetting.

I don't think that 'discredits' Orwell so much as reminds us that he was an imaginative writer. We delude ourselves if we read everything written in the first person by, say, Rudyard Kipling, H. G. Wells and George Orwell himself as being literally true. A close childhood friend of his holidays, Jacintha Buddicom, wrote a long memoir in which he appears as an 'especially happy child', a theme she repeated when she was interviewed only last year for the *Arena* programme. Her view of things may go too far the other way, but she certainly redresses a balance and at least establishes that Orwell's vacations were happy. Writers who have explained away the political warning of *Nineteen Eighty-Four* in terms of a morbid personality created by childhood traumas have built a castle on sand.

He won a scholarship to Eton in 1916, but rested on his oars when he got there. Odd-man-out and 'agin' the system, he did little formal work, although he read widely in English literature in his leisure time. Sir Steven Runciman, the great historian of Byzantium and of the Crusades, and Sir Roger Mynors, the classical scholar, were in the same class or 'Election', so too was Denys King-Farlow, who later wrote a valuable first-hand memoir; and Christopher Hollis was two years ahead of him. Cyril Connolly followed from St Cyprian's a year behind. Some very sophisticated memories are now at work on the story.

Orwell's academic indolence and poor examination results prevented him from going on to Oxford or Cambridge as most of his close contemporaries did. Instead, he was crammed for the Imperial Civil Service exams, an episode for which we have both records and memories – and chose to enter the Burma Police, a very unprestigious part of 'the Service': it is likely that he was the first Etonian to take that path. He endured Burma for five years, before resigning in 1927, having come to hate the social pretentiousness of the British and their arrogance towards both the Burmese themselves and their culture.

A fellow police cadet, Roger Beadon, was interviewed by the BBC in 1969. He has since died. Most of Orwell's fellow officers had been through the First World War, and were four or five years older than him. By the time that I began to search for and interview people who had known him – in the 1970s – they were no longer living. Peter Stansky and William Abrams had better luck in the 1960s when they were working on their *The Unknown Orwell* (London, Constable, 1972), but if they took transcripts of their interviews, they are not now available. Consequently, we know very little of what Orwell was reading and thinking about in Burma, only that he went in as a relatively conventional, if difficult, young man and came out as a rebel determined to be a writer. His first surviving and published novel, *Burmese Days*, relates to this period, but was not begun until later.

Burmese Days is often taken to be socialist in intent, but it is simply anti-imperialist. When another young writer, Jack Common, asked Orwell around 1930, 'Where do you stand?', he replied that he supposed he was a 'Tory anarchist'. He was not entirely joking. What can be gained from *Burmese Days* is the impression that he was first of all an individualist who resented one man or culture imposing its values on another. Though he sympathised with socialist arguments about capitalism and exploitation, it was not until 1935 that he was clear that anything could ever be done about such injustices.

A mixture of guilt and curiosity now led him to explore how 'the British natives' lived, to discover whether we treated our own working class as we did the indigenous native inhabitants of the Empire. Broadly, his conclusion was that we did, the beginning of the characterisation of 'the proles' he was to describe in *Nineteen Eighty-Four*. Rather oddly, he took tramps to be an extreme condition of the working class, and made journeys among them, living with them as if a tramp, sometimes for a few nights, sometimes several weeks. Sir Victor Pritchett was to describe Orwell at this time as 'a man who went native in his own country'. And all the while he was trying to write novels, at first very badly (as the poet Ruth Pitter remembers), and was only just able to stay alive by book reviewing and publishing occasional essays.

He could and did stay from time to time with his parents, who had retired to Southwold on the Suffolk coast; but neither the publication of *Burmese Days* (1934) nor *Down and Out in Paris and London* (1933) could have added much to family happiness and social respectability. Neighbours on the whole, though, tended to sympathise with them for having such a son, rather than to ostracise them. Eric Blair adopted his pen-name at this time, almost certainly to lessen the hurt to his parents' feelings. He made some good friends at Southwold, notably Brenda Salkeld and Dennis Collings, who remember those times well; Richard Peters, Professor of Philosophy, was then a small boy who, to-gether with his brother, was tutored and companioned by Orwell during two long summer holidays in Southwold.

Unable to live properly by writing, and striving for some independence, Orwell took a succession of poorly paid teaching posts in some bad private schools; and he endured poverty, both in Paris where he went to write but ended up as a dishwasher, and in and around London. While he was working part-time in a bookshop in Hampstead in 1935, he saw the publication of his second novel, *A Clergyman's Daughter*, and wrote his third, the autobiographical *Keep the Aspidistra Flying*. He received a com-mission from Victor Gollancz to go north and write about the condition of the unemployed, a journey that firmly committed him to socialism, albeit of a most critical and independent-minded kind. 'A writer,' he was to say, 'cannot be a *loyal* member of a political party.' From this time came his first meeting with Rayner Heppenstall who was to collect memories of Orwell for the BBC in 1960 and was to provide his own clever and provoca-tive account of Orwell. After several girlfriends Orwell met Eileen O'Shaughnessy, an Oxford English graduate who was trying to escape from a secretarial career by doing a postgraduate diploma in Educational Psychology. They married shortly after-wards, on 9 June 1936, and moved to a small cottage in a small Hertfordshire village called Wallington. Here they tried to live by running a village store in the mornings to augment earnings from Orwell's writing.

The Spanish War had broken out. Orwell finished writing *The Road to Wigan Pier* – the book about his journey to the north –

and then at the end of 1936 he departed for Spain, Eileen following later. 'Someone has to kill Fascists,' he told a friend. He went to fight, not to write, but *Homage to Catalonia* (1938) was the result none the less. It sold badly at the time and was harshly reviewed by Communist fellow travellers and by sympathisers with the Popular Front, the alliance of the Left against Fascism. But the book is now recognised as a classic of English prose, an extraordinarily honest description of war as seen through the eyes of the common soldier, and as one of the shrewdest and most biting polemics against the Stalinist and Communist attempt to use the Civil War for their own ends, recklessly, fatally.

Orwell was wounded and narrowly escaped arrest by the police when the Communists cracked down on the independent socialist and anarchist militias. He and Eileen, with John MacNair and Stafford Cottman, a leader and a member of the Independent Labour Party, escaped into France, encountering Fenner Brockway *en route* as he was entering Spain to protest against the Communist action and to try to rescue ILP comrades.

Back in Wallington Orwell joined the ILP, adopting not merely its egalitarian and libertarian domestic politics but also its stance of anti-militarism and anti-colonialism. Right up until the outbreak of the Second World War he maintained that the coming war was simply a capitalist and imperial struggle for colonial markets, and should be opposed. This was explicit in his last conventional novel, *Coming Up For Air* (1939). But when war broke out, he not only announced that even 'Chamberlain's England' was better than Hitler's Germany, but that there was positive virtue in popular patriotism: he distinguished love of country from vulgar nationalism. England was 'a family with the wrong members in charge'. He also thought that after Dunkirk 'a revolution is taking place in the ranks of the British Army' and *The Lion and the Unicorn* (1941) is both a profound analysis of the English national character (he never thought much about the Scots, the Welsh and the Irish) and a prophecy of the coming English revolution – which never took place, beyond Attlee's landslide victory in 1945.

After a spell in hospital in 1934 and in a sanatorium in 1938, Orwell must have accepted that he had tuberculosis, but he continued to grumble that the army would not accept him because of his service in Spain in 'the red militias'. The best he could do was to join the Home Guard, write letters to *Time and Tide* urging 'Arm the People', and to imagine the Home Guard becoming a revolutionary people's militia.

By his own account he wasted two years with the BBC writing and broadcasting to India, but in 1943 he became literary editor of *Tribune*, then edited by Aneurin Bevan (to be succeeded by Michael Foot), the voice of the left wing of the Labour Party. He was not all that good a literary editor – he said he was too soft-hearted to turn down bad poems if he knew the poet to be poor. But he wrote a brilliant weekly column, 'As I Please', in which all his favourite themes tumbled out: love of nature, love of litera-ture, dislike of mass production, distrust of intellectuals, suspicion of central government, hatred of injustice, contempt for bureaucracy, hatred of totalitarianism, advice on making, mending and growing things for yourself, detestation of censor-ship and praise of plain speaking, the good in the past and espousal of values like decency, fraternity, individuality, liberty, egalitarianism and patriotism. It was a wide span but character-istic: sport, sex, crime, travel and political and social gossip – the modern staples of column journalism – found no place in his writing. No wonder Cyril Connolly wrote in 1945 that 'Mr Orwell is a revolutionary who is in love with 1910'.

His powers as a writer and essayist began to be widely recog-nised: Arthur Koestler hurried to make his acquaintance when he reached England in 1940, and towards the end of the war, and for a year afterwards, he lunched regularly with Malcolm Mugger-idge and Anthony Powell. Cyril Connolly had recommended him to David Astor when he took over *The Observer*: they became firm friends and Orwell a regular reviewer for the paper. Some of his judgements could be hasty and unfair, but his habit of realising that he had been in the wrong was endearing, and won him the close friendship of Julian Symons and George Wood-cock, among others, as earlier it had of Stephen Spender.

Yet he was a deeply private, austere, simple-living and some-what inhibited man. It is doubtful if he had any intimate friends with whom he could unburden himself and discuss problems and difficulties (though perhaps such friendships rarely occur outside fiction). He talked to his friends about public matters: books, politics and oddities of natural history or of urban life – he could go on remorselessly about birds, and Cyril Connolly once wickedly remarked that Orwell could hardly blow his nose without suspecting and denouncing cartels among handkerchief manufacturers. He had several different circles of friends and acquaintances: poor Bohemian poets and would-be novelists in the Bloomsbury pubs; Connolly and Spender's fashionable coterie of the literary magazines; *Tribune* journalists and sundry left-wing activists; some of the British anarchists around the *Freedom Press* and bookshop; and his old Southwold circle. On the whole he kept the worlds separate, and was perhaps abnormally secretive about whom he knew and whom he didn't, but occasionally they would overlap at high tea in his flat (a meal he much favoured).

Early in the war Orwell conceived a grand design for a three-volume novel of social analysis and warning which would deal with the decay of the old order, expose the betrayal of the revolution, and describe what an English totalitarianism would be like. The work was never completed, except that his existing pre-war novels could be held to fit the first part of the specification, *Animal Farm* the second, and *Nineteen Eighty-Four* the third. Certainly the connection between these two last books is closer than many suppose, despite the difference in form and in tone. The humour and lightness of *Animal Farm* masks grim implications, is darker than it seems on first reading; and *Nineteen Eighty-Four* is not as dark and pessimistic as it is often painted. Orwell intended it as a satire and it is full of black humour about events and institutions of his time; he probably expected people to be amused by it.

Orwell had great difficulty in getting *Animal Farm* published. Three houses, at least, were nervous of annoying Russia, then our wartime ally. Fredric Warburg, to the lasting credit and profit of his firm, eventually took it on. Orwell's impending triumph was marred by the unexpected death of his wife during an operation for a hysterectomy. His single-minded absorption in his writing and neglect of her health is not entirely to his credit, as some of her friends hint in their remembrances. Not long before Eileen's death they had adopted a boy, Richard, and Orwell for a while tried hard to find another wife, companion and mother; but eventually in 1946 he went to live in Jura, a remote Scottish island, to write *Nineteen Eighty-Four* and escape from distractions. He took a young housekeeper with him who had worked for him in London, Susan Watson. Her memories are a mine of domestic detail, but she was soon frozen out by Orwell's sister Avril who was on her own since her mother's death and who determined to look after Orwell and act as if they were a family again. Orwell's tuberculosis grew worse. After finishing a first draft of *Nineteen Eighty-Four*, which was at that time called *The Last Man in Europe*, he went into a sanatorium. He was one of the first patients in England to be given streptomycin, specially obtained from America through the intervention of David Astor and of Aneurin Bevan, the Minister of Health. But he was allergic to it. He suffered much pain. Making some recovery, he returned to Jura, wrote his second draft of *Nineteen Eighty-Four* but then almost certainly damaged his health fatally by the exertion of typing out the final version himself rather than resting in bed. Neither his publisher nor his agent could find a typist willing to travel to Jura in those cold, harsh and austere post-war years.

The book was an extraordinary success. Most reviewers in Britain read it as a satiric warning against a possible totalitarian future, although a few American reviewers wilfully misread it as an attack simply on all forms of socialism. This greatly disturbed Orwell and he wrote a reply to those critics. But no one in his lifetime had advanced the now fashionable view that the book is a cry of utter despair for humanity. I think myself that this is a silly view that gives his satire a metaphysical portentiousness quite out of character with the man and the rest of his humane and humanistic writings. A random sentence in his last hospital note-book warns prophetically against 'the big cannibal critics that lurk in the deeper waters of American quarterly reviews'.

Three months before his death he had married Sonia Brownell whom he had known from 1940, first as Cyril Connolly's friend and literary assistant on *Horizon*, and intimately from 1945. They were married in University College Hospital. The doctors had given him a fifty-fifty chance of life if he was well looked after and if he was willing to settle for the life of a semi-invalid. He at last seemed reconciled to that and plans had been made for him to fly with Sonia to Switzerland; but a week before leaving, he suffered a fatal haemorrhage on the night of 21 January 1950, which killed him instantly. In fact the consultant, as I only recently learned, had lied to him; he had not, in fact, given Orwell any chance of survival, but did not see it as his business to tell anyone that Orwell was not expected to live. It was a sad irony that the great truth-teller, who set his heart on trying to be absolutely honest in literary, moral and political judgements, should have been treated in that way by a consultant.

The memories of him that follow are, of course, about the man more than about the writings. But there is a clear sense in which a writer's writings are more important than the man or woman, and Orwell had a special sense of this. He risked his own health by writing and left a request that no biography should be written. Moreover it was difficult for many years after his death to grasp the true nature of his achievement. Not until the publication of the four volumes of *The Collected Essays* in 1968 was it easy to see that the critic John Wain had been right to argue as early as 1954 that 'Orwell's essays are obviously much better than his novels'. But by that time far too many critical judgements had been made, sadly but understandably, on his last two books alone. I think that John Wain's view needs broadening to include *Animal Farm*. And I would add *Homage to Catalonia* and the first part at least of *The Road to Wigan Pier*. Jenni Calder has argued in her *Chronicles of Conscience* that Orwell's writings are at their best in the documentary tradition in which the writer himself is the hero as observer, as in his great essays 'A Hanging' and 'Shooting an Elephant' which ambiguously mix fact and fiction. Almost certainly Orwell is the best polemical writer in English since Swift, and he is moreover a typically 'English' writer. Some of Orwell's friends whom Nigel Williams, myself and others have interviewed express surprise that the Orwell they knew could have written *Nineteen Eighty-Four*, his last grim work. But perhaps they underestimate the imaginative powers of a great writer who could sometimes seem, with his commonsense demeanour and plain style, to be unimaginative. After all, it is one book among many and only by fatal accident was it his last book.

B.R.C.

Mrs Ida Blair's Diary for 1905

Ida Mabel Blair (née Limouzin) (1875–1943), married in India in 1896 a man who was eighteen years her senior, and Eric, her second child, was born in 1903. She brought her two young children back to England some time in 1904, as this diary and also photographs in the possession of a granddaughter prove. Orwell's younger sister believed that the family had returned in 1907; confusing dates is a common danger when family memories are unchecked by documentation. Unfortunately only the diary for 1905 survives. 'Bronchitis', much later diagnosed as tuberculosis, seems to have come early and one word of his early speech becomes much used in later writing. Ida Blair must have been very unlike her husband. Nieces remember her dressing in a 'vaguely artistic way', she was friendly with suffragettes, though not herself active, and might, but for her husband, have been a 'new woman' in the Anna Veronica style, as was her sister Nellie – who was on the stage, a friend to socialists, and lived in Paris with an Esperantist (then considered the universal language that would create perpetual world peace).

Monday, 6 February: Baby [Eric] not at all well, so I sent for the doctor, who said he had bronchitis. . .

Tuesday, 7 February: Baby about the same. . .

Wednesday, 8 February: Baby is better.

Saturday, 11 February: Baby much better. Calling things 'beastly'!!

Monday, 6 March: Baby went out for the first time today for more than a month.

Wednesday, 22 March: Lovely day. Baby has been out of doors nearly all day long.

Wednesday, 14 June: Baby's latest feat was to get out into the garden by the drawing room window!

Saturday, 29 July: Got a wire from Kate saying Baby was ill, got the wire at 8.30 while bathing and I was in the train at 9.10. [Mrs Blair was staying in London.]

Sunday, 20 August: Baby paddled this morning for first time, and loved it. [At Frinton.]

Friday, 1 September: Baby not at all well. I sent for the doctor.

Friday, 22 September: Eric went to his first party today and behaved very well I was told.

Saturday, 4 November: Baby worse so sent for the doctor.

Wednesday, 8 November: Baby came downstairs today.

School Holidays

Jacintha Buddicom (b. 1901) was playing one day in the garden at Shiplake, near Henley-upon-Thames, with her younger brother, Prosper, and younger sister, Guinever, when they saw a boy next door 'standing on his head'. They asked him why, and he said that he wanted to attract their attention. They all became close friends. The year was 1914. Eric and Jacintha were childhood friends, but they lost touch with each other after he left for Burma in 1922 at the age of nineteen. However, they exchanged letters the year before his death when she saw in a literary weekly that 'George Orwell' was in fact Eric Blair.

This is an extract from her *Eric and Us* (Leslie Frewin, London, 1974) and a shorter version appeared as 'The Young Eric' in *The World of George Orwell*, ed. Miriam Gross (Weidenfeld and Nicolson, London, 1971). Some critics have accused her of a 'rose-tinted' view of childhood, but it is probable that her account is well documented and accurate and should be read alongside George Orwell's account of totally miserable schooldays in his essay or polemic, 'Such, Such Were the Joys'.

There were three young Blairs: two girls with a boy in the middle, like the young Buddicoms, but the Blairs were spaced wider apart – five years between each instead of three, as we were. Marjorie, born 21 April 1898, would have been sixteen in 1914. She never played with us, and we thought her 'quite grown-up'. We did not often see her in those days, but she and I were both confirmed – according to my confirmation-class card – on Sunday 21 February 1915 in Henley. I was rather young for confirmation at thirteen, she at sixteen a more usual age.

Marjorie and her mother seemed particularly fond of each

other, with many common interests, so, except when separated by their war-work, they spent a lot of time together. As far as I can remember they looked rather alike, too. Mrs Blair had curly hair in those days. . . .

Avril, the baby of the family, was born on 6 April 1908, and was a year younger than Guiny, so the two little girls were of an age to be playmates.

Eric, born on 25 June 1903, was a year older than Prosper and two years younger than me – but fairly equivalent to us both. He was so much larger and cleverer than I was that the two-year difference was hardly noticeable: and, on the other hand, Prosper with a father and uncles around had perhaps had some better example of boyish pursuits in his home life than Eric, with only his mother and sisters till he was eight, and such an elderly father afterwards. . . .

Eric's father Richard Walmesley Blair (called Dick) was born on 7 January 1857, so belonged to the previous generation: Gran Finlay was only two when he was born, and *older* than her sister. He certainly seemed to us children to be very ancient and not sympathetic. He was not *unkind* – he never beat Eric (though he once gave Prosper a well-deserved spanking) but he did not understand, nor, I think, much care for children – after all, he hardly saw his own till he was fifty. He always seemed to expect us all to keep rather out of his way, which we were reciprocatively glad to do. This was not difficult as he was usually at the Golf Club, where he worked as secretary as well as playing a good deal of golf himself, before and after his army service in the war. Very sportingly, he joined up. It seems a bit extraordinary that they took him, since at sixty he was reputed to be the oldest subaltern in the British Army, but he even went to France. His late marriage and fatherhood carried on his family's tradition. The young Blairs never knew their paternal grandfather, the Reverend Thomas Richard Arthur Blair, who died aged sixty-five in 1867 – over thirty years before his son Richard had his first child at the age of forty-one. The timespan of these male Blairs seems fantastic: Eric's grandfather was born in 1802 – a hundred and one years before Eric. Our Grandpapa Buddicom was born in 1840, and our great-grandfather Gedye in 1833. So Eric's grandfather was old enough to have been our *grandparents'* grandfather! Both Eric's parents belonged to large Victorian families, so the young Blairs had quite a number of uncles and aunts. There was an Aunt Ivy Limouzin and an Aunt Nellie, as I remember. One or two of these aunts and their friends were

Militant Suffragettes. Mrs Blair was in sympathy, but not so active. *Some* of this contingent, Eric said, went to prison and on hunger-strike as well as more moderately chaining themselves to railings. Some of these relations of Eric's were Fabians, and he went with one of his aunts to visit E. Nesbit. As the Arden and Psammead books were among my favourites, I was rather envious of this privilege. That early Fabian influence may have been what first set his thoughts on pure Socialism: though I have not seen it recorded in any writings about him that a Fabian atmosphere was the natural habitat of some of his relatives. . . .

Eric, often accompanied by Avril, played in our garden practically every day: but we comparatively seldom played in theirs. This may have been chiefly because ours was bigger and better for playing, with a lot of wild part: the former gravel-pit was now a steep, grass-covered bank down from the road, and there was a mini-forest of fir trees. Each New Year we had a ceremony when our Christmas Tree was planted in the gravel-pit: they grew up very fast and tall – they are simply terrific now – and were augmented by a few extra ones. There was, too, the field between the Thatched Cottage and the other houses, also steep and grassy, down which we rode dangerously on our bicycles. We often played bicycle-polo on the croquet-lawn, with croquet-balls and mallets, as a change from the more commonplace game on foot: a *robber* was preferred to *straight* croquet. The Blairs' was a much more conventional laid-out garden, with a potent if unwritten notice: *Keep off the flowerbeds*.

Rose Lawn had a long garden, with the front entrance to the south on Station Road. At the far north end of the ground was a rather overgrown hedge which formed a common boundary with the Quarry House kitchen-garden. In the school holidays before Eric sat for his scholarships he had extra correspondence-coaching from one of the St Cyprian's masters. Often, when we were all playing in the Quarry House garden, Mr Blair would come down and call over this hedge to Eric, reminding him to be sure to get his homework done in time to catch the post. And if he had left it a bit late, he had to return home at once – even if it were in the middle of a game.

In all the years we knew Eric, we cannot recall his being accompanied by any friends, or any contemporaries with him in the Blair home, or his having schoolfriends to stay and exchange visits as Prosper often did in the holidays. . . .

Through all the years it would seem that his feeling for his family remained constant: it was his sister Avril he asked to come and keep house for him after his wife Eileen died, and it was for his father he named his adopted son Richard. (For Richard Rees too, perhaps: but he did not *avoid* the name because it was his father's.) He did not like his own name Eric, as it reminded him of the Victorian boys' school story *Eric or Little By Little*, a book he deplored. Again, through all the years he kept in close touch with his family: in Burma, seeing his Burma-based relations; in Paris his Aunt Nellie; and back in England often staying at Southwold or with Marjorie. . . .

The Blairs, though certainly not demonstrative, were nevertheless a united family, and their home seemed to us to be a happy one. I do not think Eric was *fond* of his father, although he respected and obeyed him, but without any doubt he was genuinely fond of his mother and sisters, especially Avril. Eric and Avril were in those days rather similar in appearance, rather plump, round-faced children – 'moon-faced' Eric described himself. He was always very kind to Avril when they played with us, and equally kind to Guiny.

Eric left St Cyprian's just before Christmas 1916, at the end of the autumn term. He spent the following spring term at Wellington, and was very glad that his sojourn lasted no longer. Having had a taste of freedom in his last months at St Cyprian's with the intensive scholarship work behind him, he expected a Public School to open the door to a wider world. So the Spartan, military Wellington, run somewhat on the lines of the well disciplined Winchester, was a cold-douche disappointment to him.

But by good fortune he was not committed to Wellington beyond this one term, and in May 1917 – a few weeks before his fourteenth birthday – he was able to take up the place now available for him at Eton. I am indebted to Cyril Connolly for explaining to me that the reason he had to wait to get to Eton was that only a dozen or so scholars were admitted at a time, according to the vacancies as older boys left: Eric, though he was successful in achieving his scholarship, was only fourteenth on the list.

The atmosphere of Eton was entirely different from that of Wellington, and Eric, good at swimming, took to it as a duck to water. The overall impression I got from him regarding his various schools was that he was indifferent to St Cyprian's, that he thought Wellington was beastly, and that he was interested and happy at Eton. At any rate, he gave us very favourable accounts when we saw him in the summer holidays of 1917.

He spent part of these summer holidays, with Prosper and Guiny, at our Buddicom Grandfather's home in Shropshire. When we were considered old enough to make the journey unescorted, we used to go up to Ticklerton for a week or more nearly every holidays: sometimes Prosper and me, sometimes Prosper and Guiny, sometimes all three of us, and on many occasions we were accompanied by Eric. I think he went with Prosper and me during the 1917 Easter holidays, and that that may have been one of the occasions when we ensured a carriage to ourselves by Eric asking Prosper very loudly whether his *spots* had come out yet. Once, when this had no effect, he swung from the luggage-rack, scratching himself and declaring he was an orang-outang: which was overdoing it, because the Surplus Lady-passenger only exclaimed that she would 'call the guard if you don't get down at once, you naughty boy!' I expect most children play these well-worn tricks. The journey to Shropshire was a popular one: the train always stopped at Banbury, where an attendant walked up and down the platform with Banbury cakes for sale. Straight from the oven, flaky, buttery, and curranty, could anything have been more delicious for travelling children? Or any traveller, for that matter.

For the 1917 summer holidays there is an informative letter from our Aunt, Lilian Buddicom, to our mother:

> Ticklerton Court
> Church Stretton
> Aug. 29/17

Dearest Laura

Thank you for your letter. I did not write yesterday because Prosper had wired.

We will take all possible care over the shooting. It is a single-barrelled gun, so there is not the risk of a boy firing off a *second* barrel while the other is running forward to pick up the game, and Ted keeps the cartridges in his pocket, only handing out one at a time. [*Ted was Ted Hall, the Estate Man who acted as keeper.*] Prosper has never been allowed to take a gun out alone, and to be on the safe side I keep all the cartridges locked up! The only further precaution we could take would be to send one boy out at a time, but they would not enjoy it so much. They went out almost directly after they arrived yesterday, with Ted – the two boys. He would not take Guinever and

I was very relieved. I could go too, but if we go five probably no rabbits would be shot – Prosper shot three rabbits, and Eric one with his second shot, which I think was very good as he has never shot before. Poor Guinever looked *very* sad to be left behind, specially as she was probably feeling a little strange. She seems such a good, quiet child. They have all been out for a walk together, and now they are at the pool together with Father, and *perhaps* some perch will arrive. [*Inserted later*] They have caught four.

The tennis ground is too wet to mow, let alone play tennis on. I hope the weather will improve. It is tolerably fine now, but it *poured* all night, and everything is saturated and impossible for the boys to tramp through the turnips after partridges. They would get *soaked*.

We are so pleased to have them here and they seem such great friends.

Eric has a bit of a cough. He says it is chronic. *Is this really the case?* I don't remember it before. . . .

'My Brother, George Orwell'

For much of her life Avril Dunn (1908–78) was very sceptical of her brother Eric's activities, blaming him for giving up a good job in the Burma Police, embarrassing his parents by living among tramps, writing disturbing and socialist books, and generally needing rather than providing support. But after his death, when she was forty-four, she read his work fully, was impressed, became more mellow, even shrewd and wise about her brother. She became interesting to talk to about his work as well as his life.

Her memory is slightly faulty. She is inaccurate about the date of her mother's return from India, and the dates of moving houses in Southwold in the 1930s are wrong. Her account of how she was asked by her brother to keep house for him in Jura conflicts with the testimony of Susan Watson (see below), who was housekeeper already. However, it is an interesting and revealing account.

The family resemblance was striking and friends say that their voices were very similar. (No recordings of Orwell survive.) They both had a dry 'home counties' monotone.

'My Brother, George Orwell' was printed in *Twentieth Century*, March 1961, which was a reprint from a Third Programme broadcast in 1960.

There were three of us. Eric was the second child and only son. He was born at Motihari in Bengal in 1903. I was born at Henley-on-Thames five years later. Five years after that, the family moved to Shiplake, then back to Henley, then to London. We lived in Mall Chambers, Notting Hill Gate.

My paternal grandfather was in the Indian Army. My father was the youngest of twelve children, so it was a very long time ago that my grandfather was born. In those days there was no Suez Canal: all the ships went round the Cape. Once, coming home on leave, my grandfather stopped off at the Cape and got to know a family called Hare and actually got engaged to one of the elder sisters, then went on home to England for his leave. On the way back, intending to marry this girl, he found that she'd already married somebody else. He said, 'Oh, well, if Emily's married it doesn't matter, I'll have Fanny.' Fanny at that time was fifteen, and I believe that she played with dolls after her marriage.

My mother's father was French. His name was Limouzin and he'd spent nearly all his life in the East – in Burma in fact, where he had teak yards. Both sides of our family had been connected with the East for several generations. Although the name was Blair, I don't think the family had any Scottish connection at all. I think it's right to say that Eric had never even been to Scotland until he went to live in Jura in 1946.

The first time that I ever consciously remember Eric was at the beginning of the First World War. In fact, I think it was actually the day war broke out. He would have been about eleven then, and I suppose I was six. He was sitting cross-legged on the floor of my mother's bedroom, talking to her about it in a very grown-up manner. I was knitting him a school scarf. He was at St Cyprian's then, and I think the school colours were either dark blue and green or dark green and blue. Anyway, it was one of those terrible garments that starts off very narrow and in some mysterious manner suddenly becomes terribly wide. I don't suppose he ever wore it.

We never played much together as children, because five years difference in age does make a great difference at that time of life, but I do remember interminable games of French cricket when he always seemed to be in and we were always vainly trying to get him out. It has been said that Eric had an unhappy childhood. I don't think this was in the least true, although he did give out that impression himself when he was grown-up.

Every summer, we used to go down to Cornwall. My mother and father used to take a house or furnished rooms perhaps, and really we used to have a lovely time down there – bathing. We had some friends down there – children – who were almost cousins, and we used to go rock-climbing and all the sort of usual pursuits. He always seemed perfectly happy.

The beginning of his writing was probably at the beginning of the First World War when he was about eleven or twelve. He wrote a poem on the death of Kitchener, who went down in the *Hampshire*, and it was printed in the local paper. When he was about fourteen or fifteen he used to be continually scribbling short stories in notebooks. He never offered to read them to us or made any suggestion that we should read them, but I know that at the time he was actually writing them.

During the First World War, we were both at boarding school, and my mother was working. Very often she used to park us out on an uncle who was a brother of her own. He was secretary of a golf club at Parkstone near Bournemouth, and there was really nothing to do except go to the local roller-skating rink, where we both learnt to roller-skate incredibly badly. Neither of us were interested in it in the least. That was on wet days. On fine days we used to walk over the golf-course, which abounded in lizards, and try to catch them. The way of catching a lizard was to put your foot on it, so that the lizard was firmly held under your instep. Then it was possible to pick it up – rather gingerly, because they bit. Our chief nourishment out of doors was picking up pine-cones, of which there are any amount there and knocking the seeds out and eating them. They tasted horribly of turpentine, but we quite liked them.

Shortly after the war, we moved to Southwold. Eric would then be about seventeen and in his last year at school. He only spent about a year in Southwold then before he went to Burma.

When he came back from Burma in 1926, his appearance had changed quite considerably. He'd become very like my father to look at, and he'd grown a moustache. His hair had got much darker. I suppose being used to a lot of servants in India he'd become terribly – to our minds – untidy. Whenever he smoked a cigarette he threw the end down on the floor – and the match – and expected other people to sweep them up.

The first thing that he did when he came back was to say that he wanted to go down to Cornwall for the month. We went down for the whole of September, and it was during that time that he told my mother that he wasn't going back to Burma; that he'd resigned his commission. Of course she was rather horrified, but he was quite determined that what he wanted to do was to write, and he wasn't going to be any kind of charge on the family. He was determined to make his way, but he was going to do it in his own way.

It must have been in the early thirties that he started teaching in a school in Hayes – a private school. When he'd been there about a year, he got desperately ill with pneumonia. He was in hospital in Hayes, and my mother was sent for, and I drove her down. He was very ill indeed, but the crisis had passed then, and he was recovering. He was very worried about money, so the nurse told us. He'd been delirious, and he'd been talking the whole time about money. We reassured him that everything was all right, and he needn't worry about money. It turned out that it wasn't actually his situation in life as regards money that he was worrying about, but it was actual cash: he felt that he wanted cash sort of under his pillow.

In about 1933 my mother had let the house that we were living in in Southwold – it was a rented house and we'd let it to summer visitors for about six weeks and she had gone away to stay with my sister. Eric and I moved into Montague House, which my mother had just bought. It had very little furniture in it, because most of our furniture was in the other house. Eric was writing away hard all day, and I was out. I was at that time working in a tea-shop in the town and came back pretty late at night. For some unknown reason, we only had two electric-light bulbs. I don't know why we didn't buy any more, but we each had one, and we used to take them round from room to room plugging them in wherever we wanted them.

When he wasn't writing, Eric was trying to distil some black treacle and water and make rum. He'd fermented this black treacle and water and was busily boiling it up in a kettle. Out of the spout of the kettle, or fixed on the spout of the kettle, there was yards and yards of rubber tubing, criss-crossed across the kitchen, slung up on chairs and draped over the sink. Every time you had to move from the gas-stove to a cupboard or to a table, it was a sort of hurdle. Eventually the stuff did come out distilled at the other end as pure alcohol. When we tasted it, it had the most frightful taste of rubber tubing.

When *Down and Out in Paris and London* was published, the family, of course, read it with great interest, but were really, in a way, rather surprised at the outspokenness of the language; not in any way shocked, because my parents weren't easily shockable, although my father was Victorian. But, in his relations with his family, my brother had always been detached and one almost might say impersonal. There was never any discussion of sex or his love affairs or anything of that nature at all. So, when all those matters came out in his book, it almost seemed as if it had been written by a different person. Although there was this element of surprise about *Down and Out* when we read it, it didn't mean that there was ever any estrangement in the family; in fact I think it would be fair to say that we were always a devoted family. Relations were always good: there were never any quarrels. When my mother died about ten years later, my brother showed great concern. We both went to see her in hospital. She was desperately ill, and he was obviously affected by the fact that she was dying and even more so by the fact that on her bed there was a copy of *Homage to Catalonia* which had come out fairly recently. . . .

In 1945 Eric went to Jura to stay. He went up to the north of the island, and he saw the house, Barnhill, standing unoccupied and immediately fell in love with it and thought that he'd like to rent it and live there in complete privacy. There was no more than a cart-track up to the house, eight miles long, and there was no telephone or electric light. It was almost like camping out. But he felt that he really could settle down and write there in peace and quiet.

He made enquiries about renting the house, but at that time the estate it was on belonged to a man who'd been killed in the war. His affairs hadn't been settled, and his executors were unable to let the house until the following year. In 1946 Eric managed to get a lease. He went up there in April and managed to collect some furniture together, which he had sent up from London, and more or less moved in that month. He had previously asked me if I'd like to go up during the summer and give him a hand with helping in the house and helping with young Richard[1] and so on. I was only too pleased. I'd just managed to escape from the essential works order – I'd been working in a factory all during the war and felt that really a spot of country air would just be about the thing I wanted.

[1] Adopted by Orwell and his first wife in 1944. Eileen died in early 1945.

We went back to London in October 1946. By that time Eric had asked me to take on the permanent job of looking after young Richard and doing the housekeeping for him, which I said I would. It was that terrible winter of 1946–7. We had no fuel, and Eric had been ill on and off during the winter with one thing and another. We even got to the point of chopping up young Richard's toys and putting them on the fire in Eric's room to try and keep him warm while he was writing.

In April, 1947, Eric and young Richard and myself went back to Jura, to Barnhill. That was a wonderful summer. Everybody thoroughly enjoyed it, and Eric was really very well indeed all the summer.

On one occasion we went for a picnic over to the west side of Jura, which is almost uninhabited. There is a derelict cottage there, in which one could stay, and we took bedding. We went by rowing boat, with an outboard engine attached, along the coast. This is an extremely dangerous bit of coast, and you have to skirt a very well-known piece of water called Corryvreckan, which I believe is the second largest whirlpool in Europe.[2] Everything went well until we set off back. I wasn't in the boat; I walked back over the hill. There wasn't room in the boat by that time: other people had joined us. Eric and my nephew and niece, aged about twenty and eighteen, and young Richard all went back by boat.

They must have gone through this piece of water at the wrong tide. The outboard engine was ripped off the boat, and there they were bouncing about in this terrible current. Luckily my nephew, Henry, managed to keep his head. He got hold of the oars and kept the boat steady. Eventually, they were washed up on a kind of island, which is in the middle of this narrow piece of water; it's really only just a rock with grass on top of it. He jumped ashore and grabbed the painter of the boat. It's in the Atlantic, and there's an Atlantic swell. As the swell went down, so the boat rolled down the rock, and they all fell out into the sea. Luckily, Eric had a hold of young Richard's knee, because he went completely under the boat. Eric managed to pull him out, and they bobbed up and got onto the island. And there they were just simply stranded in the middle of this very dangerous piece of water, perched on a rock. The only thing in the way of food-stuff that was rescued out of the boat was one potato. Somebody had a box of matches, and they managed to light a bit of dry grass, and they cooked this potato which young Richard ate. Very luckily for

[2] See also Henry Dakin's account on p. 230.

them, a fisherman – a lobster fisherman – happened to be pass-ing in his boat and took them all off.

At the end of the summer of 1947, it became obvious that my brother was ill, and we thought he'd better consult a doctor. A specialist came up to see him and said he ought to be in hospital. He went into Hairmyres Hospital, near Glasgow, at the end of the year and stayed there until the following July.

I went down to see him twice and took young Richard. They really did him an enormous amount of good. When he came out, he looked comparatively fit, but he would insist on coming straight back to Barnhill which he loved. I suppose he wanted to live there in order to go on with his writing. If he'd gone into a convalescent home then, he probably would have been cured, but as it was he came back and insisted on living a quite ordinary life. It really was extremely stupid. Several times I had to go out and take the mowing machine out of his hands and stop him from digging the garden and things like that, but somehow one doesn't have an awful lot of authority over one's own family, and he never really was one much to listen to other people.

It was during the late summer of 1948 that Eric finished writ-ing *Nineteen Eighty-Four*. I remember him coming down from his bedroom, where he did his writing. He got out the last bottle of wine that we had in the house, and he and I and Bill Dunn, whom I afterwards married, had a drink to celebrate the new book.

During that autumn of 1948 it was obvious that he was getting ill again. On one occasion he said to me, rather despairingly: 'Whatever I do, it seems my temperature rises: if I take the slightest kind of action or motion.' We both decided that he'd better be under hospital treatment as soon as possible.

He made arrangements to go away, but he didn't actually go until the following January, 1949. I was taking him down to catch the boat, down at the nearest town, or, rather, village. He was going to stay the night in the village and go away the next morn-ing. We set off rather late in the evening in our car, with Bill and Richard. The road was full of enormous potholes about the size of tables, which were impossible to avoid. We just slipped into one of these, and there was no way of getting the car out. We pushed and pulled, and eventually Eric decided to sit in the car and keep young Richard while Bill and I walked back to the farm, which was a distance of about four miles, and got out a large truck that we also had. By this time it was quite dark and starting to rain. It so happened that, just at the place where the car had got bogged, there was just room, by going well off the road and onto the peat bog, to get round the car. We managed that, and eventually we got a tow-rope on the car and managed to tow it out and complete our journey.

The sanatorium that he went into now was near Cheltenham. During the summer of 1949 I went down there to see him and took young Richard. My brother made arrangements with a friend he had locally to look after Richard for four or five weeks, so that he could see the child nearly every day. In late September 1949, he was moved to University College Hospital, London. The following month, he rather unexpectedly, to me anyway, got married again.

It's an awful long journey from Jura right down to London, so I didn't see him till the following January. I took young Richard down to see him, and we were there in London for about a week or ten days and left on about the 15th. He died on January 21st, and it was rather a shock to me, because although I knew, of course, that he was desperately ill, he was even then talking of going to Switzerland. I think arrangements had been made for him to go. But when I got back to Jura, the first I knew of his death was over the radio, on the news. Then, of course, I went back to London for the funeral.

It has been said that my brother didn't really want to go on living. I didn't form that impression. I remember him saying to me once that he wanted to live at least until young Richard was fourteen.

With Cyril Connolly at Prep School

Cyril Connolly (1903–74), novelist, critic and editor, was a contemporary of Eric Blair's at St Cyprian's, a preparatory school (the St Wulfric's referred to in the text is a pseudonym), and a year behind him in College at Eton.

After Eton, they did not meet again until 1935, when Connolly reviewed *Burmese Days*. Orwell wrote major essays for Connolly's magazine, *Horizon*, during the Second World War, and was introduced to his second wife, Sonia Brownell, by Connolly. This account is taken from *Enemies of Promise* (Routledge and Kegan Paul, London, 1938). Connolly went over the same ground again in later essays, but the memories became more and more imaginative and unreliable.

'Flip' was the nickname of the headmaster's wife at St Cyprian's, Mrs Vaughan Wilkes. Connolly says that 'Flip was a gambling metaphor, the goddess of Fortune'. 'Sambo' was the head's nickname – unhappily because he had thick lips.

I changed my handwriting and way of doing my hair, jumped first instead of last into the plunge-bath, played football better, and became an exhibit, the gay, generous, rebellious Irishman, with a whiff of Kipling's McTurk. Flip also admired the transformation and began to introduce me to parents as 'our dangerous Irishman', 'our little rebel'. At that time I used to keep a favour chart in which, week by week, I would graph my position at her court. I remember my joy as the upward curve continued, and as I began to make friends, win prizes, enjoy riding, and succeed at trying to be funny again. The favour charts I kept for several terms; one began at the top and then went downwards as term wore on, and tempers.

When angry Flip would slap our faces in front of the school or pull the hair behind our ears till we cried. She would make satirical remarks at meals that pierced like a rapier, and then put us through interviews in which we bellowed with repentance. . . .

On all the boys who went through this Elizabeth and Essex relationship she had a remarkable effect, hotting them up like little Alfa-Romeos for the Brooklands of life.

The only thing that would bring our favour back (for, woman-like, Flip treated the very being-out-of-favour as a crime in itself, punishing us for the timid looks and underdog manner by which we showed it) was a visit from parents, and many a letter was sent off begging for their aid. I was restored, after a low period during which I had been compared, before the whole school, to the tribe of Reuben because 'unstable as water thou shalt not excel', by an enquiry from Lord Meath, the founder of Empire Day. Sometimes we could get back by clinging to friends who were still 'in favour'. It might drag them down, or it might bring us up, and the unhappiness of these little boys forced to choose between dropping a friend in his disgrace or risking disgrace themselves was affecting.

I had two friends whose 'favour' was as uncertain as my own, George Orwell, and Cecil Beaton. I was a stage rebel, Orwell a true one. Tall, pale, with his flaccid cheeks, and a matter-of-fact, supercilious voice, he was one of those boys who seem born old.

He was incapable of courtship, and when his favour went, it went for ever. He saw through St Wulfric's, despised Sambo and hated Flip, but was valuable to them as scholarship fodder. We often walked together over the Downs in our green jerseys and corduroy breeches, discussing literature, and we both won, in consecutive years, the inevitable 'Harrow History Prize'. There was another prize for having the 'best list' of books taken out of the library during the term, the kind which have been only invented to create intellectual snobs, and to satiate boys with the world's culture at a time when they were too young to understand it. . . .

Thus, although I won the prize through heading my list with 'Carlyle's *French Revolution*' – and Orwell won it next, we were caught at last with two volumes of *Sinister Street*, and our favour sunk to zero.

We both wrote poetry. At sunset, or late at night, in the dark, I would be visited by the Muse. In an ecstasy of flushing and shivering, the tears welling up as I wrote, I would put down some lines to the Night Wind. The next morning they would be copied out . . . I would compare them with Orwell's, being critical of his while he was polite about mine, and we would separate feeling ashamed of each other.

The remarkable thing about Orwell was that he alone among the boys was an intellectual, and not a parrot, for he thought for himself, read Shaw and Samuel Butler, and rejected not only St Wulfric's, but the war, the Empire, Kipling, Sussex, and Character. I remember a moment under a fig-tree in one of the inland boulevards of the seaside town, Orwell striding beside me, and saying in his flat, ageless voice: 'You know, Connolly, there's only one remedy for all diseases.' I felt the usual guilty tremor when sex was mentioned and hazarded, 'You mean going to the lavatory?' 'No – I mean Death!' He was not a romantic, he had no use for the blandishments of the drill sergeant who made us feel character was identical with boxing, nor for the threats of the chaplain with his grizzled cheektufts, and his gospel of a Jesus of character, who detested immorality and swearing as much as he loved the Allies. 'Of course, you realise, Connolly,' said Orwell, 'that, whoever wins this war, we shall emerge a second-rate nation.'

Orwell proved to me that there existed an alternative to Character, Intelligence.

A Sportsman Defends the Old Prep School

Henry Longhurst (1909–78) was for forty-five years golfing correspondent of the *Sunday Times*. He went to St Cyprian's in 1915. Orwell had arrived in 1911 and left in 1917, so they had no personal acquaintance. But Longhurst's description of the school is interesting and in his memoirs, *My Life and Soft Times* (Cassell, London, 1971, and Collins, London, 1983), he set out to defend his school against detractors like Orwell; he had obviously read Orwell's 'Such, Such Were the Joys', which I argue in my *George Orwell: A Life* is a polemic against private education rather than a literally accurate memory of Prep School. None the less Longhurst's account of being made to eat up a bowl of porridge into which he has been sick may indeed be a defence of the 'character forming' ambience of the school, but as a defence I ventured to call it 'an own goal'.

Morning revealed St Cyprian's to be a vast, gabled, red-brick house with a sunken playing-field, complete with cricket pavilion, known as the Armoury, and twenty-five-yard rifle-range. On the far side was a high bank; then the road; then another bank, and above it the first fairway of the Royal Eastbourne Golf Club. . . . At that age you don't ask many questions. You take life for what it is, and on the whole, by today's standards, it was pretty spartan, not only from the point of view of washing in very cold water and having to do a length of the swimming-pool every morning, followed by P.T., which put me off every form of artificial physical exercise for life, but also because the food rationing was far less expertly managed in the First War than in the Second and the Wilkeses must have had a hard job feeding a hundred appetites made ravenous by the sea and downland air, to say nothing of 'runs' the whole way to Beachy Head and back.

It is one of the more merciful dispensations of providence that one tends to forget the hard times and remember the good – hence 'time the great healer', which it is, and 'your schooldays are the happiest time of your life', which they assuredly aren't. Some of the scars remain, but not many. Among them I should put the cold pewter bowls of porridge with the thick slimy lumps, into which I was actually sick one day and made to stand at a side table and eat it up. . . .

Looking back at what I hope I have now become, namely a 'freethinker', all passion spent, all bitterness gone, I conclude that St Cyprian's was a very good school indeed, despite the fact, to which I shall return, that three of my more celebrated contemporaries, or near-contemporaries, have written so vitriolically about it as to make one wonder whether we are writing of the same institution. It is true that Mum Wilkes's dominant and sometimes emotional character caused one's whole existence to depend on whether one was 'in favour' or otherwise, and indeed the expression became a normal part of one's daily life without, so to speak, the inverted commas. If you were in favour, life could be bliss: if you weren't, it was hell, and no doubt this should be chalked up on the debit side. On the other hand it taught you the hard way one of *the* lessons of life – that, if you don't 'look after Number One', no one else will.

This was somewhat confirmed by one of the three critics I have in mind, Cyril Connolly, a fellow-contributor, though on more elevated subjects, to the *Sunday Times*. The other two were George Orwell, of *Nineteen Eighty-Four* and *Animal Farm* fame, whose real name was Eric Blair, and Gavin Maxwell. Writing on Orwell's *Collected Essays* in 1968, Connolly said: 'There one is, back again, among the cramming and the starving and the smells, a little boy in corduroy knickers and a green jersey. Horror upon horror – and yet we are determined to survive.'

Connolly went on to admit that later, on getting possession of his school reports and Mr Wilkes's letters to his father and his own letters home, they 'revealed a considerable distortion between my picture of the proprietors and their own unremitting care to bring me on'. Orwell, he added, 'rejected not only the school but the War, the Empire, Kipling, Sussex and Character' – hardly perhaps an endearing 'reference' for one's hero. Orwell himself sank from Eton via service in Burma and the Spanish Civil War to a life among the down-and-outs in Paris, and those who have read his book about it may share the charitable opinion that by this time he was mad.

Christopher Hollis on Orwell at Eton

Christopher Hollis (1902–77), Conservative MP, author and Catholic intellectual, wrote *A Study of George Orwell* (Hollis and Carter, London, 1956). Hollis entered Eton in the Election of 1914 (pupils at Eton were organised into Elections by the year they entered, irrespective of precise age) and Orwell joined the 1916 Election late, when a vacancy occurred after Christmas; he had already spent a term at Wellington. The social distance between boys separated by two Elections was vast; so Hollis did not really know Eric Blair at all well. Most of his book consists of rather ordinary critical pronouncements on Orwell's books, and he was perhaps tempted to exaggerate his personal acquaintance with Orwell to give his judgements more authority; certainly their contemporaries suggest that some of the anecdotes are stock stories of schoolboy resistance to masters rather than things that specifically occurred to Orwell. But Hollis's description of the College at Eton is excellent. The College was that part of Eton where the scholars or scholarship boys lived, the rest of Eton being divided into Houses. It was an intellectual élite inserted into a social élite.

People vary greatly from one another in the vividness of their recall of their schooldays, nor can any just generalisation be made of what sort of people we recall most vividly. There is, it is true, the bore who lives in his schooldays because he has never grown out of them and never come to the mentality of an adult. But such a description would be by no means just of all those to whom those early days are vivid. Nor, though it may be a general truth that the mind retains that which it has most enjoyed, is it universally true that those remember their schooldays best who enjoyed them most. The retentive mind of Sir Charles Oman held to the last, as he showed in his *Memories of Victorian Oxford*, every detail of the ill-treatment which he had received at Winchester half a century before, and Bismarck in his retirement lay awake, hating the schoolmaster of his youth. From time to time I meet again over the arches of the years one who was at school with me. Sometimes I find, as Mr Connolly has shown the world in *Enemies of Promise* to be the case with him, that every detail of Eton life is vivid to the mind. With others – by no means necessarily the stupid or unobservant – I am almost embarrassed to see how completely the picture and arrangement

37

of the life there have passed from them and how they have forgotten the part that they themselves played in incidents that are still utterly familiar to me.

Mr Connolly was certainly not one who found nothing to complain of in his Eton life, and a superficial critic might say that he was certainly not one who remembered it because it was pleasant. In the latter judgement the critic would, I think, be wrong. Although Mr Connolly's story is in large part the story of a battle, it was a battle which, as he himself would confess, he greatly enjoyed. The life of personal relationships meant much to him. He wrote, 'Were I to deduce anything from my feelings on leaving Eton, it might be called The Theory of Permanent Adolescence. It is the theory that experiences undergone by boys at the great public schools are so intense as to dominate their lives and to arrest their development.'

To Orwell personal relations of that sort meant little, and therefore it was natural perhaps that his attitude towards it should be polemical, that, excellent as his humour was in general, there should be throughout the whole of 'Such, Such Were the Joys' no hint that there was ever any joke in the life of Crossgates. To a strong solitary such as Orwell there was little that school could do to him save not interfere with him. It was therefore perhaps natural that to him – a rare case – his preparatory school remained more vividly in his mind than his public school. It remained more vividly in his mind because he was interfered with more. He wrote little about College at Eton because he was little interfered with there. But it does not follow from that that Eton had little influence on him.

It was at Eton that my own path and that of Orwell first crossed. I was of the Election of 1914, Orwell that of 1916. But, as I have said, I was a twelve-year-old of my Election and he a thirteen-year-old of his. So there was not much difference between us in age. But in the curious hierarchy of College they were not years of age which counted at all. All was reckoned by the years of Election. The bottom Election – that of those still in their first year – was the Election of the fags. Those immediately above them gave themselves great airs, called themselves the Senior Election, and would not speak to the Junior Election at all or spoke to them only with great condescension. They were continually on the alert for any sign of the fags 'giving themselves airs'.

It is, I think, a universal experience of school that in his first year a boy soon gets to know by name almost everybody in his school or house. His seniors are more prominent than he and there is every cause to discover who they are. In fact he had better know – for many reasons. But, as he goes up the school, he comes to know fewer and fewer by name. It is only for some special reason that he has occasion to know by name boys junior to himself. As a result, when we of our Election attained to the seniority of a third year we soon indeed formed some confident general judgements about 'the scruffiness' of the new fags, but we were very content to pride ourselves considerably on not knowing one from another. So some weeks went by before I knew that there was in the new Election, recently arrived as a late reinforcement to it, a Blair, K. S. – or at least before I knew which of the fags Blair, K. S., might be.

And the first thing that I got to know about him and the way I got to know about him was this.

There was in my Election a boy – today a distinguished peer. We will call him Johnson – Johnson major. In the ordinary way we would have had no means of knowing what were the topics of conversation in the underworld of the fags, but it so happened that Johnson major had a younger brother who was then a member of the fags' Election – who is today a scholar of world renown. There was not the rigid ban on conversation of brother with brother which ruled among the generality of the unrelated. One day Johnson minor reported to Johnson major that there was a boy in his Election of the name of Blair, who had taken a most violent dislike to the elder brother, and, lacking wax and wishing to give effective expression to his dislike, Blair had made out of soap an image of his hated enemy. He had extracted all the pins out of his returned washing and stuck them at odd angles into this soapen image. I do not remember that we ever saw the image. It was reported to us that it was not a very recognisable likeness but that, in order that there might be no misunderstanding on the part of either boy or demon, Blair had labelled it 'Johnson major' and stuck it upon the bracket below the mirror in his cubicle or 'stall' as it was called.

We made some enquiries as to the reason for this so great hatred, for Johnson major was not conscious that he even knew Blair by sight. Blair, it transpired, did not pretend that Johnson had ever done him any harm, but said that he detested him because he was so 'noisy', as indeed he was. Clearly it was a case of

I do not like thee, Doctor Fell,
The reason why I cannot tell

– and this was more or less admitted.

It was on Friday that Johnson minor told this tale to his elder brother.

Now the régime in College in those days was a régime of fairly rough justice. The Colleger had to expect to be beaten a number of times during his first two years. It was thought to be good for him, and, even if he did not commit an offence, some offence would probably be fathered on him quite without malice and for the good of his bottom and general entertainment. But, after these two years of novitiate, unless a boy had won for himself a reputation for being 'pretty awful', it was possible with a little trouble to avoid punishment. Perhaps a blow would descend once in a while – just to remind even those in Upper Division that they were not yet exempt – but apart from such a mischance those in their third year or beyond could usually escape.

Now it so happened that by what was, I dare say, little more than happy accident Johnson major had during his first two years been more fortunate than most and had won for himself something of a reputation of being magically protected by the gods against such indignities. But on the next Monday he was suddenly and unexpectedly summoned before Sixth Form. He had, it seems, come in late for lunch that day and, when asked if he had got leave from a member of Sixth Form – as was the obligation – had replied that he could not find anybody to give him leave. It appeared – so the Sixth Formers alleged – that there were several Sixth Formers about. He was told that he could easily have found somebody to give him leave if he had taken a little trouble, that this was casual behaviour, that there was a great deal too much of such casual behaviour and that it was time that something was done to stop it. Before he knew where he was he was being beaten.

That was on Monday. On Tuesday there was a field day, from which we had to return by train. Johnson was the senior boy in his carriage. During the journey a boy in that carriage, with great folly, threw a bottle out of the window as the train was passing through Reading (West). The matter was reported. There was a great row. The culprit was discovered. He was summoned before Sixth Form on the Wednesday and, not surprisingly, punished, but while he was about it, the Sixth Former who was the head of the College contingent of the Corps thought to ask also who was the senior boy in the carriage. It was Johnson major of course and he – a little harshly perhaps – was beaten into the bargain.

The news was carried back to the fags. Blair accepted it with a smile of wry triumph, but that evening just before lights out – so Johnson minor told us – the soapen image slipped into a basin full of hot water and was dissolved. Blair did not re-erect it on its bracket. It was a symbol, we comforted the damaged elder brother, that the jealous gods were no longer athirst and that the curse had been expiated. And so indeed it proved, for he had no more troubles in his immediate future.

This tale convinced me that Blair must be 'an odd fellow' and that it would be amusing to get to know him and find out what were his ideas. It was always at school my hobby to defy as far as might be possible the bans of convention and to talk to amusing people wherever I might find them. I did not, needless to say, believe in Blair's magic, but even a bogus magician was better than no magician at all. So the next time that we passed each other in the passage I said to him 'Hullo, Blair' – which was an outrageous thing to say to a fag. He replied 'Hullo' and smiled a little feebly.

There are limits to daring, and for the moment I could think of no more to say. So after stopping and staring at one another we both passed on without a further word. It was our first conversation, and it left on me the impression that here was a boy of a peculiar humour – a saturnine perhaps and not wholly benevolent humour but above all a humorist. So he certainly was. It is as such that I primarily remember him – as a boy saying and doing funny things. It is well to set this against his own picture of himself at Crossgates [St Cyprian's] and at Eton in which humour plays no part.

Mr Noel Blakiston, who was a few years Orwell's junior in College, has told me of his first meeting with him. Mr Blakiston was fielding in a cricket match. Orwell came up to him with a paper and pencil in his hand.

'I'm collecting the religions of the new boys,' said Orwell. 'Are you Cyrenaic, Sceptic, Epicurean, Cynic, Neoplatonist, Confucian or Zoroastrian?'

'I'm a Christian,' said Blakiston.

'Oh,' said Orwell, 'we haven't had that before.'

My other early memory of him is at Chamber Singing. In their first Michaelmas half, a few weeks after its beginning, all new boys in College had one by one to stand upon a table in their dormitory which was known as Chamber and each to sing a song. Orwell sang – not very well – 'Riding down from Bangor', about which he was some thirty years later to write one of his *Tribune* essays. At the time that he wrote the essay he had no copy of the song at hand and had, he said, to quote from memory – the memory no doubt of Chamber Singing.

For my next memory I move on some three years. I was then a junior member of Sixth Form. A fellow Sixth Former conceived, rightly or wrongly, that he had been cheeked by the members of Orwell's Election in a complicated dispute over the borrowing of some tennis balls, and the whole Election was summoned before Sixth Form and told that they were all to be beaten. There was a tremendous argument whether they had insulted him or not, and in that argument Orwell stood out as the spokesman for his Election – first, maintaining that there had been no insult and then, with melodramatic gesture, that at least there could be no point in beating the whole Election. It would suffice if there was a scapegoat and for that he offered himself. The argument was to no purpose, and the whole Election was in fact beaten. The incident only remains in my mind because I noticed that Orwell's trousers were more shiny than those of his fellows – and that was certainly the only suggestion that ever came to my mind during his schooldays that he was perhaps poorer than the rest of us.

It certainly was not true that he was unpopular with his fellow Collegers. It certainly was not true that he was insignificant among them or what I might call superficially solitary. As for work, he may not have worked as hard as he could. Indeed it is true that, in an order, based upon marks obtained in Trials, or the term examination, he sank to the bottom of his Election, but these marks were given predominantly for proficiency in Latin and Greek, in which he was not especially interested, and he was in competition against the most expert mark-grubbers in England. He was a science specialist. Mr A. S. F. Gow, now Fellow of Trinity College, Cambridge, was his tutor when first he went to Eton. When he became a science specialist, he was attached for a time to Mr Christie, of Glyndebourne, but that was, it seems, little more than a formal connection, and he soon went back to Mr Gow.

Orwell maintained that, as an Etonian, he was an anarchical prig, an idler and despised by the other boys for his poverty. Let me deal with these claims.

As for anarchy, it is certainly true. 'We all thought of ourselves,' he wrote, 'as the enlightened creatures of a new age, casting off the orthodoxy that had been forced upon us.' 'I was against all authority. I had read and re-read the entire published works of Shaw, Wells and Galsworthy, at that time still regarded as "dangerously advanced" writers, and I loosely described myself as a Socialist.' Mr Connolly confirms this. He speaks of Orwell as 'immersed in the *Way of All Flesh* and the atheistic arguments of *Androcles and the Lion*' at the age of fifteen. He was, I remember, known as 'the Election atheist'.

But the operative words in these extracts are 'We all'. Orwell records how in a division of sixteen, fifteen nominated Lenin as one of the ten greatest men of the age. The period was the period of Woodrow Wilson and of reaction against tradition and discipline, the period of the years after the armistice of 1918. What Monsignor Knox – then by no means Monsignor – speaking of an earlier crisis, called in his leaving entry, in College Annals, 'a healthy wind of antinomianism' was then blowing over almost all schools in England. Certainly it blew like a gale at Eton and particularly in College. Anarchical opinions by no means made Orwell isolated. They made him a notable leader. They put him in the fashion. As Mr Brander truly says, the anecdote about Lenin proves that Orwell was by no means peculiar in his opinions. He was only peculiar in that he was solitary and that he did not, as Mr Connolly truly says, throw himself into the conflicts of College politics by which so many of the rest of us were absorbed. Perhaps there was in his rebellion against authority a kind of obstinate and puritan sincerity which contrasted a little with the more light-hearted ragging in which at any rate the greater number of the escapades of the rest of us were conceived. 'Well, Blair,' said the Master in College, 'things can't go on like this. Either you or I will have to go.' 'I'm afraid it'll have to be you, sir,' answered Orwell. It may be – I do not know – that some of the masters felt that he was a serious danger, where the rest of us were merely silly nuisances. I fully accepted the whole grammar of anarchy about no discipline and no punishments and was always delighted to find pretended abuses and tyrannies to denounce. But there was a custom at Eton by which boys touched their caps to a master when they passed him. It seemed, and seems to me, a very harmless courtesy and, questioning all else, I had never thought to question that custom, but I remember discovering to my surprise that Orwell resented passionately the indignity of this servile action that was demanded of him.

Orwell tells how the boys ragged the peace celebrations in School Yard in 1919. As he records it, 'We were to march into School Yard, carrying torches and singing jingo songs of the type of *Rule Britannia*. The boys – to their honour, I think – guyed the whole proceeding.' The reason why we guyed the proceedings was that they were organised by the Officers' Training Corps, and the OTC in those post-war years was a very unpopular institution. Mr Fyvel [Tosco Fyvel, see p. 212] cannot believe that Orwell's account of the deriding of the OTC and the mocking of the flag was not exaggerated and even confesses to the strange belief that Orwell himself 'rather enjoyed serving in the OTC', which is certainly not true, whatever Orwell may afterwards have pretended. Both then, as later in the Home Guard, it was one of his curious whims to pretend that he was an efficient soldier, but it was completely untrue. He was appallingly untidy and, rebel as he was, not even he would have dared to carry eccentricity so far as to have enjoyed the OTC in the early 1920s. But Orwell's account of the peace celebration is not at all exaggerated. Antinomianism that would not have been tolerated at any other school in England was, and I hope still is, tolerated at Eton. But the rag was to most of us, I think, a straightforward rag. There was not the element of principle in our protest which Orwell imports.

It may seem both from this narrative and from Mr Connolly's *Enemies of Promise* that life at Eton was a very vapulatory business. And so, indeed, in general it was. But it so happened that shortly after those of us who held after the new ways came into power in Sixth Form and as a result, for better or for worse, beatings became an extremely rare thing. It is true that at the end of Orwell's time there, after we had left, there was a certain reaction, as one result of which Orwell, according to Mr Connolly, was, at eighteen, beaten by a boy of substantially his own age, for being late for prayers. But on the whole, far from suffering brutality at Eton, he had an easier time than the average public schoolboy. Nor indeed did he ever deny this. If it is true that his interests even during his schooldays were not bounded by the world of Eton, Eton, I think, deserves some credit for this. The general freedom of Eton life combined fortuitously with the special freedom which the régime of College allowed him. There was a kind of insolent carelessness about what was taught at Eton, arising from a confidence that the pupils would not attend to it very much anyway, that could not be found, I imagine, anywhere else. I remember in 1920 having to write an essay for Mr Aldous Huxley, then one of the masters, to explain how there could never again be any dictators in the modern world. A good many of the things that were taught there were palpably untrue, but they were very well taught. Indeed this was substantially Orwell's own verdict. He wrote in an article in

The Observer, 'For Ever Eton', on 1 August 1948:

> Whatever may happen to the great public schools when our educational system is reorganized, it is almost impossible that Eton should survive in anything like its present form, because the training it offers was originally intended for a landowning aristocracy and had become an anachronism long before 1939. The top hats and tail coats, the pack of beagles, the many-coloured blazers, the desks still notched with the names of Prime Ministers had charm and function so long as they represented the kind of elegance that everyone looked up to. In a shabby and democratic country they are merely rather a nuisance, like Napoleon's baggage wagons, full of chefs and hairdressers, blocking up the roads in the disaster of Sedan.

But he added:

> It has one great virtue . . . and that is a tolerant and civilised atmosphere which gives each boy a fair chance of developing his individuality. The reason is perhaps that, being a very rich school, it can afford a large staff, which means that the masters are not over-worked; and also that Eton partly escaped the reform of the public schools set on foot by Dr Arnold and retained certain characteristics belonging to the eighteenth century and even to the Middle Ages. At any rate, whatever its future history, some of its traditions deserve to be remembered.

And indeed, like most other Etonians, he owed many of his opportunities in later life to his old schoolfellows – in his case, to Mr Connolly and Sir Richard Rees.

In his essay *Inside the Whale*, Orwell takes Mr Connolly to task, with some ridicule, for suggesting in the passage already quoted that an Eton career is likely to be a permanent formative influence in the life of an intellectual – 'five years,' as he put it, 'in a lukewarm bath of snobbery.' But I think that Mr Connolly was right and Orwell wrong. The great mark of most iconoclasts is their lack of self-confidence. Attacking society, they yet need somewhere where they can feel the security of support, and thus it follows that, criticising the evils of society at large, they allow themselves a blind spot to the evils of the particular organisation to which they belong. If you wish for the self-confidence not to need this support of an organisation I think that it helps a great deal to have been an Old Etonian. Orwell was so wholly unique a character that if, knowing nothing of him, I had been shown his work and asked to guess whence he had sprung, I should not perhaps have known how to answer, but if I had been told – which would not have seemed to me an improbability – that he was a public schoolboy, I should certainly have guessed that he was an Eton Colleger, for I think that at Eton that peculiar excess of individualism is more kindly treated than elsewhere. An Old Etonian is far more likely to 'dare to be a Daniel' than is a Non-conformist. Class privilege has seldom been effectively attacked except by a writer who has to some extent benefited from it, as Orwell, whatever he may have pretended, naturally did.

I would not say that he was a typical Old Etonian, but then it is the especial mark of Eton that it is peculiarly easy for an Old Etonian not to be a typical Old Etonian. His private school may, for all that I know, have played its part in driving him to spiritual loneliness, and this loneliness certainly was sharpened and embittered by a life in Burma, in which none of his fellow Europeans were people at all sympathetic to him, but I think that Eton had a good deal to do with the unique courage with which he gave expression to that spiritual loneliness. Eton left him free to develop his own interests without constraint to a degree that he might not have found equalled at any other school in the world. . . . If it be true, as Orwell tells us, that during all his early years he always assumed that all his enterprises would inevitably end in failure the sense came from an accident of his temperament – perhaps from his ill health. In fact his career was averagely successful. Of direct literary work during his school-days he writes, 'Apart from school work, I wrote *vers d'occasion*, semi-comic poems which I could turn out at what now seems to me astonishing speed – at fourteen I wrote a whole rhyming play in imitation of Aristophanes in about a week – and helped to edit school magazines, both printed and in manuscript. These manuscripts were the most pitiful burlesque stuff that you could imagine, and I took far less trouble with them than I now would with the cheapest journalism.' These verses gained, I remember, a reputation for wit among his schoolfellows and I should be surprised if they were not better than he pretended. But I cannot quote any of them at this distance of time. So there is no way of proving my point.

But as for his main grievance against Eton, that he was a poor boy among the rich, it was, I am sure, entirely a grievance of his own imagination. Eton is about as completely a classless society within itself as can be imagined. The Etonian of my day was childishly arrogant about anyone who was not at Eton – Marlburians, Hottentots, barrow-boys, Americans and what-have-you were all dismissed with sweeping gesture as beyond the pale. But his very arrogance meant that anyone who was at Eton was accepted. At Leeds Grammar School there certainly was much more awareness than there was at Eton whose parents were rich and whose were poor and which lived in the fashionable and which in the unfashionable parts of the town. The only vestige of what by any stretch could be called internal class-feeling in Etonian life was the contempt with which some years before Oppidans, who paid for their schooling, used to treat Collegers, who got it free. But, just at the time when Orwell and I were at Eton, this feeling of contempt had quite died down, and Collegers had far more than their fair share of members of Pop, or the Eton Society. 'Probably the greatest cruelty one can inflict on a child,' wrote Orwell in *Keep the Aspidistra Flying*, 'is to send it to school among children richer than itself.' It is an absurd exaggeration. To one who sees things in proportion it is not by any means an unmixed evil to be brought up in sufficiency but in the company of somewhat richer children. By far the greater number of notable achievements of man, I should say, have come from those who have had such experience in youth, and to one who has common sense there is no better discipline in economy. By the side of the advantages the few incidental embarrassments are trivial.

Orwell complained of himself and of the rest of us that we were snobs. 'When I was fourteen,' he writes, 'I was an odious little snob, but no worse than other boys of my age and class.' We must use words carefully. It was of course true that, while we were still at Eton, we had not at all learnt how to be at ease with those who did not come from a public school. It was not that we claimed superiority. On the contrary, in our anarchical mood we indulged in a good deal of frothy egalitarian talk. It is true, of course, as Orwell says, that we wanted to have it both ways – that while we clamoured that the workers should have better opportunities, we never faced the corollary that this would in any way mean that we should have worse opportunities. In an illogical fashion we looked forward to an unprivileged society in which we still had all our privileges. But what is that but to say that we were still very young?

Orwell in *The Road to Wigan Pier* claims that class conscious-ness is a reality and that the hypocrite who denies it deceives himself. Everyone, he argues, on either side of the fence as a general rule does prefer to associate with those who were brought up to the same habits as himself, and, if we want to lessen class distinctions, we must be content to hasten slowly. Otherwise our well-meant folly will only succeed in accentuating them. This is sensible enough. We shall certainly never succeed in building the classless society so long as we are always talking about it. We can only begin to move towards it, when we can school ourselves to talk and think about more interesting and more important things.

Class consciousness in Orwell, as he claims, showed itself during his boyhood most clearly in his conviction that the lower classes smell. This conviction remained with him for years even after he left school, and indeed it is not quite clear, from the pages in *The Road to Wigan Pier*, whether he ever abandoned it. It is far from clear whether he thought even in maturity that this was a vulgar prejudice which snobbery had imposed upon him or whether he agreed with Mr Somerset Maugham that they did smell but that, considering the circumstances of their life, it was neither unnatural nor reprehensible that they should. But if we are to pursue this peculiar topic – and, as Mr Quinton argued in an interesting broadcast on 'Orwell's Sense of Smell', delivered on 16 January 1954, smell played so large a part in forming his opinions that we must pursue it if we are to judge Orwell at all – it is important to see his crudity in perspective. At the time when he was most insistent that the lower classes smelt – the time of his own schooldays – he also firmly believed that he smelt himself. As he writes of his schooldays in 'Such, Such Were the Joys', 'I was weak. I was ugly. I was unpopular. I had a chronic cough. I smelt. . . .'

How keen was Orwell's sense of smell it is difficult to say. His whole point about the soldiers with whom he served in Burma and of whose smell he speaks in *The Road to Wigan Pier* is that he thought that they smelt and said that they smelt because that was what prejudice had taught him to expect. He never thought of smelling himself to see. . . . No doubt, like the rest of us, Orwell did not think very much about the working classes when he was a boy at Eton, but I do not think that he had any deliberate prejudice which could justly be called snobbery, nor, even though he thought as an intellectual proposition that they smelt, do I believe that he thought about it very much.

He was reasonably good at games. He was in the College Wall Eleven and played against the Oppidans on St Andrew's Day. He played at goals, and the College Wall book in a number of places commends his cool and skilful kicking, both on St

Andrew's Day and throughout the season. 'Blair made some neat kicks.' 'Blair kept his head and stopped the rush,' I read in the Wall book. In the Wall game the common score, corresponding to a rugby try, is a shy. When a shy is scored, the scoring side, as in rugby, attempts to convert it into a goal. A goal is scored at the Wall game by throwing the ball at one end against a garden door, at the other end against a mark on a tree. The throw is inordinately difficult and for years on end no one ever scored a goal. But Orwell scored one in a match played on 29 October 1921. He threw the ball to Robert Longden, afterwards Headmaster of Wellington, who passed it on to the door. Mr John Lehmann, who was a new boy at the time, remembered it happening and on looking the game up in the College Wall book, I was delighted to discover – what I had, I confess, quite forgotten – that I was playing in the match on the side opposite to Orwell.

Much in Orwell can be explained by the acute sense of sin by which he was haunted. Sometimes, as in his criticisms of Mr and Mrs Simpson, this discomfort of sin made him attack those who had caused it. He tried – and failed – to relieve himself of it by denouncing its alleged irrationality. Elsewhere, where a genuine moral judgement led him to acclaim the goodness of equality, he attacked those, such as the masters of the totalitarian states, who preached equality but practised inequality. He thought it necessary to punish himself for his privileges by voluntarily embracing the lot of the 'down-and-outs' in London and Paris or of the Spanish revolutionaries, and in the same spirit he did not care to talk much of his Eton life, not because it had not had influence on him, but because he had enjoyed it and, since it was an inheritance of privilege, he felt it wrong to have enjoyed it. He was willing to talk about Crossgates because he genuinely disliked Crossgates. When it came to the planning of the education of his adopted son, Orwell argued, as Mr Fyvel tells us, that it would be a good thing if the public-school system should have come to an end before he had to go to school, but that, if there were still public schools, he should go to one.

In various places throughout his books there are scattered and incidental remarks about the public-school system – condemning it for its inegalitarianism – and various scattered and incidental remarks about classical education – which he disliked professedly because it diverted the mind of the pupil from the real problems of the day – which he disliked in truth perhaps because all his own interests were in the present and the future and he did not care greatly about the past, whether of Greece or

Rome or of any other land or period. But the nearest that he comes to a systematic criticism of the place in society of the public school is in his study of the stories of *The Gem* and *The Magnet* in his essay on 'Boys' Weeklies'. He there notes two important truths – first, that England is the only country in which there is a large, continuing market for the school story – second, that such stories are invariably about expensive and exclusive public schools but are generally read by boys of humble origin who have never had any hope of going to such schools. The stories themselves are, if considered realistically, both fantastic and outdated and he submits their absurdities to a witty analysis. But the lesson that he draws from this analysis is that there is an enormous proportion of the unmoneyed youth of the country who are living 'fantasy' lives as pretended public schoolboys. For this reason the public schools receive an absurd and adventitious aid in their struggle for survival. There is not the unqualified hostility to them which one would expect on pure egalitarian principles. He analyses the financial ownership of these papers, and finds that they belong to the Amalgamated Press and suggests – I do not think quite seriously – that Lord Camrose deliberately flooded the market with this literature for reasons of Conservative propaganda. The truth is, I think, less subtle. 'What I have seen of our governing class,' he more justly writes in *The Road to Wigan Pier*, 'does not convince me that they have that much intelligence.' Lord Camrose and his associates did not invent this strange English mentality any more than the producers of Hollywood taught the American public to worship wealth. But they astutely observed its existence and exploited it. Whether it should be so or not, in fact the English is not an egalitarian nation. It is rare to find among the English those who care greatly about equality, so long as the grossest injustices are avoided. Where we do find an English egalitarian we find him sometimes indeed among the unprivileged, but more often among those who have themselves received privileges and are made uncomfortable in the possession of them by a sense of sin. Which makes for the greater general human happiness – equality or a frankly unequal society with a comparatively easy ebb and flow between class and class – what Pareto called 'the circulation of the élites' – is a question with which Orwell was to spend the rest of his life wrestling and to which, like the rest of us, he never found the certain answer.

A Contemporary in College

Sir Steven Runciman (b. 1903), the historian of the Crusades and of the Byzantine Empire, was an exact contemporary of Orwell in College at Eton. The incident in which he criticises the accuracy of the late Christopher Hollis's memory concerns Orwell's vindictiveness towards another boy.

I interviewed Runciman five years ago, and took notes, but did not make a verbatim record as is given here. My impression of Sir Steven was of an historian who was professionally very sceptical of memory, even his own excellent one, if it was unchecked by documentation. Moreover, his testimony to me was in effect the same as in this recorded conversation with Professor Yasuhara Okuyama of the University of Waseda which is reprinted in Okuyama's book *George Orwell* (Tokyo, 1981), here shortened and edited. It is more bold and brief than Hollis's piece because Runciman will only speak from direct knowledge and refuses to embroider.

. . . First he went to Wellington and then he came on to Eton for the Summer Half. And so those of us who had been there a bit longer were patronising. We were, so to speak, at home, but he was certainly able to look after himself from the beginning, and was obviously a character. In those days, at that age you don't formulate things properly, but to me in those days he was much the most interesting personality. I enjoyed his company. His mind worked in rather different ways, his reactions were different from ordinary schoolboys.

He read a lot of rather odd books. Rather haphazard. I cannot think there could have been any scheme in his reading. I had read a certain amount of odd books myself and it was wonderful to find someone who had read a whole lot that I hadn't – and was amusing about them.

Shaw and Wells and Samuel Butler?

I'd read those things already earlier, but that was really through being a younger son. But certainly Eric had read a lot of very unusual books and he loved airing his knowledge particularly to the masters who were slightly shocked to find someone so well read in books which they thought a bit too grown up for the young. So he was very good company from the beginning. And he rather knew that I had a taste for fantasy in many ways, and he loved and he encouraged that. So the first two years I think I saw more of him than I saw many of my other colleagues.

What was his character like?

It's awfully difficult to be honest about that when you are thinking back over so many years. I don't think I ever thought him a
very kind character. I don't think he was very kind. And, in a way,
I suppose his company was rather stimulating because you didn't
feel confidence in his friendship, you got worried all the time.
You'd really got to be interesting enough to be worthwhile.
Well, that's rather good for one!

So he was rather egotistic?

Not egotistic, just not affectionate. I don't think those sort of
affections ever meant much to him. I don't think he was really
interested in friends as friends. He was interested in friends as
company, as stimulants, as people who might be doing things
that were worthwhile; but simple friendship, I wonder whether
he was really capable of it: what was stimulating about his
company was that you couldn't count on it quite. We were all a
bit like that. The College at Eton is a sort of nest of clever boys.
You don't get there unless you've got your scholarship. And
clever boys are apt to be a bit, well I wouldn't say on edge, but
never frightfully relaxed: it wasn't a very relaxed atmosphere. . . .
I was going to say no sentimentality. But he did have a sentimentality about Burma. He had hardly known it, but he always
used to talk about it. That was where he wanted to go back to. And
when he got back there, he was disillusioned, chiefly by the
British in Burma. But it was at the back of his mind . . . I think all
through his school days. I mean it was one reason why he didn't
want to go to university. He wanted to get back to the East. I think
that was the only thing he really, in those days, felt sentimental
about. Otherwise, he was wonderfully free of sentiment for good
or for ill, but wonderfully free.

He writes in his essay on his prep school and also in The Road to
Wigan Pier, Part II, *that in his school days he was so miserable
because he was very poor.*

I thought it dishonest of him to talk about being miserable
because of being poor. College at Eton was full of clever boys who
hadn't got particularly any money, and there were others there,
who were every bit as poor as he was. And there was no conscious-
ness of being poor.

I think possibly if you were rather better off, or your parents
were, when your parents came down to see you, they could take
more of your friends out with you to lunch or to whatever it was.
But Eric's mother used to take his friends out and I quite frankly

don't believe he was as poor as that. And that was part of the legend about himself that he began to create.

He also writes that he felt he was ugly. Did the boys around him think that he was ugly?

No, I don't think so, but I know he rather made a point of saying [that] he was ugly. But I always thought he did it rather almost with enjoyment. And he wasn't. Most boys at that age are apt to be pretty ugly, except for one or two angel-faced ones. He wasn't ever good-looking, he was never beautiful, but I really cannot think that his looks ever affected his life except he chose to think so.

Your brother, Lord Runciman, was at Eton with you and Eric Blair. Did your brother tell you something about Eric Blair when you were back home?

No, because my brother was barely conscious of Eric Blair's existence.

Did Eric Blair sometimes come to stay with you?

No, he never did. I asked him more than once. Once he was going to come, but he never did. I don't in a way think he wanted to really. I don't think he liked being in an atmosphere which was very different from his. . . . I think Eric would have disliked feeling he had got to conform to – a code of manners is putting it perhaps a little bit too strongly – to the behaviour. And I think he would have felt a little bit out of place and therefore tempted to behave badly. And to be quite frank, I think I was rather relieved when he didn't come.

Could you tell me more about Aldous Huxley in your classroom at Eton? Did you have some private conversation, for instance, with Huxley after the class?

No. He was only too anxious to get away from us all. He hated it all. So much so that even in later days, when I used to see him fairly often, it was no good trying to get him to talk about it. It was a check on his life that he wanted to forget.

How did Eric Blair behave in Huxley's classroom?

Oh, he behaved perfectly courteously. He wasn't the one to behave badly. It wasn't his style to behave badly in the classroom. And also he rather stood up for Huxley because we found him interesting. . . . Huxley used phrases that rather impressed us. Eric was the only person I remember discussing Huxley's words with. I suppose we all were rather interested, but Eric certainly was. Whether it had any later effect in his writings, I don't know. He was interested in words at that time.

After Eton, Eric Blair went out to Burma to be a policeman. Did he tell you something about this rather unorthodox choice?

No. . . actually, I left Eton a year before he did. I got a scholarship to Cambridge . . . and I delightedly left Eton. Eric stayed on. I saw him only once or twice during that year. And then he was determined to go to Burma, and the Burma Police was those days quite a good job, quite a well-paid job. You started on quite a good salary, unlike a great many jobs and you started with what obviously attracted Eric, a certain amount of independence and responsibility. You were on your own quite a lot. And I think that was what attracted him. I always knew that he had no intention of going to the university. He had no wish to. And again all this talk of him being too poor to go to university . . . that was all nonsense. He wanted to go to the East. He had a sort of sentimental side. This nostalgia for the East which he can hardly have remembered.

But Miss Jacintha Buddicom writes that really Eric Blair wanted to go to Oxford but his father was adamant and did not allow him to follow his study at Oxford.

I don't think that was true. Eric rather took the line of slightly despising us for going on to the university.

But was it not his rationalisation?

It may have been that, but I don't necessarily think so. He used to talk about going to the East. I'm very doubtful whether he really wanted to go to the university. I don't think he did.

Eton Days with George Orwell

Denys King-Farlow (1903–82) entered Eton in the same year as Orwell in the College, the House for the scholars and scholarship boys. He was later an executive in various international oil companies. The first part of the following is an unpublished account that he wrote in 1967 in reply to questions from Ian Angus about Orwell's schoolboy writings, when Ian Angus was editing *The Collected Essays* with Sonia Orwell. But by the time that he wrote this, he had not merely read Orwell's writings but several pieces about Orwell. I suspect that his references to Orwell's 'self-pity' and his 'sadistic side' are written with hindsight. The snapshots of Blair at Eton to which he refers are splendid and have been often reproduced, notably one of Eric in school uniform smoking: smoking alone could then have led to temporary expulsion, and to photograph the offence was real bravado.

The second part is an extract from King-Farlow's contribution to Rayner Heppenstall's BBC Third Programme production of 2 November 1960, 'George Orwell, a programme of recorded reminiscences'. The 'wet-bobs' referred to were those at Eton who chose rowing and other water sports, whereas the 'dry-bobs' were those who took field sports. OTC was the Officer's Training Corps.

Recently I came across a lot of long-lost snapshots taken on my 1A Kodak of contemporaries at Eton just before and after the end of World War I. Some show George Orwell – his real name, never changed by Deed Poll or Royal Licence, being Eric Arthur Blair – at the age of fifteen or sixteen. He arrived in College the same day as myself. From 1917 to 1921, he and I, two of seventy King's Scholars, shared with a really rather extraordinary generation, the munificence of the blessed Henry VI. Annual fees for tuition, lodging, board and recreational facilities totalled just under twenty-five pounds. 'Exorbitant,' Blair always insisted.

With these snapshots there was an *Election Times* dated 3 June 1918, a hand-written periodical brought out by Blair, myself and Roger Mynors, later brother-in-law to Sir Alec Douglas Home, who was knighted in 1963, for remoulding the New Testament nearer to his heart's desire. Contributors included Steven Runciman, later historian-diplomat, also knighted, in 1958, a shyly genial host envied for invariably procuring fine weather for his annual garden party: and Bobbie Longden, who was probably the best-liked, certainly the best-looking of the Oxford dons, during the thirties, and who was killed Headmastering Wellington in a 1940 air-raid.

Sixpence was charged to members of our Election, which was fourteen strong, for perusing this magazine (editorial, stories, verse, correspondence column, illustrations). The return seems rather laughable contrasted with the £128 that Blair and I netted from publishing *College Days* No. 4, heavy with snob-appeal advertisements, in 1920 for the Eton-Harrow Match at Lord's. Nostalgic names from half a century away, 'The Hot Spot Chalmers America's Favourite Six', 'De Reszke, the Aristocrat of Cigarettes', 'Erasmic Shaving Stick', 'The Sizaire-Berwick Automobile', 'Palmer Cord Tyres – the highest price tyres – and deservedly so' – and of course, 'Pears Soap'.

We inherited *College Days*, launched in 1919, with contributions, written and drawn by both of us, from our considerate senior, George Binney, who was later to direct United Steel, having won his knighthood (1941) and DSO (1944) in World War II.

Several snapshots show bathing parties at Athens, where the Thames runs fast and deep round a sharp bend, opposite Windsor race course. Blair loved swimming (as appears often in his writing) but never bothered about swimming or diving with any style. Always obsessed with smells, he claimed Athens had a subtly delicious exhalation of its own. Apart from swimming and fives, Blair in 1919 was unenthusiastic about games – but he loved to go fishing for pike in Jordan (a small tributary of the Thames) – at Eton then not at all an approved pastime. He was also rather a good shot with the service rifle of that era in the school Officers' Training Corps, a useful training for shooting that mad elephant, years later in Lower Burma and, years later still, for the Aragon front. At just sixteen, Blair would insist, self-pitying, that, although 5 feet 7 inches, he was undersized and puny. By summer 1921, he had filled out and grown fully 8 inches! This considerably altered his attitude towards athletics and, before leaving Eton, he played for College at the Wall. On the compulsory football field, he sometimes showed the sadistic streak that was normally confined to spiteful truculence in conversation – the will to give offence and to really hurt. Blair's extraordinary physical growth was something I myself watched with envious amusement. . . .

Blair, knowing [Cyril] Connolly from preparatory school, hoped the new association might alleviate Connolly's unhealthy snob obsessions. He warned we could expect to hear plenty from Connolly about a 'Connolly' (*probably no family connection*) who married in 1758 the second Duke of Richmond's third daughter. We did. In 1936, I met Blair again after fifteen years. He mentioned casually that his really tough time a few years before had become tolerable only through Connolly's encouragement and practical sympathy. . . .

Proficient cricketers welcoming occasional non-serious games with wet-bobs included Chris Hollis (Conservative MP for Devizes 1945 to 1955). His quickfire banter to encourage catch-dropping or stroke mistiming was as enlivening as anything heard in the Commons after 1945 or read in *Punch* even after Chris joined its Board; and John Wilkes, another brother-in-law to Sir Alec but rumoured to have declined three offers of a mitre.

He was a man capable of smiling with sincere good humour at 'Such, Such Were the Joys', Orwell's ferocious pillorying of John's parents' stewardship of a would-be fashionable preparatory school, beside which Connolly's outrageous account of the school in *Enemies of Promise* seems lenient caricature. Jackie O'Dwyer, birched by the Headmaster for idleness (this was a rare experience among Collegers), was later reported to have become the model of a modern major-general. In these non-serious games, Blair (pseudo-wet-bob) sometimes batted and fielded with unsuspected expertise. . . .

In 1920 Dadie Rylands brilliantly produced *Twelfth Night*, the first play staged in College for many years, in which Rylands was an unforgettable boy Viola. Blair derided the venture but at the last moment agreed to be a non-speaking 'officer'. In 1921 he was easily co-opted a 'shepherd' for our *Winter's Tale*. . . .

Comrades with Blair on Spanish battlefields and in the St John's Wood Home Guard have commended not his military efficiency but the excellence of his military mucking-in ability. As early preparation for this, Blair's Eton experience included the modest rigours of two OTC camps on Salisbury Plain. In College he always enjoyed playing the lone wolf: so it seemed odd to discover that he was such an admirable stablemate under dripping canvas.

With some exaggeration, Blair wrote, 'I did no work there' (at Eton). That he did not share O'Dwyer's experience was thanks to Andrew Gow. This quiet but dynamic young Fellow of Trinity, Cambridge, was Blair's tutor (Director of Studies) and, mercifully, mine. Gow recognised in the stubborn, wilfully unattractive embryo-Orwell qualities for which most other masters had no time, finding him indolent and often 'dumb insolent'. He set out to encourage and make Blair compose, not the weekly essays exacted by most tutors, but fables, short stories, accounts of things liked and detested.

Blair himself seldom admitted to any warmth for Grannie Gow ('*praeceptor idemque amicus*'), disparaging his love of Homer as sentimentality, his erudition in Italian painting (Gow later became a Trustee of the National Gallery) as escapist posing. One of his ribald songs dealt also with obvious physical targets in 'm'tutor', tufts on the cheeks in the naval manner, a characteristically cautious way of sitting down:

Then up waddled Wog and he squeaked in Greek:
'I've grown another hair on my cheek.'

Crace replied in Latin with his toadlike smile:
'And I hope you've grown a lovely new pile.'
With a loud deep fart from the bottom of my heart:
'How d'you like Venetian art?'

Crace was the Master in College, whom Blair always treated with barely concealed contempt. . . .

TRANSCRIPT OF THE BBC PROGRAMME MADE BY RAYNER HEPPEN-STALL

In June 1936 I did at last get round to dropping him a line and invited him to come to a birthday party. He replied rather touchingly.

> Of course I remember you. I only got your letter this morning. I'm afraid I can't possibly come along on the eleventh much as I would like to. First of all, because it's always difficult for me to get away from here; secondly, because like the chap in the New Testament, I have married a wife and therefore cannot come. Curiously enough, I am getting married this very morning. In fact, I am writing this with one eye on the clock and the other on the Prayer Book, which I've been studying for some days past in hopes of steeling myself against the obscenities of the wedding service. When exactly I'll be up in town I don't know. This place, The Stores, Wallington, near Baldock, Herts., as you see, used to be the village general shop and when I came here I reopened it as such. The usual little shop stocking groceries, sweets, packets of aspirins, etc., it doesn't bring in very much, but it does pay my rent for me and for a literary gent that is a consideration. On the other hand, it makes it very difficult to get away from here, but if you're ever passing anywhere near, do drop in. It's not much off your track if you're going anywhere in a north-easterly direction or, e.g., to Cambridge. I should always be at home, except on Saturday afternoons or sometimes on Sundays. I should love to see you again. I hear you've been in the USA a long time and are very rich and flourishing. I've had a bloody life a good deal of the time, but in some ways an interesting one. Please excuse this untidy scrawl. Yours, Eric A. Blair

I left a decent interval to allow for his honeymoon and then I drove down one Sunday to the village, which I found a couple of miles off the main road from London to Cambridge and quite out of sight of the road, set in a rolling sort of agricultural country, very few trees about. The Stores was a typical village shop and there was in the garden and on the verge by the road-side, room for a couple of goats and also for geese and chickens which he and his wife were rearing. He came out and croaked a warm welcome at me in that curious voice of his that I remember very well, rather bored and slightly apologetic. He'd shot up another couple of inches after he'd left school and gone out East. I should think he was about six foot four; he was burnt a deep brown and looked terribly weedy, with his loose, shabby corduroys and grey shirt.

His wife, Eileen, came out too. She was pretty and dark-haired . . . I thought she had rather an Irish look. I think we then had some cold lunch and some very good pickles that Blair and his wife were very proud of, that they'd made together, and then Blair offered to take me for a walk. He began to tell me about a new hobby he'd just embarked upon and that was prison visiting. As he'd been a Police officer in Burma, of course, it had been easy to get appointed as a prison visitor, but he'd only done one visit so far. He said quite kindly that he supposed a lot of what he was saying must be quite incomprehensible to me, who probably never had to work outside a comfortable office and never had to do a job of any sort with my hands. I asked him whether he'd ever had to do any work with his hands, apart from washing a few dishes in French restaurants, which I'd read about in his book. I didn't regard traipsing about England as a tramp as manual labour. Still less living in comfort in a miner's family imbibing local colour. He said, well, he had done quite a number of odd jobs with his hands from time to time, and he was, of course, now running this store and raising chickens. I said I'd raised chickens since I was a boy and I never regarded that as manual labour, and then I went on with some pleasure to tell him that when I first went out to Texas, I had worked for two years in the oilfields as an oil roustabout, doing every sort of odd job as a tool dresser, then as a driller's help, then as a truck driver and later a much softer job, working as a service station attendant.

I used to come down to see him on Sundays several times and I was very much interested in what he had to say about what was going on in Spain. There was a bit of a gap and then he dropped me a line one day, saying that he was going to do some journalism abroad, saying, 'I leave you to guess.'

One day I was going down to Cambridge and I thought I'd call in – oh months and months after, and look up and see if there was any news of Blair, see if perhaps he'd come back. And I found Eileen at the stores, entirely by luck. She'd come down for the day and was apparently packing up, the geese had been sold and the goats and the chickens gone to somebody else and she was really locking up the whole place. She told me that they'd both been out in Spain and that Blair had been wounded in the throat in some engagement and had had a very bad time in hospital. He got away, I gather, with her help, with great luck, while still wounded, into France. Blair, was, she told me, in a sanatorium down in Kent, somewhere near Bearsted. She gave me the address, which was at the old Victorian stately home of Lord Bassie, a terrific place looking rather like St Pancras station. And there I went one day, with my wife, and with my father and mother who remembered Blair very well at school, when we'd been out together on various outings.

I don't think they would have been very pleased at some of the things that he'd said about them after they'd taken him out to lunch or tea when we'd been at school.

He seemed to be recovering rapidly and really in pretty good form. He'd always had a rather peculiar voice and now as a result of this trouble with his throat, he spoke very huskily and he wasn't allowed to raise his voice. He wrote to me once or twice from the sanatorium and then I had a line from Eileen in London, who told me that after having recovered apparently pretty thoroughly, he'd had a sudden relapse and was again in a sanatorium. I went down with my wife and looked him up. After that, I had some meetings with Eileen, but I didn't see Blair again until the outbreak of war. He came to see if I could help him get some work of national importance because he felt that with his background in Spain, having fought on the left side, he was rather a suspected person. He'd been refused for the Army and for any sort of service. We all went home and had some drinks together and soon after that, I'm glad to say, I got my call-up and went to France. I got out of France in June after the French had declared an Armistice. He turned up the day that I returned to London. We had some very amusing times together. I did meet him once afterwards at the Westminster Theatre when on leave, but that was about the end of my friendship with Blair. After the war, I had hoped to see a lot of him, but like a lot of those things, that didn't come about.

At the Crammers

Mr R. G. Sharp (b. 1905) sent me this letter in 1972, describing the period when he was a fellow pupil with Eric Blair at a crammers in Southwold. 'Little go' was the traditional name for the first part of the BA examination at Cambridge or Oxford. The reference to the rat is almost the first time we came across the animal which Orwell used often in his writings.

In January 1922, at the age of sixteen-and-a-half, I went to a coaching establishment: Craighurst, Southwold, Suffolk to be 'crammed' for 'Little go'. . . . Eric Blair, whose father – I think he was a retired Indian Civil Servant (anyway he had been for years in India in some civil capacity) – lived in Southwold with his wife, son and daughter and Blair (I think that I had better stick to his surname and one never used Christian ones in those days) was being coached for the Indian Police. Rather odd, perhaps, for one who had been a King's Scholar of Eton as the Indian Police exam was, I imagine, not much harder than 'Little go'; but it may have been that he was weak in Maths. . . .

Towards the end of the summer term of 1922, Blair and a rather wild young man who had, I think, been expelled from Malvern, somehow fell foul of the Borough Surveyor, Mr Hurst by name, and, I don't know how, found out the date of his birthday. By way of a present they sent him a dead rat with birthday greetings and signing their names. Poor old Philip Hope [headmaster of Craighurst] . . . decided to make an example of them both, and they were expelled. This didn't worry Blair at all: he was living at home, had passed his exam, and was just 'ticking over' till term ended.

. . . I have always thought that the above story was a bit out of keeping with Blair's character, but I may well be wrong as I think he had, in fact I know, a very determined streak in him. My mother went to live in Southwold and I saw him when he returned from Burma in, I think, 1927, but I don't remember any special conversation and I never saw him again.

Blair was very tall, very shy, as I have said, and rather untidily dressed. Although I am going back a great number of years, I can still remember his voice: a kind of quaver in it, and he was slow and deliberate of speech. . . . I also remember Blair's father, a rather meek and mild sort of man who must have been horrified when his son left the Indian Police.

An Old Burma Hand

Roger Beadon (1901–76) met Eric Blair in the Training School of the Burma Police. He plainly thought that Orwell's novel *Burmese Days* had let the side down. There was something odd about an old Etonian being in such a second-rate part of the Imperial service, and he distrusted Orwell's interest in the natives and native languages.

Beadon was interviewed on 5 December 1969 by Pamela Howe of the BBC, Bristol, and the following is taken from the full transcript of the broadcast.

In 1922 having passed into the Indian Police – my father being in Burma – I chose to go to Burma. I went out to the Mandalay Training School. I was actually a fortnight earlier than the other two gentlemen who came and so later I went down to meet them at the railway station. There was Eric A. Blair, who we now know as George Orwell, and a fellow called Jones. After we met them we took them back to the mess, and that's how I first came up against Blair.

We were known as probationary police, assistant superintendents of police, we had one pip and thought ourselves very important. This would have been soon after Blair had left Eton, I think. . . . He didn't speak very much about his past. I mean, he was very quiet.

What was your impression of him?

Well he always looked as if his clothes would never hang on to him properly, he was long and thin and always, I felt, rather lugubrious, very tall for his age. You couldn't make him tidy however hard you tried. He was a very pleasant fellow to know, but kept very much to himself. I was very fond of going down to the club and playing snooker and dancing and what have you, but this didn't seem to appeal to him at all. He was not what I would call a socialite in any way; in fact I don't think Blair went to the club very much.

What did he do in his spare time?

Read mostly. He stayed up in his room and read or possibly had a few drinks in the mess in the evening. I don't remember him being one of the bright boys of the club, or anything like that.

Did you in fact have much to do with him socially?

We were in the police mess and that naturally meant we saw each other every day; we attended instructions in Law, Burmese and

Hindustani, and we used to do an hour's Burmese and then have to switch straight over to Hindustani which we found a little difficult. But what shattered me more than anything else was that, whereas I found it very difficult, it didn't seem to worry him at all. I mean, when we should have been attending class, Blair was probably up in bed reading; so whether he had a flair for continental languages or rather Eastern languages, I don't know, but he certainly could speak it extremely well because I'm told that before he left Burma, he was able to go into a Hpongyi Kyaung which is one of these Burmese temples and converse in very high-flown Burmese with the Hpongyis, or priests, and you've got to be able to speak very well to be able to do that.

The two of you went on one or two trips, didn't you?

I had a small two-stroke motor-bike and Blair had an American one; a most incredible looking thing, I'd never seen the like of it before. It was very low, and he was about 6 foot 6 and when he sat on it his knees came up round his chin.

Once we were in Fort Dufferin, which is the square mile fort in Mandalay and we wanted to get out. I suddenly realised that one of the gates wasn't open, so I shouted, 'Look out! This one isn't open,' and pulled up, but he didn't react, he didn't quite know what to do. I don't think he was very mechanically minded, so he just stood up and the bike just went straight on between his legs and hit the gate. However, no damage done.

And then another time I said, 'Would you like to come out for a tiger shoot?' He thought it was a good idea. Heaven knows what made me do it, but I had a Luger Parabellum Automatic and we borrowed the Principal's shot-gun and went out about fourteen miles from Mandalay and asked a man if we could borrow his bullock cart because we wanted to go after tiger. The gentleman very kindly produced his bullock cart, it must have been about nine o'clock at night, and as dark as you could make it. We got into the back of the cart and he drove round about, me with my Parabellum cocked and Blair with the other gun. But we didn't see a tiger and I had a sort of feeling that the gentleman in charge of the bullock cart never intended that we should. I think if we had, possibly Mr Blair or Orwell would not have existed and I don't suppose I should either.

Another time my father, who was, of course, in Burma and had been for many years, came up to Maymyo, which was the hill station. I got leave to go up and I asked Eric Blair to come up with me, and we had quite a pleasant time; we played golf and we went down to the club, but you know he didn't mix very much. I mean, we enjoyed ourselves but, as I say, I was probably very extrovertish and he was probably entirely the opposite. I don't suppose we really had very intelligent conversations beyond what was going on and why, and when we were going to be posted and whether we should get through the exams and just the ordinary sort of run of events that one does. I don't think we ever got on to a very high-flown level. I mean, I certainly wouldn't have thought that he was a person who was going to write or anything like that, at least not in those days . . . and it came as a complete shock to me when I read his *Burmese Days* and realised that it was the same chap.

Was this when you first realised that the Eric Blair you knew was George Orwell?

Well, of course, *Burmese Days* was rather an extraordinary book, I mean, it was to me. I read it with my tongue in my cheek and thoroughly enjoyed it because from what I can make out he obviously was rather 'agin' everybody and I don't think he cared very much for the Europeans. He thought that most of the Burmese were corrupt, which is rather unfair – although again, some of them were. And he seemed to have picked up all the bad ones he could find and pushed them into one district which, of course, was an impossibility, and made a very good story out of it. I may say, however, that Mr Stewart, our Principal, who's a big Scotsman who didn't drink and didn't smoke – he was about 6 foot with a large moustache – was first class when we had a mess night. I mean, he was in the thick of the scrum on lemonade. How he did it I don't know, but I'm told that when he read this book he went livid and said that if he ever met that young man he was going to horse-whip him.

There must be a lot of people like yourself who have by chance met somebody in their youth who later became famous and I wonder if looking back now you can honestly remember anything about him which indicated that he might become a great radical writer?

No, I honestly can't, but I can see possibly why, say, he turned in the way he did, because whether I'm right or wrong, I have a feeling that he had to serve in one district – and I couldn't tell you which it was – under a certain District Superintendent of Police, who treated him very badly. I think that this fellow was rather an extrovertish type himself while Eric was very retiring. They were as different as chalk and cheese, and he took it out of Eric and that was, I think, the main reason why he chucked it and left the police in 1927. The only other time I met him was when he was down as headquarters assistant in Insein, and I went there and as far as I can remember he had goats, geese, ducks and all sorts of things floating about downstairs, whereas I'd kept rather a nice house. It rather shattered me, but apparently he liked that . . . it didn't worry him what the house looked like and as for female company, I don't honestly think I ever saw him with a woman; he certainly was not like me – I had an eye for anything that was going – but I can't say that I think he did.

When you read Burmese Days *you didn't think of writing to him?*

I read *Burmese Days* out in Burma, I think, and in those days when it came out, I didn't even know where he was or why he was or what he was. But I felt, well, fancy old Eric Blair, just like him, and I think that's about as far as I went. So as far as I was concerned, to find that George Orwell was Eric A. Blair, as I say, was rather like seeing a flying saucer arrive at your front door and wondering what it's going to do.

An Evening on the Verandah

L. W. Marrison (1901–81), research chemist and noted writer on wine, was employed by the Burmah Oil Company, where he had this chance encounter with Eric Blair which he recalled in a letter to me dated 24 October 1972.

I met George Orwell briefly in 1924 and although my memories of him are trivial and our conversation trivial, I offer you them for what they are worth.

I was a young chemist (eighteen months older than Blair) employed by the Burmah Oil Company; I arrived in Burma in April 1924. It was some time in the summer of that year that De Vine and Blair, two policemen, were so to speak billeted with me. . . . This was at Syrian, the BOC refinery and tank farm village near Rangoon (but separated from it by the Rangoon River). De Vine and Blair would normally have stayed at the dak bungalow, but this was for some reason not available and the oil company offered them accommodation. They stayed with us for only a few days and of those De Vine was, after the first night, usually absent.

De Vine, a tall, dark, lean man with a strong aquiline nose, was Blair's superior and introduced Blair to us as 'a highly educated sort of chap, ha, yes. Blair was eaten and brought up – ha, sorry, brought up at Eton.' Blair took this with the sort of blank expression which indicated that he had heard it before. I imagine De Vine and he, although obviously incompatible, got on reasonably well, for De Vine seemed to me no worse than rather insensitive. (Here you are depending on the judgement of a very callow youth, remembered after nearly fifty years.)

That first evening we (Blair and De Vine, the two other chemists – J. A. Sutherland and H. S. McLeod – and myself) sat on the verandah in pyjamas after dinner, drinking and singing. That singing was quite unusual and was, I think, started by Blair. I am not a singing man and I can remember only one of the songs – the student song about 'zipping Zyder through a straw-haw-haw'. One remark of Blair's I do remember distinctly: he deplored the fact that 'there weren't any good bawdy songs about nowadays'. He did give me the impression that he was a very typical public school boy . . . devoid of snobbery, but with a slight pose of nonchalance under all circumstances, deprecating enthusiasm.

He told me he wanted to get in some revolver practice and asked me if I would like to go with him. We found some waste land and a tin can and started. As I remember (but I hesitate to be very positive) he wasn't a very good shot and the practice did not last long. My recollection is that he was piqued that I was a better shot than he. . . .

I had been reading a novel by Aldous Huxley (*Chrome Yellow*) and a year or two before, I had been considerably impressed by *Leda*. Blair made no literary judgements that I remember, or betrayed any desire or determination to write himself; he told me two facts that I didn't know – that Huxley had been a master at Eton and that he was nearly blind. We did not discuss writing as a career.

He showed no sign of holding any particular sociological or political views, and I never saw or heard from him afterwards. . . .

If I may be permitted an observation of my own, I would say that there are two sorts of reformers: those whose sense of justice is outraged, and those whose hearts bleed, and I think Blair's heart did not bleed except in such extreme situations as the death of the elephant.

'He Didn't Really Like Women'

Brenda Salkeld (b. 1903) met Orwell in 1928, after his return from Burma, at Southwold where she worked as a gym mistress. They became good friends and remained friendly for the rest of his life, though they often did not see eye to eye on important matters. She admired the writings and philosophy of George Bernard Shaw and was a firm rationalist, while Orwell professed to think that Shaw was shallow, and plainly had some ambivalences about religion at that time, which he concealed from her. Some of Orwell's best extant letters are to Brenda Salkeld.

She recorded this for Rayner Heppenstall's BBC Third Programme of 1960.

I think it was before 1929 that I met Eric, but I really got to know him in 1929, when his family were living at 2 Queen Street, in Southwold. There was the father, rather a charming old boy, and the mother, fond of bridge, and Eric and Avril. The other sister married and was away with a family at Middlesmore up in Yorkshire, and she occasionally came down. Then later they left this house – it's now turned into a dress-shop – and they lived at 36 High Street, Montague House.

I was working in Southwold, but my home was at Bedford. What we used to do mostly was to go for long walks, talking – discussing books, like *Ulysses*, and he would rail against Roman Catholicism. But we used to bird-watch as well; we used to take my field glasses and once we were walking back across a railway – a disused railway bridge across the Blyth river – and the glasses slipped out of his hand, dropped into the river, which was tidal of course, and I had to stand on one of these precarious sleepers, while he went down and waded into the water almost to his waist to find the glasses. We did find them eventually. He had very good eyesight and really could watch these birds from very long distances. There was a Roman barrow on the common, and he got permission to dig it, but they found nothing except a soldier's button which was appropriately made of bronze. Another thing we talked about, what would happen if you ever got entirely lost on some moor. If you were cut off from food by some enemy you would have to grow your own vegetables – he was very keen on a vegetable garden. Of course, he never grew flowers, and I remember that he grew an enormous vegetable marrow which he'd fattened up for the local harvest festival. He was very fond of swimming and the early summer always tempted him in, but it was always terribly cold and far too cold for me to enjoy bathing, so he used to rather crow that he could get in before I could, though he said women had far more fat on them than men and so wouldn't suffer from the cold. We also went riding occasionally, but he rather disapproved of my playing golf, though his father was very keen on golf.

He never understood people. He didn't really like women; I used to bring up the women who I thought were good writers, and he would very occasionally praise their writing, but he used to say it stuck in his throat to have to do it. . . . He was a sadist and that was why he had this feeling towards women. He was tone deaf; he didn't enjoy music or concerts; in fact, he always had something rather against musical people altogether. . . .

He was summing up his life at twenty-eight – financially, of course – and he said that through writing he'd made a hundred pounds, and through teaching or tutoring, he'd made 200 pounds, and dish-washing twenty pounds; other jobs, twenty. In the Indian Police he'd made 2000, but he hated it, and he thought perhaps if he could find something he really loathed still more, he might become quite rich.

He really felt he ought to get down and really know what life was like without anything so he became a tramp and walked about; one time he turned up at my home at Bedford in the morning, having stayed in the local workhouse. We gave him a bath before he came to breakfast. But, of course, we always argued about this, because he said he was getting to know what it was like to be a tramp, but I felt quite certain that just putting on tramp's clothes and walking, does not make you a tramp because you knew you could always get back home; that it was the attitude of mind that was much more important.

I remember when his first book *Down and Out* was accepted, he wrote saying: 'Do hold your thumbs to be sure it's a success – and by that I mean 4000 copies.'

'Like a Cow with a Musket' or 'We cruel girls laughed'

Ruth Pitter (b. 1897), the poet, described Orwell as being 'like a cow with a musket' when he first tried to write, but she was impressed by his perseverance and eventual mastery of English prose. She was a friend of the Blairs and especially of Marjorie, Eric's older sister. Orwell had met her briefly before going to Burma and then sought her help to find a cheap room in London when he returned there in 1928. She and her friend found him a room next to their pottery workshop in the Portobello Road.

The first part of the following is from a tape-recording made of an interview which I conducted with her in 1974; the second extract is from a BBC Overseas broadcast made in 1956.

Well, he was seventeen as I dare say you know, when I first met him. I knew at once that he was an interesting person. He told me afterwards – he looked at me with his keen look, he had a very keen look – his eyes were an exact pair – he told me afterwards with all the impudence of Eton – Eton for ever when it comes to impudence – he was only seventeen and I was twenty-two – 'I wonder if that girl would be hard to get. . . .'

So you first met him when he was a schoolboy at Eton?

Yes. It all came quite casually in the way of social contacts you know. A lifelong friend and former business partner had a flat in Notting Hill Gate. They were working-class flats – the earliest block of working-class flats in London. The architect built them to accommodate his work people when he was building the Albert Hall. They were called Mall Chambers. Now, put yourself on the spot in your imagination. You turned out of Church Street and were approaching Mall Chambers. You stop when you get to it and there is (or was) a sort of alley on your left called Rabbit Row. And the ground floor flat on that corner is where I first saw Eric Blair. His sister and her husband owned a little flat – they were only a few bob a week but we were all so poor then. It was my friend's parents who recommended that the Blairs go to Southwold, and so they did. And then, of course, as soon as he left school he went off to Burma and I didn't see him again until the end of his first five-year stint and then, of course, he chucked it. He was pretty sick then. And he wrote and asked me if I could find him a cheap lodging. We found him one in the old Portobello Road, next door to our workshop, with a mews at the back. It was awful – I'm sure it's gone now. Oh, he must have been uncomfortable, he wasn't well, and after the heat of Burma it was as cold as charity. They were only thin buildings, you know, with no source of heat. He would sometimes warm his hands at a candle before he would start to write.

And do you know, he wrote so badly. He had to teach himself writing, he was like a cow with a musket; it was sheer hard grind. He put in a fair number of rude words in those days, and I had to correct the spelling for him. You would think an old Etonian would know every rude word and a few more. But he certainly couldn't spell the London rude words correctly.

And we lent him an old oil stove and he started to write a story about two fine girls who lent a writer an oil stove! Oh dear, how we cruel girls laughed. But people were inclined to laugh at him then.
What else was he writing about?
I remember one story that never saw the daylight. It began '*Inside* the park the crocuses were *out.*' Oh dear, I'm afraid we did laugh. But we knew he was kind because he was so good with our old sick cat. And we used to ask him for a meal occasionally. I've thought recently, oh dear, why didn't we ask him oftener, but I think, you know, we tended to look on the Blairs as rather tatty. Nellie Limouzin [Orwell's aunt] also lived in the Portobello Road. Yes, I remember we went to supper with Aunt Nellie once. Ooh, what a supper it was. She was living with some old Anarchist, I think. She was a coughdrop. She gave us some fearsome dish such as one would have in Paris if one was a native Parisian and dreadfully hard up. You know the sort of thing? Oh dear, poor old Aunt Nellie.
Coughdrop? I don't think I know that one.
It means *type.* You know the sort of thing. A person is a coughdrop, or a proper cure.
I wonder why he came straight to you when he came back from Burma to get him a room. . . .
I don't remember. I remember feeling rather surprised that he had written to me. But you see, he knew we lurked round there, and people knew Mall Chambers, and so we were likely people to know of something in the vicinity. Handy for Aunt Nellie and all that. It was the neighbourhood probably that made him write to us.
I suppose he thought of you as a model of a young writer, did he? Did he look up to you as someone who had already been published?
No, I think he felt a bit snooty. You see, I'm rather an Establishment poet, and all right with David Cecil and all right with Rab Butler – people like that. I've been in the mainstream of tradition to them, you see. You ask Dr Leavis and you'll know all the difference. Ha, that's why I kept away from the current literary scene, because I'd got just that much intuition, that's the way it went; what on earth is the use of grafting it into another stream

of thought and feeling – which is all you've got. Keep away, don't get bent if it's all you've got.

But he was in that sense a very traditional writer himself. . . .

That's what I always saw. His socialism was a kind of conscience socialism. So many young men with his kind of education went that way, didn't they?

When he came back from Burma, did he talk politics? Did you think he was a socialist then?

I didn't see all that much of him. My friend didn't fancy him that much; having chucked his Burma job filled us all with holy horror. It was like turning down a cheque for 5000 or 10,000 pounds. His mother had thrown everything, all she had, into getting him up to be somebody in the British Raj, which was already crumbling. You see, her people were in love with Burma. Her own people settled there. His father had been in the Burma Police [sic] and his mother had had him too cruelly crammed, as we know, to go to that particular prep school which was so good at getting scholarships, so he got to be a King's Scholar at Eton – in those days we rather looked down on scholars; though not now. Altogether we thought it was a scruffy thing to do. And anyhow, Mrs Blair was not a conciliating person, you know, Mrs Blair was very kind to anyone poorer than herself, but if you had tuppence more, God help you.

What sort of person was she?

She was very intelligent . . . but was she widely read? – that's what I don't know. But I do know she had a very penetrating wit. There's no doubt any satirical, any attacking moods in her son would have come from her rather than his old man. Because although he had a deep-seated grudge against life, and I know he had, there was nothing militant about him in any way, old Mr Blair. But Mrs Blair was different. She was small and dark and, don't forget, half French. And you know how militant they can be! So she had dark eyes and hair, thin features, and an acute mind. Her degree of culture I never knew, but it was an acute mind. Oh, but we did enjoy her society; there were occasions when she has given one a jolly good meal and she was a jolly good cook, too. I was young and poor and I think there was a bit of snobbery on my own part, because coming from the suburbs as I did, I thought them very grand people and thought an Old Etonian a very grand person. My father was a schoolmaster in the East End, you know. So this to me was rather dazzling society. I was rather enamoured of it than otherwise. . . .

I can't have received more than half a dozen letters from him in my life and those apparently I did not keep. I think they must have been very short, the merest notes. I lost touch with him at the beginning of the war, I think. He got in with a very different set of people. Not that the set of people mattered to me at all, but my 'in touch' with him depended much more on the family and social relationships than his friends whose interests he really shared. He still asked me to go out with him now and then. I remember those times. Yes, I don't think it was often, and there was a great deal of misery to it because he never had sufficiently warm clothes on. Going out in all weathers without so much as a muffler, you know. He had several attacks of pneumonia but he seemed to get over them in the end.

I remember going to see him in hospital – that was before the penicillin days; it was somewhere Ealing way, when he had that schoolmastering job, and dreary to get at – and I remember the sister telling me this ward full of men with pneumonia, that those with red faces were ill and going to die, all those with pale faces would get over it. He had four or five pneumonias altogether. He paid no heed. Really, it was as if he had a death wish. This annoyed my common sense, this annoyed my affection too, because I had a great affection for him. I always loved interesting people. I remember saying to my father once 'I wish interesting people were not such freaks', and when one feels one has a bit of talent oneself and yet never asked for any tolerance, you know, paddles one's own canoe, it annoys one to see others going on like that. You know, he would go out and hadn't any money, and was fit to die of chagrin if I put my hand in my pocket and put money in his hand. He hated it, poor soul.

There's a long passage in one of his novels (Coming Up for Air) *where he goes for a walk in the country with a girl and then they decide to get a cup of tea and the only cup of tea is in a pretentious place – a set tea – so he had to borrow money to get home.*

Must have been that time. There was thin, melting snow on the ground and we went for an awful long walk all around the countryside. . . .

What impressions did you form of him then? Was he a young man obsessed with an older girl, or a man who liked many girls?

Oh, I don't think he was obsessed with me. I didn't see enough of him for that to be true . . . a straightforward sexual attraction, you know. If he was obsessed he would have been round oftener. I think he thought of me as a person, someone sufficiently distinctive to be interesting, quite apart from other considerations. I had a tenderness for him but never forgot the gap, the age gap. I was born in 1897 and he was born in 1903. A girl of that age was much more grown up.

What did he look like then?

Rather intimidating. I remember him coming back to Portobello when we had got him his lodging. He had several great valises, and was still wearing one of those great spreading hats. Made him look very imposing, a great spreading hat like that, yes, and the children in the street followed him. Much he cared, this straight Swordsman look from under that great imposing hat – you know, 6 foot 3! He looked defiantly at us and brought his great bulging valises into our workshop to unpack – there was no room in his little room. He defied us to laugh – you know, he was always like that, he would defy people to think him funny.

In his tramping days he left his traps at our workshop and would sometimes send for them *poste restante*. He came to change into his rags at our workshop once or twice. He looked daggers at me as if to say laugh if you dare! But we did laugh a lot. In fact a sister of mine called him the Dirty Beau. I came across a letter from her the other day in which she said, 'I see young Dirty has had a very good review. . . .'

What did you think of his tramping?

I thought he was doing it at society in general. And I always thought there was one thing he missed. It was the sporting spirit of really poor people. Because when you were as poor as people were then, you haven't much to lose, you can't fall very far. Life might turn up trumps, even if only in a small way, so you were rather like Mr Micawber; and he made great tragedy of their lives, much greater than they would have made themselves of it. Poor people on the whole were very devil-may-care, and if they could afford a trip to Southend, they'd go. They didn't take a tragic view of their lives at all.

A bit lacking in a sense of humour, was he?

A bit, yes, a bit. . . .

There's a paradox. Portraits of women in his novels are very flat, yet most of his best friends seemed to be women. He was never confidential with men.

He loathed old women, though, he said so. But there was one old woman he was rather pleased with. She let rooms, a Mrs Saddell. She was fabulous, like a rag picker who does a sideline in stolen goods. One of those bloated faces that look like they are made of something viscous. She was an old terror. I remember he came to see me sometimes and she said, 'Bring your boyfriend in, I want to see him.' So I took him in there and he seemed to like her very much. I was amazed at that. She said, 'He's like a long, very clean stick of celery – take him away and scrape him!' Poor soul. . . .

What did he say to you about his tramping?

He didn't say anything, just gave us that defiant look. We just took it for granted and sent the odd pair of socks when requested. . . . He came down once to a little cottage my family owned in Hainault Forest and I often think of that little, poor, decaying cottage right in the middle of the forest, and nobody there knows that this world-famous man slept there. It's very strange. He shared a bedroom with my brother, and afterwards my brother said that Eric's body was very beautiful. . . .

How often did you see him in the thirties?

We saw him at Southwold quite a bit. When he came back from Burma he wasn't at all well, he had a nasty foot. The old woman who lived next door used to be very kind and good to him, but he wasn't at all grateful to her, I thought. She bathed his foot for him and did it up.

Did you find that he was ever deliberately awkward or difficult?

He had a cruel streak, he could be spiteful. He could be very spiteful. He might give one a cruel pinch and he could say very cutting things too at times. Very true. His mother, you see, was waspish. He's bound to have inherited a touch of that. I think waspish is a fair description. . . .

EXTRACT FROM A BBC OVERSEAS BROADCAST

Gradually we saw less of Orwell, and then war came. I only saw him once between about 1935 and the time of his death in January 1950. It would be in the early autumn of 1942. By then, of course, he had been married for some years to Eileen O'Shaughnessy, who died before him. I had met her at the BBC, where he also was working, and she'd asked me to supper. They were living in a damp basement flat. She was worried about the rent – a hundred pounds a year – which she said they couldn't afford. He was known as a writer now, but not to the extent of getting much out of it. Eileen was a small, slender woman with nice Irish features and rather curly, dark hair. She told me about his recent illness – she had not realised what a sick man he was, and the sudden severe haemorrhage had terrified her. The last straw was that when he had been got off to hospital, she looked for the cat to hold in her arms for a little consolation, but it had disappeared, and she never saw it again. Eileen had been through a bad time, and was soon to die herself; she didn't have much of a share in Orwell's brief time of success. When he was wounded so badly in the Spanish War, she actually managed to get out there. She took a job in Barcelona and, I supposed, earned some sort of living for both of them. He would have had his army pay, too, of course.

While we were talking and working away at cooking supper that evening (I remember it was apple-pie, and she was nervously anxious not to leave a scrap of core in the apples, as she said he disliked it so), while we were working and talking, Orwell came in. Like a ghost. No doubt he was showing the effects of his recent illness, and of course he did live another seven or eight years, but I thought then that he must be dying. The emaciation, the waxen pallor, the slow, careful movements, all shocked and distressed me. But he seemed cheerful, fetched some beer, and went out again to see if his mother would come in – she was living close by. I had brought with me two things impossible to buy in London at that time – a good bunch of grapes from my mother's home in Essex, and a red rose – two rare treasures. I can see him now, holding up the grapes with a smile of admiration and delight on his face and then cupping the rose in his wasted hands, breathing in the scent with a kind of reverent joy.

That's the last vivid image I have of him. After that evening I never saw him again – I never knew him as the immensely successful author he became. How he did adore life! His nature was divided. There was something like a high wall right across the middle of it. A high wall with flowers and fruit and running water on one side, and the desert on the other. I think he was much more fastidious and conventional than one might think from his work – more than he knew himself. Not liking any core left in the apple-pie, for instance; and do you remember in *Down and Out in Paris and London* how he threw away the milk which was the only food he had, simply because a bed-bug had fallen into it? Too fastidious for a starving man. And his anger at the idea of letting a woman pay – that was very conventional.

His funeral was the orthodox Anglican ceremony, and he was buried by his own wish where he had passed his early youth.

Orwell's great virtue, it seems to me, was that he would not let things go by default, as we nearly all do. He threw all his forces into the battle for truth. Once he was convinced that we had no business in Burma, out he came – never mind the sacrifice of his career. Time-serving in any form he hated and rejected with all his force. His was a pure, scientific honesty which is very rarely found in literature.

75

Southwold Days

Dennis Collings (b. 1905) was a friend of Orwell from 1927 onwards; his father was the Blairs' family doctor. He read Anthropology at Cambridge and became assistant curator of the Raffles Museum in Singapore. He married Eleanor Jaques in 1934, another friend and correspondent of Orwell's.

This is an extract from the 1984 BBC TV *Arena* programme *Orwell Remembered*. He is interviewed by Nigel Williams.

Dennis Collings, there's an edition of Down and Out in Paris and London *in your bookshelf inscribed with many thanks for bothering to buy this book. Did you buy it?*
I don't really know, yet I must have done if it says so. Either I did or my wife did, I can't remember which. But it was, you know, one of Eric's . . . Oh, I'm sorry, George Orwell's.
Are they two different people?
Yes, they were two different people. Well there's Eric Blair and well, there's George Orwell, and somehow or other the George Orwell came to the top and even now I think of him as George Orwell rather than Eric Blair.
Can we talk about Eric Blair to start with. When did you first meet Eric Blair?
In 1920 soon after they came to Southwold. He'd come back from Burma and he was living with his parents and his uncle. I can't remember his name now, very nice man, who was on his mother's side – he lived in Queen's Street. And they all fitted in very nicely, you know. Southwold in those days was quite different to what it is now.
In what way?
Well there were people who lived here, did things, you know what I mean. Many more shops competing with each other and if you didn't like the price of a lettuce in one shop you could go to another one and get it a halfpenny cheaper and all that kind of thing.
You became friends with Eric Blair didn't you?
Yes.
What brought you together do you think?
Well, I don't know. It's just one of those things. We had things in common. He, of course, had been in Burma and myself in Africa . . . yes, I had been in Malaya then. The East, the Far East and all that kind of thing.

And did you agree about certain things concerning British rule out there?
Not altogether, no. I never did get to the bottom of what his
objections to it were because he seemed rather involved in this, it
was a very personal matter with him. And he was just 'agin' the
government a bit over it.

Did he speak about his experiences in Burma to you at all?
Oh yes, used to talk about when he went out as a cadet in the
police and of the things he had to do. He couldn't stand the
Buddhist monks because they were all very political. Burma is
the only part of the Far East where Buddhism is political. I think
he thought we ought not to be there but he was pro what we had
done for the country. The wars had finished and people had to
live in peace and security. And before that, you see, the various
tribes and nations in Burma were all fighting each other. And
when we went in of course that ended. There was a battle or
two . . . and everybody lived happily.

*But he speaks in one of his essays about hanging a man in Burma. Did
he talk to you about things he'd had to do as a policeman?*
Yes he mentioned that. That was one of the initiations they had
to go through when they first went there as cadets. It didn't refer
to him in particular, it was a sort of standard thing.

They all had to see a man hanged?
Yes, if there was one available. Some murderer or other dacoit or
somebody of that kind had been condemned and a cadet had to
be there. There had to be a police officer there in any case. And
the cadet was always assigned to that kind of thing.

You can remember Eric Blair telling you he'd had to shoot an elephant?
Yes, indeed, but he wasn't happy about it. He didn't like to have
to shoot the elephant, you know. He didn't want to take life. But
at the same time he knew he had to.

He liked animals didn't he?
Oh yes, he was very fond of them. He had a very gentle nature
and he was a very . . . mature kind of person.

*Did he say anything else about Burma? That experience seems to have
had a very strong effect on him.*
Yes, it did. He didn't like . . . well one of the things . . . was that
on arrival at your station you had to go out fully dressed with a
sword and God knows what, in a little horse-drawn carriage with
a driver, and you had to drop cards on all the people you ought to
drop cards on. It was literally a load of tosh. And yet on the other
hand it was a sort of initiation ceremony. . . We thought about
things. Both he and I, we wanted to know why, the whys and the
wherefores, of whatever was going on. And what we thought

should be and what we thought shouldn't be.

What did he think should be?

Well now, here again there's a great mystery, because, you see, he didn't really know what he thought should be. That was his trouble.

You mean he would talk to you about politics.

Yes. Oh we'd talk about politics but he hadn't got any substitute for the politics that were going on at the time or politics which might turn up in the future. He had no use for a Labour government for example.

Really?

None whatsoever. Because his idea was that they were not trained. They hadn't been brought up in the right way to run a government. If you could have got the right kind of well-trained leaders, that would have been all right.

It was during the time that he knew you, after he came back from Burma to Southwold, that he started to go off tramping, wasn't it? Can you tell me how that started, or how you came to know of it?

Well, he told me about it. He was a down-to-earth chap in many ways. And he felt he couldn't write about the down-and-outs unless he was one himself. So he became a down-and-out, to all intents and purposes. The famous time of sleeping on newspaper in Trafalgar Square, where people did all that kind of thing. He said how uncomfortable it was, he'd never do it again. Policemen kept coming along wanting to know who he was and moving him on to the next bench, you know, and you try to go to sleep and then somebody else would come along and move him. I don't know how he got his old clothes, but he got them, and he was on the tramp. He put up at the Spike at Blythburgh, which is now a sort of old folks' hospital or something. And he thought of coming on to Southwold and putting up at the White Horse which is just up the road and which was a tramps' workhouse, a tramps' lodging house. And then he thought, well no, I couldn't possibly do it, if my father were to see me it really would kill him. And so he never came.

Was he fond of his father?

Yes, oh yes. They were rather silent with each other, you know, there was not a lot of talk. But he was very fond of his family. And his sister was very nice, the younger sister that is. I hardly knew the elder sister. And Mrs Blair was very nice.

Did he talk to you about his writing at all?

Yes. He used to sit down at nine o'clock in a little back room, where there was a table and writing things, and he used to write till twelve. And at twelve o'clock he'd throw everything down and go out and have a beer. Well it didn't matter what he wrote as long as he wrote. He was forcing himself to write. Anything that came into his head he wrote it.

Did he show what he wrote to you?

No, I never saw that at all. But it was anything; it could be something he'd read in a paper or a thought that had come to him or a book he'd read, whatever it might be he would write about it. I had no literary ambitions and still haven't. But I think that there are some things that should be written. . . .

Did you lose sight of him after he went to London or did you still keep in touch with him?

Oh yes, yes. And the last time I saw him was when he was living at Wallington which is just outside London, in Hertfordshire. You got off the main road and you drove up this little lane that went straight up over the hill, and then over the other side was a little village and a very nice church. I've got a picture of him in the churchyard. And he had the village shop and he was selling everything he could sell. He was selling everything off so he wouldn't have anything more so it wouldn't be a shop any longer. And then the war came and I went back to the Far East. I didn't see him again after that.

But when he was in London did he talk to you about going to Spain?

Yes he did. But not so very much. Going to Spain, and fighting, was an eye opener to him. And he never realised the crookedness of his comrades.

Was he a humorous man?

No, no, he was not humorous. He took things rather seriously. And he was very factual you know. And of course he had that rather unpleasant time when he looked after a batty boy in Walberswick, who really was, poor child, he was incapable, there was something wrong with his brain. He had to try and teach him something. He did it in order to get a bit of money. And that affected him very much. The sight of this poor child, incapable of improvement in any way. And that was when he saw the ghost in Walberswick churchyard, which I think he's written about. He was sitting in the ruins of Walberswick church, you know the old part, and he was sitting down there, I think, making notes for something that had come into his mind, and he suddenly saw a man walk past him, giving no heed to him whatsoever. This was about three o'clock in the afternoon. Now he was not given to spiritualism in any form, he rather despised it, I think. But nevertheless he saw that ghost all right. . . . He took the cares of the world upon himself. Which I suppose you can admire a person for doing, but if you can't do anything about it then you're only wearing yourself out. His father was not interested in politics, didn't want the matter discussed. I think quite rightly because he'd only show his contention. Especially as George Orwell was not on the same side in politics as his father. And his father was very nice and so was his mother but they had a different outlook to George Orwell. And I think father and mother were not really very happy about this. Not that they weren't very fond of him and all that but he seemed to have gone off the rails slightly. Why did he want to go messing about in dirty old clothes talking to these horrible people?

It must have been very odd for somebody from a quiet Suffolk village like this to suddenly dress up as a tramp and disappear. Didn't you think it absolutely extraordinary at the time?

Well, no. I thought it quite reasonable. If you are making an investigation you've got to do it so as to be as inconspicuous as possible.

When he talked to you about the people he met on his tramps did you get the impression he liked them or do you think he was, as some people have suggested, rather anti the working class?

Yes, because for this reason; quite a number of the tramps were professional tramps. They had no need to be tramps at all. All they had to do was to get themselves a job, but they didn't want a job. It was more fun going about begging. There were some genuine ones, of course, but very few. It was a métier for them, you know. I'm a tramp, so what.

How was he supporting himself at this time?

Well I really don't know, but he had a bit of money. And he was able to buy himself nice clothes as Jack Denny will have told you. . . .

When you read George Orwell do you recognise the tone of voice of Eric Blair?

No I don't. In fact I don't recognise Eric Blair.

Really. You think they're two different people? How are they different?

Well, Eric was a professional down-and-out, if one might use that word, 'agin' the government and all that kind of thing. That was his profession. But in fact he wasn't. Everybody disagrees with governments; there were some things he agreed with and some things he disagreed with. But he was not a revolutionary in any shape or form.

So you're saying Eric Blair wasn't a revolutionary but George Orwell was?

In a quiet way. . . .

Dennis, why do you think Eric Blair seemed to have such a hard time with women?

I don't know. I think he was just one of those who happen to be that way. His was a happy family and he was very fond of his sisters and all that kind of thing. I just think it somehow wasn't within his nature. It may have been that he, I'm making this up now, but it may have been that he always had the glorious fairy in front of him, in his eyes, at the back of his mind, who never appeared on the scenes at all. I think he rather sought perfection and, of course, there never is perfection. I'm making this up but it seems to me now you've asked the question that it may have been the answer.

But that was what you felt, that he idealised people?

Yes. . . . He had an ideal in his mind, I think, which was never lived up to. I don't know anything about his wives except his first wife was a very charming, sweet person.

You met her?

Yes. Very nice indeed. But she was very much the wife to George Orwell as distinct from, in my opinion, George Orwell's wife, if you know what I mean.

You mean she ministered to a reputation?

Yes, yes. She effaced herself and, well, he was a sort of God about the place. That is the impression I got. I may be quite wrong. It wasn't what I would call an ordinary husband and wife set up.

How interesting. And he was rather dominant with her?

Yes, but not unpleasantly dominant. You'd never notice it as such. And he was not a dominating kind of person in any way. But if a woman was going to sort of worship him, then of course the onlooker sees a rather difficult situation. But it was not Eric's intention, I'm sure of that.

You did disagree with him about a lot of intellectual things didn't you? Why did he go into the Burma Police? It's a mystery isn't it?

It's a mystery to me and it's a mystery to his father, who wanted him to go into the ICS, the Indian Civil Service, which he could have done with the greatest of ease.

So why did he choose the Burma Police which is an outpost and a grim job?

I don't know, I don't think anybody does know. And I don't think he really knew. Except he wanted to get away from it all, this is my feeling. He didn't talk about his reasons, but he would often talk about the unpleasant jobs he had to do . . . and the difficulties and the orders that he would get, such as quelling riots and all that kind of thing, that used to be stirred up. And they were all political rackets. The Burmese were perfectly harmless people but riots used to be stirred up and they had to put them down. And chaps would get beaten over the head. . . .

Some people have said that he enjoyed violence, that there was a sadistic element in his nature.

No, far from it.

I've asked you about your memories of Eric Blair as a friend. Can I finally ask you what your opinion is of George Orwell, the writer and thinker?

George Orwell the writer. Well the only word I can think of is karma, the Indian word. He imagined himself in a karma in which he had to do all these kinds of things. It was his destiny. He never thought of it as such, of course, but looking at it from the outside. . . . You see he never achieved anything really. He achieved literary fame but he didn't achieve anything else.

What do you mean by achieve anything?

He didn't alter the state of affairs in this country.

Which you think he wanted to do?

He wanted to but he also, I'm quite sure, knew he couldn't do.

Why didn't he go into politics? Did he ever talk about going into practical politics?

I did mention this to him once and he said, 'Oh no, that was no good at all.' He said he wouldn't be bound to anybody to, you know, carry out certain things. No, he was not a politician, he was far too honest to be a politician. If you know what I mean. It's nothing to do with money . . . you know, trimming his sails.

He never involved himself in local politics did he?

Oh no, no, no, no.

He sounds very remote, almost . . .

He was, you said it, he was very remote.

Were you fond of him?

Yes, I liked him very much. In fact everybody who knew him liked him very much. He was a very likeable fellow. But it was always rather a mystery to people – his disappearing for six months or so and then appearing again. Finally it would leak out he'd been tramping to somewhere or other. And this hop-picking business. Now I can understand him going hop-picking. . . .

But he wrote to you all about it, didn't he?

Oh yes, he just decided. The poor took their holidays from the East End of London to go hop-picking. It was the great thing;

the whole year you looked forward to it. And they made quite a lot of money. But he used to write me little postcards, you've probably seen all that stuff, and he always used to say 'please enclose stamp for reply'. Well a letter was three halfpence then, I think. He was posing, you see – that he couldn't afford three halfpence.

His Tailor's Testimony

Jack Denny (b. 1911) is Southwold's leading tailor and men's out-fitters. When he says 'we', he speaks for the firm and his late father, so his is a kind of collective or family memory. Orwell is not famed as a snappy dresser, so it is a surprise perhaps to find him having trousers and sports jackets made to measure at all; but it throws light on the habits and precise social standing of what Orwell had famously called, 'the lower-upper middle class', that is, the upper middle class without money. They inclined to a 'few good things', which were 'made to last' and were not 'off the peg', rather than conventional fashionable attire.

This is an extract from the 1984 BBC TV *Arena* programme *Orwell Remembered*. He is interviewed by Nigel Williams.

Mr Denny, how did you come to know George Orwell?
Well it dates back to the 1920s when we first made clothes for him here. He had then left Eton and I suppose he'd be a man of about eighteen or nineteen. But from that time we went on making clothes until he died. He kept in touch all the time. Of course, there was a period, the Spanish Civil War, when there might have been a lapse. I had some notes actually on the times we made clothes for him. And right through 1922 and then from '22 to '26 there's a blank. I think mainly because my records are missing for that period. And then 1927 was the next period and of course I would have known him better then because I had finished being away at boarding school and was back in South-wold and starting in the business. We made him a lot of flannel trousers over the years. I've got a record here actually when he paid thirty-two and sixpence, thirty-two shillings and sixpence in old money, per pair of West of England trousers. But when you compare that of course with the average wage of this part of

the country at the time, thirty-five shillings was probably almost a working man's weekly wage.

What impression did he make on you at that time?

Well, slightly aesthetic, a very tall man, and slim. I don't think he ever really lacked for money even when he wrote *Down and Out in Paris and London*, because he was always, as most tailors like to know, a good payer. I mean we never had any financial trouble with him of any sort over the years, in sickness and in his more robust days. He disappeared from time to time, of course. And I think it was to do writing. He loved writing, would do anything for the sake of writing. But we never looked upon him then as a writer. And of course I think he rather upset the old girls of the town because in *Paris and London* he mentions his association with homosexuals and this was very taboo, naturally. But his father and mother were living in the town. His father was ex-colonial. Obviously not in the army because anybody who was in the army in those days they made a play on it and, of course, had to have their full titles. He was a quiet old boy, his father. And so was Eric, as I knew him. And he used to appear at local functions, dances and probably, I suppose, the odd whist drive that one had in those days. But he never took a great active part. You'd see him standing around, I think, a little bit shy in many ways.

And he still kept up contact with you long after he'd left Southwold?

Oh very much so. He was very friendly with the front shop manager we had in those days and used to write to him pretty frequently. In fact they kept a pretty good correspondence right until Orwell died in 1950; my manager died in '51. But he had all sorts of clothes, overcoats. We made him a cord suit once. We made him a linen suit. I suppose he was going off on one of his trips somewhere. And then for a time he'd be missing from the scene and suddenly roll in again. Or we'd get a letter from him asking us to make more things for him.

It's very much the part of the English gentleman to have your tailor make clothes for you; it's part of a vanished world now really, isn't it? It's not something one associates with Orwell, who was a socialist after all.

To a degree. No, he was scruffy in a way. As long as he'd got a pair of flannel trousers on I don't think it mattered much what they looked like. I mean we turned him out decent stuff and of course we kept patterns for him here so if he wrote in and said he wanted anything specially made, well they were just made straight with out fittings and sent off to him.

What was the last thing he had made at your shop?
The last thing we made him was a sports jacket in April 1949.
He wrote to you from Jura?
That's right, on several occasions. He wrote to my then manager
and told us that he was very ill and confined to his bed and we
sent off pyjamas and things that he ordered for that time. And
you never know at that period how you're going to assess them.
*Do you think the town's taken any interest in him really? Did he make
any impact?*
No, I don't think so, no. I think he was just taken as one of the
community and he wandered about as anyone else would, as I
said before, looking a little bit on the scruffy side and not taking
part much in the social life of the town, such as it was. And I don't
think anybody in the town, until *Down and Out* appeared, took him
seriously in any way as a writer.

His Niece's Memory

Jane Morgan (b. 1923) is the daughter of Eric's older sister,
Marjorie. She wrote a letter to me in September 1976, containing
these memories. She also sent me the diary of Ida Blair, her
grandmother (see p. 19). She now lives in Ardfern, Argyll, just
across the sound from Jura, her uncle's last home.

'Ricky' is Richard Blair, Orwell's adopted child, and Lucy and
Henry were her sister and brother. Henry's account of the 'ship
wreck' is on p. 230.

My impressions of my grandmother Blair's houses in Southwold
are of extremely comfortable, well-run establishments. Quite
small but rather exotic. The furniture was mostly mahogany,
perhaps second-hand, but everything blended. Rainbow silky
curtains, masses of embroidered stools, bags, cushions, pin-
cushions done by my grandmother, interesting mahogany or
ivory boxes full of sequins, beads, miniatures. . . . Fascinating for
children.

Most of the work of the house was done by my grandmother
with the able assistance of a tiny Suffolk woman. Grandmother
and Aunt Avril took breakfast in bed, one at the head, one at the
foot. Earl Grey tea, toast and Patum Peperium. The dachshunds
usually sat on the bed, which delighted and scandalised us. We

85

Dakins went to Southwold fairly frequently for Christmas and summer holidays.

One of the Christmas holidays must have been around 1930–3. Eric had been staying with us for quite a long time and I think must have been writing *Down and Out in Paris and London*. Only two authentic memories of that visit stay with me; one of the typewriter endlessly tapping in the small end room, and the other is a very clear picture of the start of the journey [to Southwold]. The car was a small Rover. Canvas top, celluloid windows. (My sister had almost died after birth as she could retain no food. Someone suggested goat's milk so my father rushed off and came back with a goat, and it was an instant success. So we kept goats and often had young goat kids.) In the front of the car sat my mother with Lucy on her knee, in the back sat my brother aged about four, myself aged about seven or eight, our pug dog, our cat, two or three guinea pigs and a kid goat called Blanche in a straw fish basket with her head sticking out. Rugs and food baskets and the usual clamour. And behind the driver, on the back seat, sat Eric, quite unruffled and amiable although dissociated from any responsibility, with his knees up near his ears, reading French poetry. . . .

I think he quite liked us children, but unlike most adults he didn't interfere, talk down, try to be jolly or in any other way treat us in a patronising manner. I remember a walk he took me once to see sea anemones on an unused pier at Walberswick. He liked walking but not as an exercise. He noticed plants, frogs, tadpoles, birds and was amused by animal behaviour, so that a walk with 'Uncle Eric' was more fun than with most adults.

On a par with this kind of walk was a time when he collected any small barb-like growths on trees and hedges. He carved them to look like faces. And I think it was Eric who told us in a ghoulish way about skeleton hands with rings on them that one might find washed down from the churchyard at Dunwich – covered by the sea.

He had the knack of getting a lot of pleasure from the country-side without any expenditure at all. A good thing, as he was usually hard-up. . . .

The usual picture given of Eric deliberately trying to repudiate his family doesn't conform with my impressions. When he was ill his mother took him over, when he wanted to write his first book his sister, my mother, offered him accommodation, and later, when his wife Eileen died, it was his sister Avril who took over his house and made a welcoming home for his friends and relatives.

During the 1939–45 period we were quite separated as a family. I was in the Land Army in Lincolnshire, with one week's holiday per year. One was with Avril and my grandmother who lived in an upstairs flat in St John's Wood, not far from where Eric and Eileen were living in a semi-basement. I can't remember anything much except that there was masses of talk, as always in any Blair/Dakin meeting, and that Eileen made delicious meals in a nonchalant way, mixing pastry while joining in the conversation in the sitting-room, smoking constantly.

My second visit was after Eileen's death and Avril and Eric were in a top floor flat in Islington. It was most inconvenient as there was no lift and poor Av had to haul Ricky's [Richard's] pram up and down endless stairs. I think that Eric was dramatising *Animal Farm* at the time. When he was writing he worked hard for long periods at a time, but he liked a complete break at meals. Av also was a marvellous cook and Eric enjoyed good food, especially puddings. Suet puddings, fruit pies, etc. Good, solid, tasty puddings. He relaxed at meal times and had time to catch up on gossip and make plans for any outings. He smoked a lot, very strong cigarettes, and liked to live in an unbearable fug in the winter time. I expect that smoking, stuffy, fuggy rooms and hunching over a typewriter for hours at a time must have aggravated his chest condition.

It occurs to me now that Eric never discussed his work when he came to meals. He enjoyed a relaxed atmosphere and liked and made jokes. He had a very distinctive laugh, rather high-pitched and cracked – not a good description as it was a very pleasant laugh. His jokes often took the form of a succinct remark or observation or addition to general conversation which was so apt that we all laughed, Eric as well as he liked his own jokes in a surprised, modest sort of way.

Not long after this, Eric must have moved to Barnhill. At first he went with Ricky. Avril went up to Jura and made her usual efficient job of the house. This was not easy as Barnhill was four miles from the nearest hamlet and one-and-a-half from Donald and Katie's [Darroch] croft, where Av often bought milk. I suppose that Eric must have been better off financially at this time as there always seemed to be plenty to drink. He never worried about furniture or elegant clothes or cars, etc., but he did like food, and after fishing for mackerel or saithe in the evening, or walking to get the milk in a Scotch mist, there were cries of 'brandy and milk, brandy and milk', and people sat around the kitchen talking and drinking.

Although such a remote place, Barnhill must have been one of the most sociable of Eric's houses as there were constant streams of visitors, especially during the summer. My sister, brother and I went up sometimes together, sometimes on our own. Even my father paid visits. . . .

Eric had always liked gardening, Avril as well, and this was invaluable at Barnhill where veg. were impossible to buy.

At about this time, Eric was writing *Nineteen Eighty-Four* but although he worked hard he also seemed to be around more – gardening or walking – and even took a week-end off one year when I was there for an expedition to White Sands Bay, on the other side of the island. I suppose that Henry will have told you of that adventure. Although it ended in near disaster, and I think Eric was deeply annoyed with Avril and myself, we really had a lovely time. There was an empty croft where we slept on bracken. Eric liked fishing and he and my brother went off and caught some trout in a lochen nearby which Av fried with bacon. Also probably mushrooms which grew well on Jura. We put one end of a log in the fire and kept pushing more in as it got burnt. It was warm enough to bathe. When it was time to return, the boat looked so full and unsafe that Av and I elected to walk home, not very difficult as Jura is long and narrow and it was not far across. And although everyone had warned of the whirlpool on the flood tide, no one had mentioned the danger on the ebb, which was when Eric and party were almost drowned.

Av and I had assumed that they had missed the tide when they did not appear, and were helping Donald and Katie with their hay when Eric, Henry, Lucy and Rick came walking over the top of the hill. I felt then that he thought we ought to have got up a search party, but he didn't say so. He didn't usually comment on what people ought to do in that sort of way. It was typical of Eric to have been so interested in making the best of life on a rock – roasting the one potato and contemplating roast puffin – and not to have checked the Tide Tables which would have been really practical.

One summer there were quite a number of snakes on Jura. Av and I screamed when we saw even the most minute specimen. It was very brave of us to rake the hay when snakes might be under any swathe. Eric was walking with me down the field to Barnhill one day when I screamed loudly at the sight of quite a long snake ahead of us on the path. Av screamed too, but Eric just put one of his enormous feet on the snake, got out his pocket knife and cut off the head. Then he tossed the body away over a wall!

Without a word. We were most impressed.

Eric took a twelve in shoes. There is a family story which may or may not be true that on an occasion when he was to meet H. G. Wells he tried to hide his huge feet under his chair, while H. G. Wells was doing the same thing with his extra-small pair.

While I remember it, another of Eric's habits was to make a highly satisfied sort of squeaky whine, rather like a puppy, if he was eating pudding that he really enjoyed! After Eric became really ill and had to leave Barnhill I only saw him once -- in the remarkable sanatorium in Gloucestershire.

I think petrol was still rationed at that time, as we went from Southwell (Notts) in a motor bike and sidecar. It was great fun in the sidecar – we couldn't go very fast and so had a good view of banks and hedges with wildflowers.

I vaguely remember meeting some odd people who lived in a sort of nature retreat, and we visited a woman whose house was actually a converted hen-house; or so my father said. As far as I remember, the 'sanatorium' was a series of hut-like buildings, but I may be wrong.

Eric was quite cheerful, as usual, and hospitably offered us some highly-illegal drink – either rum or brandy. Having spent many Sundays visiting a TB friend in a sanatorium near Nottingham, where rules were rigid, I was horrified but Eric waved away scruples and we drank whatever it was.

The room seemed rather cluttered and Eric was surrounded by books and papers. Whether or not he was working I don't know.

You say that you want to give a true picture of Eric's character, or as true as possible. I remember him as cheerful but usually somewhat abstracted in manner, as if what was happening reminded him of something else. I can't remember him grumbling about his health or financial problems, although he frequently fulminated against general dislikes like false teeth or unpleasant body odours. He loved useless practical pottering, although he also enjoyed gardening. When he was writing he worked very hard, only emerging at mealtimes, which as I said were regular.

Through the Eyes of a Boy

Richard Peters (b. 1919), formerly Professor of Philosophy of Education at London University, was one of three boys whom Orwell tutored at Southwold in their school holidays in 1930.

The reference to Orwell's perhaps surprising predilection for the 'Cavalier' rather than the 'Roundhead' at this period is confirmed by other witnesses.

This is from a script prepared for a BBC broadcast on 9 September 1955.

Most of you must have wondered what sort of a man it was who created those morbid and savage satires – *Animal Farm* and *Nineteen Eighty-Four*. Books have been written by Orwell's friends sketching his progressive disillusionment with man as a political animal and his despair for the future of human decency. I have no intention of adding to these comments on Orwell's later years. I wish purely to present to you a picture of George Orwell at the beginning of his literary career as he appeared to a boy of ten. For I knew him when he was writing his first book – *Down and Out in Paris and London*. I leave you to draw your own conclusions about the man who conjured up Big Brother, the Thought Police, and rats released at human faces.

It was in the late 1920s and we were living in Southwold on the East Coast. My father was in India and I, together with my two brothers, were proving rather a handful for my mother during our long school holidays. She therefore arranged with an Anglo-Indian friend of hers, a Mrs Blair, that her son Eric should act as holiday tutor to us. We gathered that Eric Blair, who later wrote under the name of George Orwell, was rather a strange fellow but very nice. He was very kind to his mother and helped her with the washing up; but he had given up a very good job with the Burmese Police and had chosen to do a year's trip as a tramp without any subsidy from home. He had done all sorts of dreadful things, like sleeping in doss houses and acting as a bottle washer in a Paris hotel. But he had stuck it out for the full year and now he was writing a book all about it. You can imagine that we felt a bit apprehensive when the day arrived for him to take us out for our first walk.

I vividly remember the first impression of him as he came up the garden path . . . a tall spindly young man with a great mop of hair waving on top of a huge head, swinging along with loose, effortless strides and a knobbly stick made of some queer Scandinavian wood. He captivated us completely within five minutes. He had a slow disarming sort of smile which made us feel that he was interested in us, yet amused by us in a detached, impersonal sort of way. He would discuss anything with interest, yet objectively and without prejudice. We knew nothing of politics and cared less. I have only the vague impression that he thought most politicians wicked people and that making money entered into it rather a lot. But his remarks on these subjects were without rancour. He commented on the actions of politicians in the same sort of way as he commented on the behaviour of stoats, or the habits of the heron.

He was a mine of information on birds, animals, and the heroes of boys' magazines. Yet he never made us *feel* that he knew our world better than we knew it ourselves. He loved H. G. Wells' scientific stories – especially the one about the schoolmaster who got into the fourth dimension and was thus able to observe that the boys in the back row were cribbing. And it was as if he entered unobtrusively, like Wells' schoolmaster, into our world and illuminated it in a dry, discursive, sort of way without in any way disturbing it. He never condescended; he never preached; he never intruded. I remember him saying that he would have sided with the Cavaliers rather than with the Roundheads because the Roundheads were such depressing people. And I can now understand what he meant. For temperamentally he was a Cavalier, lacking the fervour and fanaticism of the Puritan. Like most people who have thought out clearly where they stand, he did not make a fuss about it. He was never noisy and lacked the dogmatism of the insecure. I can only remember him getting indignant on one occasion when he told us how he thrashed a boy whom he caught blowing up a frog with a bicycle pump.

His attitude to animals and birds was rather like his attitude to children. He was at home with them. He seemed to know everything about them and found them amusing and interesting. Perhaps he thought of them like children, as uncorrupted by the pursuit of power and riches, living for the moment and caring little for organised exploitation of each other. He infused interest and adventure into everything we did with him just because of his own interest in it. Walking can be just a means of getting from A to B; but with him it was like a voyage with Jules Verne beneath the ocean. He had, of course, nothing of the hearty technique of the adolescent scoutmaster or the burning mission of the enthusiast. Neither had he the attitude of the guide on a conducted tour. A walk was a mixture of energy, adventure, and matter of fact. The world, we felt, was just like this. And it would have been absurd not to notice all there was to see. He even assured us, in a matter-of-fact sort of way, that he had seen a ghost in broad daylight in Walberswick churchyard. He saw a figure of a man in brown come up the path and thought nothing of it until it disappeared behind a derelict pillar and failed to come out on the other side. The way he spoke of this even made it as much part of the natural order as the movements of birds and boats.

These walks had often a definite purpose. Perhaps we would walk along to a nearby broad [estuary of the River Blyth] to attempt to get near a swan's nest or to find plovers' nests, on the hillside that overlooked it. On another day we would walk inland to Blythburgh to look at the heronry there. Some days we went fishing in the mill-pool at Walberswick and managed to catch roach or rudd with bent pins and bread pellets. I can still remember the smell of wild peppermint or spearmint which formed a background to his exposition on the properties of marsh gas. He also told us how he used to kill eels by firing at them with a 12 bore shot gun. But he never demonstrated this method to us. He initiated us into the delights of catching white-bait from the cross-beams of the old pier at Southwold and claimed that the beams were a very good place to have a sleep on a sunny day. We helped him, too, to dig a couple of tumuli in a search for prehistoric remains, though I think that all we found was a soldier's button. His attitude to nature was symbolised in the prodding of his stick. There was nothing of the romantic about him. If he had met Wordsworth's leechgatherer he would have been interested in the leeches and in how the old boy made a living.

But of all the activities which we indulged in with him, the one that stands out in my memory most is the making of bombs. We used to call him by the somewhat irreverent title of Blarry Boy and we coined a kind of war cry which was later to make my mother and grandmother tremble – both literally and metaphoric-ally. 'Blarry Boy for Bolshie Bombs' would echo through the house and my poor mother would look anxiously out of the window to see which part of the garden was going to disappear next. My grandmother, I remember, nearly had a stroke when a grassy mound blew up just by the sitting-room window. George Orwell taught us a very special way of making gunpowder and he had a patent firing mechanism which involved tipping a test-tube of sulphuric acid from a distance by means of cotton on to a fuse composed, as far as I can remember, of chlorate of potash and sugar. The same energy and detached interest went to making and firing a bomb as to looking for a redshank's nest. We had to get every detail just right; we must not hurry; we must get into a really safe place before we pulled on the cotton. Nature was intriguing but predictable; we had to learn the way she worked or we would suffer.

We had another game in which he would also join with quiet nonchalance. We would stalk each other in the sand-dunes armed with small sand-bags. His calm precision was formidable. This was our world and it also seemed to be his. He was merely the boy who played the game with his head.

I suppose the nerve and quiet confidence with which he played this and other games was the quality in him which we admired most. Courage can be a dashing demonstrative business. With him it had a quality of coolness and resourcefulness which I have never since encountered. I have no doubt that it was with this calm courage that he later went to fight for the Republicans in the Spanish Civil War. The picture I shall always carry of him is of a tall, loveable man striding nonchalantly across a girder about 18 inches wide on which the old disused railway bridge at Walberswick was suspended. I must confess that I was pretty frightened just jumping from sleeper to sleeper with the river swirling through the mudbanks about 30 feet below. But there he was, walking as calmly as you like up to the apex of this girder miles above our heads. He told us that he had often wheeled a bicycle across. And I am sure that he had; for it was not in his nature to exaggerate or to strive to create an impression.

And was not this the core of George Orwell – a lonely, courageous figure passing with detached honesty and without rancour across the mudbanks of corruption? The tide of tyranny and double-think was rising. Human decency must have seemed to him to be in decay like the disused bridge. Children and animals, perhaps, were as yet uncorrupted. But what could they do against the organised idiocy of man? Perhaps Orwell was a man of extreme sensitivity like Rousseau who found the conventions of the city too cramping and the stupidity and power seeking of bureaucracy intolerable. Perhaps he was really *at home* only with animals and children. I cannot say; for he passed out of our life for ever. All I can say is that to us he appeared as a thoroughly loveable and exciting companion. The world, it is said, is never ready to receive its saints. Perhaps children alone can readily recognise them for what they are.

A Great Feeling for Nature

Mabel Fierz (b. 1890), occasional reviewer for *The Adelphi*, life-long activist in good causes and seeker after truth, met Orwell in the summer of 1930 while on holiday in Southwold. She and her husband were thereafter of considerable help to him in good, small ways – a meal and a bath for a poor and hungry writer, a bed for a few nights at their home in Hampstead Garden Suburb, helping him find a flat in Hampstead and Kentish Town, storing his tramping clothes, giving him introductions to other young writers; but most of all she rescued the rejected and abandoned manuscript of *Down and Out in Paris and London* and found a literary agent who had faith in Orwell's writing.

This is from a transcript of an interview made for Melvyn Bragg's BBC *Omnibus* programme of 1970.

We met him at Southwold. We had a little cottage on the beach. He'd been in the habit of sketching from there. And he turned up one day with his painting brushes and his colours, and he said, 'I'd no idea that this place had been let. I've been in the habit of sketching from here.' So we said, 'Oh well, don't let that worry you, we shall be very pleased. Come whenever you like.' Which he did. And when we left there we came home to London, Golders Green, and we said, 'Any time you wish to come to London about your book' – he'd then just finished *Down and Out in Paris and London* – 'we'll always be pleased to have you.' So he came frequently for weekends, and, as you know, he left his book with us. It had been rejected by three publishers. And I thought one day I'd try and get it published. So I took it to an agent in the Strand, Christie & Moore, and I badgered that man. He said, 'Nobody knows your friend; I couldn't possibly publish this book.' So I said, 'Well, you read it.' In fact I stayed so long and persuaded him so hard that in the end he kept the book. And after three months, Orwell had a letter to say, I've sold your book to Gollancz and you will get thirty pounds on the day of publication.

And he was thrilled of course, he'd no idea it had even been taken to the agent.

What would you say about his life?

It was rather a sad life, very lonely. He was always writing. . . . He saw Rees [see p. 115] now and again. And he came to us. But when he was working in the bookshop he had a pretty dreary life; he didn't care for the people who owned the shop with whom he lodged. He found them very uninteresting. But later he lived in his own room and he was able to write more freely. He was still working at the bookshop but at any rate he was living on his own. And he was pretty lonely during that period. He had girlfriends, girls who used to come to the bookshop. He got to know several of them. But there was nothing serious; he didn't care much for any of them. In fact on the question of girls he once said that of all the girls he'd known before he met his wife, the one he loved best was a little trollop he picked up in a café in Paris. She was beautiful, and had a figure like a boy, an Eton crop and was in every way desirable. Apparently he came back to his room, and this paragon had decamped with everything he possessed. All his luggage and his money and everything. So I said, 'You would never have married this girl, would you?' And he said, 'Oh yes I would.' It was just typical of him. She was desirable and a nice girl and he liked her; he cared nothing what her background had been.

What pressure did his parents bring to bear?

Well, the pressure was that he must make money. He must make the grade. And when he left the Burma post, his father was very disappointed. And looked upon him as a sort of failure. He felt that deeply. But his mother and I were very good friends, and she said to me, 'You know, Eric loves his father far more than he loves me.' And I said, 'No, I don't think he does – he wants his father to acknowledge him as a successful son.' The son who couldn't make money in old Mr Blair's concept was not the right sort of son.

Do you feel he wanted to make money from writing?

It was a curious thing about him, that he had always this timidity of being downgraded, of being thought less of than he felt he deserved. He always had that feeling, so that he was urged on to do more, write more, write better, in order to establish himself. He had great ambitions. Had he lived longer, he would have written far more and far better because he deepened very much during the last five or six years of his life. . . . He used to say he would have given anything to have written *Lycidas*. He really adored good poetry, and Latin poetry he used to know by heart. Yards and yards of it. I think he would like to have been a poet, but he felt he wasn't equipped for it.

A would-be poet writing a bestseller on working-class life: does that surprise you?

Very much. But not as he was. He identified himself with the working class utterly. When he went hop-picking, they all called him by his Christian name. And he was perfectly happy among the hop-pickers. Except it worried him that he could never have a bath. He always had these little remnants of upper-class life you know; must have a bath every day, must wash your head every day. . . . He was so warmhearted and he had such a sympathy and such pity for the working class and their sufferings; that started in Burma. When he saw how unhappy the people were under British rule. And he showed that in the essay, 'A Hanging'. And that started him; when he came to England and Paris he still felt that he wanted to know exactly how the working class lived. And he felt deeply what the working class suffered. Poverty, bad housing, all these things were a great concern with him. In London he'd only mixed with tramps. But in Wigan he saw how the poor lived. He tells about the woman who used to wash the stone steps on a cold morning on her knees. That sort of thing used to hit him hard.

Did he change after Wigan?

He says he became a socialist as a result of *Wigan Pier*. But my recollection of him was he always was a socialist. . . .

What was Orwell's relationship with his family like?

On his part it was a relationship of loyalty. But absolutely no warmth of contact. They hadn't the vaguest idea of what he wanted to do, or what he felt. He used to say, 'My mother would forgive me whatever I did.' Well, that polished her off. And his older sister, he felt she was spiteful. She thought, of course, he never made money, he was no use. And the young sister hadn't much time for him either. They were a solid British respectable middle-class family. . . .

He suffered very much when he went to his prep school. All the boys had more money than he had. And then with the scholarship to Eton, in the scholarship house that was another thing. And at Eton the boys had more money than he. And he used to say, 'If only I'd been sent to another school, a freer co-educational school, I should have been much happier than at Eton.' He didn't really care for Eton. . . . He felt that he had a bad deal in the sense that everyone has a bad deal, has less money than they need to live a decent life. He identified himself with socialism as against the capitalists. He used to say, 'Britain is made safe for fat little men.' That was the epitome of his dislike.

What do you think kept him going over those seven or eight years?
This urge to make the grade and to affirm his own potentiality. And to convince his father that he was worth something; his one idea was to convince his father of his own worth, because he loved his father and he wanted his father to love him.

Did his father ever read a book?
I doubt that he read anything until Orwell became generally accepted. Then he became interested. He may have looked at *Down and Out in Paris and London*, he may have read it, I'm not sure. I was in Southwold the day it came out. But the family didn't seem to show much excitement. They were not interested in books or literature. Any of them.

Would you say his life changed when he met Eileen O'Shaughnessy?
No, I don't think it did, because he always wished to find a good wife who would be a companion, and a presentable wife, pretty and intelligent. He would never have allied himself to anyone less than that. So he was very happy with Eileen. He thought a lot of her and she thought a lot of him. But they weren't idyllically happy as far as you could tell. But they made the grade. And then, of course, one of the things he felt very much was that he had no children. He always wanted a child. So he adopted this boy, and it fell very hard on his wife because she was working then, and running the house, and looking after him. And I think that militated against her recuperating. She got very low in health.

Orwell never took much care of his health?
Not the slightest. He always wanted to make out that he was tougher than he knew he was. He knew – he must have known instinctively – that he wasn't tough. But he always wanted to make out to himself that he was tough. . . .

What was the spark in your relationship?
I think it was that he felt he could tell us anything, as he didn't have to keep up an image of being a perfect gentleman and really wonderful, which you do when you're with young people your own age. He felt entirely at ease with us and he would tell us anything. He knew that we liked him and were tolerant, and he felt entirely at home in our house. He and my husband used to talk endlessly about Dickens. He loved that. . . . And he was an interesting man to go for a country walk with, because he knew the flowers and the trees, he knew the names of all these things.

Pity he hadn't done more botany; he would have excelled in that. He had a great feeling for nature. Real warm feeling. . . . If he'd had a brother he'd have been much happier. And then there wasn't a great deal of harmony in his family between his parents, and he grieved over that. . . . He was less unhappy at Eton, but he always, always felt it wasn't the school for him; there were so many regulations. And there were things there that he felt. For instance Aldous Huxley was a master there and was almost blind. And the boys used to tease him. Well, that worried Orwell a lot. He thought, 'How can anyone tease a blind man?' That was just typical. I don't suppose many boys would have noticed it, would they? But he noticed it and he felt it. And then of course in Burma he was very lonely; there was no one worthy of him to talk to. He was rather isolated, among the whisky-drinking, rather, you know, usual Indian bosses. And he never made friends much in Burma. He was pretty lonely. So when he came home on leave, he decided he just couldn't go back. And, of course, his parents were terribly upset. He was landed in England without a penny. That was a serious problem.

Hampstead Friendship

Kay Ekevall (b. 1911) ran a secretarial agency and lived near the bookshop on the corner of Pond Street, Hampstead, where Orwell worked part-time in 1934–5; and being of literary tastes, she got to know him by talking about books. They were friends for nearly a year. This is the time when Orwell was writing *Keep the Aspidistra Flying*. He met Eileen O'Shaughnessy, who became his wife, in Hampstead, and his affair with Kay came to an end. She refers to Rayner Heppenstall (see p. 106), one of their circle, and Michael Sayers, who, with George Orwell, were the three members of Mabel Fierz's 'Junior Republic'. She persuaded the trio to share a flat in Kentish Town.

This is taken from a transcript of the 1984 BBC *Arena* programme, *Orwell Remembered*. She is interviewed by Nigel Williams.

Mrs Ekevall, when did you first meet George Orwell?
I believe it was the end of 1934, in the bookshop at the foot of

Pond Street. I had a typing bureau up at the top of Pond Street. I used to haunt second-hand bookshops all my life. I didn't know the Westropes personally but I knew the shop fairly well and bought a lot of stuff from it. And when I went in one day, I saw this tremendously tall man and I thought, how handy, he can reach all the books that we can't. Most booksellers in Hampstead in those days were very interested in what you bought, you know. They weren't indifferent like a lot of them now. And so we started discussing books and it was 'have you read this' and 'do you like' so and so . . . that kind of thing. And I went in several times afterwards and we went on discussing books. Then he said would I like to come and meet some of his friends who were also interested in books. So I went up to his place at Parliament Hill. He used to live above Westropes but he'd left there by that time. And so I met Rayner Heppenstall and Mike Sayers, Mrs Fierz, several other people who were his friends. We began to meet quite regularly. Went around together and used to go for long walks over the Heath, which was great fun because he was very knowledgeable about country things. I think he'd been brought up in country areas. And then, of course, he knew all about the Far East and he was fairly colourful about the landscape there.

He talked about Burma to you didn't he?

Oh yes, yes. He was fiercely anti-colonial of course, as most of us were then. And we discussed politics generally, but none of us were very well-versed in politics at that time, except Mike Sayers who had read a lot and wrote political articles. He was very knowledgeable but the rest of us were all for the underdog so to speak, but didn't really know any theory or anything like that. There was an organisation, I think it was – something Commonwealth. And I think G. K. Chesterton had put the idea forward. And he was quite interested in that and we used to discuss it quite a lot among all our friends.

So he was involved with the Democratic Commonwealth?

Well, he wasn't involved with it but he was interested in it. . . . And he was fairly keen to do a sort of epic on history from Chaucer – because he was very keen on Chaucer – continuing up to the present day. He did the first part of it, which he wasn't very satisfied with – and it wasn't particularly good – then I think he decided that poetry wasn't in his line and gave it up.

Oh it was a poem?

Yes.

A sort of epic poem.

Yes. But I don't think he really was cut out for poetry. Maybe I'm a bit arrogant about that, because I wrote poetry myself at the time. I mean he was a really very interesting person but he had a tremendous amount of strange prejudices, you know. One of them was against Scotsmen, which was very odd.

All Scotsmen?

Yes. Now this was what was so silly. I knew Edwin and Willa Muir, who lived just round the corner from him. And they used to invite young writers to their house every so often. And I invited our crowd, Eric and Rayner and Mike along to one of these dos. And Rayner and Mike came but Eric wouldn't come because Edwin was Scots. And he would cross the road rather than be introduced to him. I used to fight him over this. I said, 'Edwin's the most mild kind person, and in any case,' I said, 'he's Orcadian and they don't call themselves Scots.' But he just had this blind prejudice because of what he called the whisky-swilling planters in Burma that he'd met. So he lumped all Scotsmen together. Must have got over it towards the end of his life because he was in partnership with a Scots farmer up in Jura. But probably that was his sister's doing because she married the Scots farmer.

He really hated Burma didn't he?

Oh yes. That's really why he opted out of it, because he just couldn't take it any more. And of course the conditions in the colonies were pretty awful in those days.

Had he published any books when you first met him?

He'd published *Down and Out*. Mabel [Fierz] was responsible for getting him introduced to the publishers for that. She knew a lot of publishers, she was in that kind of field. *Burmese Days* had come out in America and they were considering it over here and it came out just at the end of the time when I knew him.

Did you like Down and Out?

Yes I did. I thought that was a very honest sort of book. Of course it had been done before by Jack London. Orwell was the sort of person who always wanted to get first-hand experience of anything that he wanted to write about. He tried to get himself imprisoned once in order to study prisons. I heard in the end that he became a prison visitor.

Was that when you knew him? How did he try and get himself into prison?

He bashed a policeman or something like that when he was drunk. But they told us to take him home and look after him. He was very honest in that respect, he always wanted to have first-hand information about everything. And that's why I think he wrote so well about Burma and about Spain, because he was really there. But of course that didn't work with *Wigan Pier*. I think probably because it was a commissioned book and he was seeing everything from the outside . . . absorbing all his preconceived prejudices into it. You see he had a sort of predilection for the sordid. He tended to gravitate towards that side of things rather than see both aspects of a place.

When you read Keep the Aspidistra Flying *did you recognise that. . . ?*

Oh yes, well I think most of the people who knew him in those days felt that there was something of themselves in that book; because a lot of the incidents were things that I recognised, like the party when he spent all the money he'd got for an article or something. There were about five or six people there and he treated us all to a great slap-up meal and then he got completely drunk – that was the time he assaulted the policeman.

In the book there is a great feeling of shame and insecurity. Was he like that as a man?

He had a phobia about money. I didn't think he was that poor, but he thought he was terribly poor. And I used to say, 'Look, you've got enough to eat and a roof over your head, what more do you want?' But he had this sort of feeling that he wasn't sufficiently capable. For example, this slap-up meal which he'd got some money for, he seemed to want to cut a dash a bit. Especially with women. He hated you to offer to go dutch with him. He thought this was a very unmanly sort of thing. And all his girlfriends used to argue with him about it. I mean, we were all earning about as much as he was, so why not?

In Keep the Aspidistra Flying *that nagging sense of not having money is one of the strongest, most pervasive things in the book.*

Yes, and he exaggerated it so, because he wasn't as hard up as he made out. He lived quite comfortably.

Can I talk about his socialism now because you knew him just before he went to Spain and just before he went to Wigan Pier, is that right?

Yes. We'd always agreed that if we met anybody else we'd be open about it and our relationship would just fade out. And he told me that he was keen on Eileen and so I said OK, that's it, cheerio. Rayner in his *Four Absentees* makes out that we quarrelled about it, but we didn't actually. But Rayner's not very reliable in that respect.

Do you think that it surprised Orwell, that you had this rational attitude towards relationships, while he was rather a romantic in some ways?

Oh yes, he was a bit old-fashioned in that respect. But most of my friends and I thought of ourselves as free women and *avant-garde*; at twenty-three you do. But he, I think, found it hard to take. He liked women to be interesting and intelligent, but I think he found it hard to take that they could give back as good as they got. I mean there was never any question of marriage or anything between us, we were just friends. I didn't want to get married anyway; I wanted to knock about a bit and see more of the world. But I think he would have liked children very much. It's sad that he didn't have any . . . I once talked to him about children and he said he would like to have some but he didn't think he could. So I said, 'Why not?' 'Oh,' he said, 'I don't think physically I could have children.' So I said, 'What makes you think that? Have you ever tried?' So he said, 'Well . . . I've never had any. . . .' So I think that's why he adopted Richard, because he was so keen to have children. I don't know how Eileen felt about it. I think maybe she was a bit worried that they wouldn't be able to cope. Because neither of them had particularly good health.

Did you know Eileen at all?

I only met her twice, at Rosalind's [Henschel] house in Parliament Hill. That's where Eric met her, of course. She was a charming person, from what I knew of her, but you don't know a person very well when you've only met her twice at tea parties.

What did you think of The Road to Wigan Pier?

Oh I thought it was really a terrible book. I thought it denigrated all socialists; it put the working class in a terribly sordid light. I mean, he admired the miners for their physical prowess but not for any sort of political commitment they had. And the miners were very political in those days; they were more or less the vanguard of the trade union movement. And he seems to have ignored anything that was happening on the positive side of politics and just concentrated on all the sordid aspects. And, of course, there is the second half where he rails against all the different kinds of socialists he conjures up, which are mostly Aunt Sallies, and not like any of the socialists I ever met. . . . He was against feminists, vegetarians, pacifists, people who drink fruit juice, people who wear sandals, oh practically every Aunt Sally he could conjure up. But these groups didn't represent socialism at all. I mean, they might have been on the fringe of it; there was one dreadful passage where he describes two old men getting on to a bus, and he assumes, of course, that they're socialists, immediately, because they were wearing khaki shorts and khaki shirts and they're fat and old and one of them's bald. And he talks about him being obscenely bald. How on earth one can be obscenely bald I can't imagine. It was a really childish, schoolboy sort of ranting against people. And he didn't know what they were – nobody seems to have heard their conversation, so he didn't know, but he immediately assumed they're socialists because they're a bit odd looking. They could have been scout masters or anything but this is the kind of thing he did, he imposed his prejudices on people without finding out what they really were.

When you read Wigan Pier *had your own political attitudes altered?*
Oh I'd got much more political by then and mixed with real socialists, real working-class socialists. Not the kind that Eric seemed to know. He doesn't seem to have met any of the kind I knew.

He wasn't really a political writer in the sense that he was involved in politics was he?
No. No. I think Mike Sayers was the only political person in the group that I knew. I don't think any of the others were really dedicated. They were more dedicated to becoming writers.

But isn't Orwell's testimony as a writer who was involved in politics still valuable?
I think it has value up to a point, but I think it also has a distorting perspective, it's so one-sided that it doesn't give any value to any other reality. And people tend to have adopted it as gospel. Especially now that they use *Animal Farm* and *Nineteen Eighty-Four* in schools, and I think *Wigan Pier* is considered to be a picture of the thirties, which it isn't.

One accepts that people will take a writer like Orwell and try and make him fit into their own particular cause. But in a book like Homage to Catalonia, *surely the value of what he said about what had happened. . .*
I think that is one of his better books. I don't agree with his point of view in it, but at the same time he was writing from factual experience. And while that experience tended again to be very one-sided and knocked anybody that wasn't in his group, at the same time it was a very valuable picture of the terrible conditions they had to fight under in Spain. But I don't think it was all the fault of the other groups that the conditions were terrible. I think they were just terrible because of the Fascist intervention.

But one can see that because he happened to be in a POUM Unit (see p. 146), that was the way he felt. . . . His relationship with Communism is crucial to the way in which intellectuals interpret the whole history of the left. Don't you think there is an element of value in his statement of the personal experience of politics, as experienced by the ordinary person rather than the practical politician?

Yes, I think a lot of his stuff is valuable but it tends to be accepted – because it happens to suit the establishment – as gospel instead of as a statement to which there is another side. This is what I became worried about after *The Road to Wigan Pier*. I began thinking he turned so rabid that nobody else got a look in except the people he approved of.

Did you write to him about Wigan Pier?

Yes. But I didn't get a letter back. I wrote a very fierce article about it because he was slating all the people I knew as genuine good socialists, and guying them. And so I wrote him what I thought about it, and according to my folk in London – I was in Scotland by that time – he sent a letter there and my mother had opened it by mistake. She said she'd sent it on but, of course, I was moving around and I never got it. Unfortunately, as I would have liked to have read what he said about it.

Gollancz, of course, wanted him to change the second half of that book didn't he?

I think he was only worried about the libel aspects of it. But I don't think he really wanted him to change it. I think Gollancz was sufficiently powerful to have made him change it if he'd wanted him to.

Do you think Orwell was a reserved man?

In some respects. He would only discuss things with people that he felt he had some rapport with. I don't think he would just expand to anybody. I mean, he talked very readily in the bookshop to people that came in. And I got talking to him because of books, I don't think he was all that reserved. I think perhaps he was just a bit cautious about what he said to people. But lots of people say that he was very secretive but I must say I never found him so. He talked very readily about any subjects that came up. I thought he was quite open and a very honest person. I mean, he wanted to really know about things and I think this is why he did the down-and-out business. If you've got a background to fall back on it's not easy to put yourself in the place of somebody who's really experiencing difficulties. But I think that was a very good factual book and he really learned a lot about people. . . .

You think that he was a middle-class Englishman who faced up to his own prejudices?

Well I don't think he faced up to a lot of his prejudices. I think he preserved them rather carefully. But at the same time he thought that he must know about people's lives, that you can't be a good writer unless you really delve into it. And this was his way of doing it.

He had this obsession about smell didn't he?

Oh he had an absolute phobia about it. He used to talk about places that he'd lived in and they all smelt of cabbage and this kind of thing. But he kind of overdoes it all the time, I feel.

Yes, the sense of smell and the phobias about things is very strong in his work isn't it?

Yes, it comes out very strongly in *The Road to Wigan Pier*, all the smells of everything. But I think he always exaggerated this kind of thing. I think he just had a sordid imagination.

Did you talk about literature at all?

Oh yes, it was literature we talked about.

Who were the writers he admired?

Dickens of course; he was crazy about *Gulliver's Travels* – Swift, he was very keen on him. He quite liked some of Thackeray's work but he felt he was a bit pedantic I think. He didn't like Scott and neither did I. We had quite a few people in common that we liked.

Do you think he really liked people?

Yes I think so. I think he had a capacity for friendship, but there again I think he was a little bit cautious. Maybe he'd had some bad experiences in Burma and . . . his background was a little difficult, you know. He seemed to have had bad experiences at school and at Eton. I don't know about those, of course.

He didn't talk about them?

He pretended to slate public schools and that kind of thing, as if they were dreadful.

And his family?

He didn't say much about his family. He said he hadn't got on very well with his father until the end of his life. He seemed to think of himself rather as a rebel – which he was, of course. I mean he questioned middle-class values all the time and wanted to identify himself with a more working-class background, but I don't think he could ever quite make it. He found it very hard to talk to anybody who wasn't on his level of education.

What do you think of Animal Farm?

Animal Farm, I thought, was quite amusing but, of course, it's been done before. I mean Swift did it, Anatole France did it in *Penguin Island*, Aristophanes did it long ago. It's been done quite a lot before so it wasn't as original as people acclaimed it to be.

And I did feel that it was very slanted to what everybody thought at the time – of the Soviet Union – that it was bad propaganda.

He had a hard job getting it published because we were still allied with the Soviets at the time. You can understand people being cautious politically I suppose. But I just didn't think it was all that clever. People think it's very clever but it didn't strike me as being very original. And, of course, *Nineteen Eighty-Four* is a ghastly book because it's so hopeless. I mean Jack London wrote *The Iron Heel*, which is a very similar kind of theme. But at least he brings you up to a hopeful situation. According to Orwell we're all damned and doomed and that's it. What's the good of struggling?
What's your fondest memory of him?
I think the walks we used to have over the Heath when we used to talk about birds and animals. . . . He was a very self-sufficient person. He could cook and mend his clothes and all that kind of thing. And I admired him for that a lot. But I think I enjoyed most of all what I learned from him. Because I was only twenty-three and I hadn't had much experience of life. And I felt that I was absorbing an awful lot of new ideas.

Rayner Heppenstall Remembers

Rayner Heppenstall (1911–81), novelist, critic and BBC producer, first met Orwell through Mabel Fierz, and she persuaded Heppenstall and Orwell to share a flat together with Michael Sayers in Kentish Town. They remained friendly until Orwell's death, Heppenstall even casting a horoscope for Orwell's adopted son, Richard.

Heppenstall commissioned radio scripts from Orwell, notably an adaptation of Darwin's *The Voyage of the Beagle* and later produced two versions of *Animal Farm*, one scripted by Orwell and the other – far better – scripted by himself. In 1960, he produced *George Orwell: a programme of reminiscences*, an invaluable record made before too many memories had decayed or too many early friends of Orwell had died.

This extract is from his book, *Four Absentees* (Barrie and Rock-cliffe, London, 1960), which is a study of four men he had known: Eric Gill, George Orwell, Dylan Thomas and Middleton Murry. It is a minor classic and a most neglected book.

However, it is fair to point out that memory over twenty-five years can be helped by a novelist's skill, and there are signs of jealousy as well as the perspective of hindsight in this memoir. He was angry when I cast some doubt in my biography *George Orwell: A Life* as to whether the description of his being struck by Orwell was not, while something like it undoubtedly happened, coloured by subsequent knowledge and resentments.

It was during this period that, at Bertorelli's in Charlotte Street, dining with Richard Rees, we had met a tall, big-headed man, with pale-blue, defensively humorous eyes, a little moustache and painfully snickering laugh. This was Eric Blair, who had published two books under the pseudonym 'George Orwell', one about Burma, where he had been with the Indian Police, and one about Paris soup-kitchens and tramps. Dylan and I had gone to Bertorelli's already pretty well stoked-up on Henekey's cider. There was a good deal of nonsense that evening, too, but nothing which casts much light upon either Dylan [Thomas] or 'George Orwell'. . . .

He lived on the ground floor of a house at the top of Parliament Hill Road, in a room he rented from a Jewish woman psychologist of, I fancy, Adlerian persuasion. Michael Sayers and I had dined with him there. He had cooked for us himself. He gave us very good steak, and we drank beer out of tree-patterned mugs, which he was collecting. I had also met him in restaurants. There he would order red wine, feeling the bottle and then sending it away to have the chill taken off, a proceeding by which I was greatly impressed. I had never seen it done in France, but then my French experience, like most of my English experience, had been provincial, while Eric had worked as a *plongeur* at restaurants in Paris.

Eric went to play-readings at the house of T. Sturge Moore, a white-bearded poet in a skull cap whom A. E. Housman had characterised as 'a sheep in sheep's clothing', a pleasantry later misattributed, like so many others, to Sir Winston Churchill and said to have been used by him to describe Earl Attlee. Eric had invited me to one of these play-readings, and Mabel [Fierz] was there. So far as I ever gathered, Eric himself had met Mabel through his present landlady. I also understood that Mabel had paid for the typing of his first book, *Down and Out in Paris and London,* and touted it round the publishers. . . .

Orwell found a flat in Kentish Town and Michael Sayers and I moved in. . . . The new flat was at the top of a house, but these were small, yellow-brick houses. Two couples lived below, both evidently childless. The ground-floor husband was a tram-driver, the basement one a plumber.

We had three rooms, a kitchen and a lavatory, compactly disposed. One of the two rooms at the front was very small, a mere boxroom. I, able to pay least rent, had this. Michael had the other front room, but seemed likely to spend little time in it. Eric had the big room at the back. In it, all eating was done, at a big, scrubbed table. . . . I borrowed a mattress from Mabel, who called the new household the Junior Republic, a denomination which none of its members thought witty enough to adopt. This mattress I rolled up during the day and spread a rug over it. My desk stood in the window.

It was a quiet, pleasant street, called Lawford Road. We were at number fifty. Across the way lived two pretty sisters whose young men called for them in the evening and on Saturday afternoon with motor-bikes. We fetched our beer from the Duke of Cambridge, at the corner. In the main road were public baths. Orwell used these. I still went to Mabel's, taking one bus to the bottom of Highgate Hill and another up it and into the Garden Suburb.

In the afternoon, Orwell worked in the second-hand bookshop at the bottom of Pond Street in Hampstead. His new girl, Jo [Kay], had appeared there as a customer. In the mornings, he wrote *Keep the Aspidistra Flying*. He wore baggy grey flannel trousers and a leather-elbowed sports coat, with a khaki or dark-green shirt and pale, hairy tie. He continued to favour this style of attire in the days of his prosperity, ten years later. On the other hand, the portrait he somewhere gives of himself as the harassed author, unshaven and in a dressing-gown, is false. *I* cheerfully loafed around like that when I was working. Then I would shave and go out. Orwell was astonished that I could do this. *He* felt, unshaven and in a dressing-gown, that he was unworthy to write. He was always up first in the morning and called me for breakfast. I am afraid he did most of the cooking at other times, too, if only because he was better at it. Sometimes I would bend the spaghetti into boiling water. Usually, I fetched the beer.

There was a curious lack of strength in that tall, raw-boned frame. My own physique is quite unimpressive, but it was always I who had to unscrew the difficult bottle-stoppers and jar-lids. The Indian Police and possibly the OTC at Eton had set Orwell up for life with something in the nature of a military bearing, but the vaulting of his shoulders betrayed a poor chest, and he was liable to bronchitis.

'George Orwell' was eight years older than I and nine or ten older than Michael Sayers. He would then be thirty-two, which seemed to me a great age. It was perhaps a little odd in itself that he should have wanted to share premises with us rather than with men more precisely of his own generation, among whom, it is true, he did not seem to have many friends, except Sir Richard Rees and, I suppose, Rees's assistant editor, Jack Common. The disparity in age will, I hope, in itself partly excuse some deficiency in my appreciation of Orwell at the time. I shall not much exaggerate if I say that both Michael and I regarded Eric as a nice old thing, a kindly eccentric. We liked him, but we did not always take him seriously. For my own part, I even tended to exploit him a little.

Our backgrounds, too, were quite different. To me, as to Michael, Southwold was little more than an outer suburb of London. Eric had been at Eton, but had received less formal education than either Michael or I. To us, indeed, he seemed ill-read. In the worst possible sense, we were both very high-brow. The kind of novel Eric wrote seemed to us not worth writing. I thought of myself as a poet, and, to Michael, prose, to be really interesting, had to be at least as experimental as James Joyce's. To us, Eric's tastes were peculiar. We did not really care for Samuel Butler, though Henry Miller was not bad, we supposed. I had assiduously read *The Magnet* until twelve years ago, and at Blackpool long ago I had been amused by the picture-postcards, but I thought it odd to make a cult of these things in adult life. It did not seem to me to matter very much whether Edgar Wallace was a Fascist or not, since I was not tempted to read his books.

I can see that I am in danger of overdoing this. Certainly, no conversations ever took place between Michael Sayers and myself in which we compared notes and decided that between Eric and ourselves there were such-and-such differences. Nor, in fact, did I at the time enunciate in my own mind a single one of the sentences above. I liked Eric. The situation suited me. There was always something to talk about. There seemed no kind of fundamental clash. I was aware of never having any money. I was aware of Eric not having much more. The difference in background would seem greater today. The provincial universities seemed more respectable then, and nobody thought Eton *chic*, for we were still in the era of the public-school, ex-Army-officer vacuum-cleaner-salesman. I did not hold his unfortunate social origins against Orwell. He lived them down pretty well, I thought.

The difference in background was in fact less than the difference in attitude towards one's background. I was not much interested in mine. Eric seemed curiously involved with his. . . . The distinctness of print meant a great deal to Orwell. He would praise or condemn people on the evidence of a single sentence they could be shown to have written. In this he was more literary than either Michael Sayers or myself. To us it was a curious mind, satirically attached to everything traditionally English, always full of interesting and out-of-the-way information like *Tit-Bits*, but arid, colourless, devoid of poetry, derisive, yet darkly obsessed. There underlay it all some unsolved equation of love and hate, some memory of childhood nursed through Eton, through Burma, taken out and viewed secretly in Paris kitchens or upon the thresholds of doss-houses. The fondness for country parsonages, comic postcards, *The Magnet* and *The Gem*, anecdotes about Queen Victoria and bishops, all betrayed something quite inaccessible to us.

Orwell, too, had recurrent, worked-out jokes. One concerned what he claimed to be his publisher's way, in advertisements and on wrappers, of quoting bits of reviews with words missed out, so that, for instance, if a reviewer said, 'This is by no means a masterpiece', the statement would appear on a jacket as, 'This is . . . a masterpiece.' Another of Orwell's jokes was about replying to American women readers of one's books. They always, said Eric, sent him a questionnaire, and the first question would be, 'What do you consider the most worthwhile thing in life?' To this, said Eric, he always replied, 'The love of a good woman.' Now, both these are perfectly good jokes. They would have been better if Eric himself had not laughed at them and if he had told them less often and more *à propos*. In the case of the second joke, I found myself wondering how many fan letters Eric in fact got from America and whether more than one of them had asked him what he considered the most worthwhile thing in life.

By one of his observations I was shocked. I showed him some photographs of Uday Shankar and Raden Mas Jodjana, asking him which of the photographs he thought would go best in my book of dancing. He said that he could not judge, as he found Indians physically repulsive.

So there he and I were, our daily lives very much bound up with each other, remote from each other at deeper levels. There was no overt intellectual disagreement. It was rather a matter of where the weight of emphasis would have lain. Orwell was already contemplating a guide to working-class life. With my information on this subject he was dissatisfied. He wanted leaky ceilings and ten in a room, with scrabbling on slag-heaps if possible. Himself he hankered after the simple life. He compared the process of writing, unfavourably, with that of making something *real* like a chair, on which you could then sit down. I thought him a wonderfully nice man, but confused. . . .

Orwell's letters had made it plain that the important person now was Eileen O'Shaughnessy. . . .

Though in her late twenties or early thirties, Eileen O'Shaughnessy pursued some course of study at London University. I was in favour of her and had ventured to say as much to Eric. Her complexion was a bit muddy, her manner a bit forced and girlish, but she was prettier than Jo, and Eric considered her family background more suitable. Though she occasionally came to dinner, Sunday was Eileen's day. She and Eric then went for long walks in Surrey, and on Sunday mornings Eric left the house carrying a shooting-stick which he had recently bought. Eileen, presumably, also possessed a shooting-stick or borrowed one of her father's, and the two would sit propped side by side to view the scenery of the Home Counties in the manner in which I supposed that public school men were accustomed to view scenery, what time cads and bounders sat on raincoats. . . .

Orwell was again showing signs of his winter bronchitis, but on Sunday morning he went off with his shooting-stick and a rucksack. . . .

That evening, when I got home from the Mercury, I was exceedingly drunk and feeling rather weak. This was not altogether my fault. I had been plied with the management's whisky. Having in my pocket the money with which I meant to pay Orwell some arrears of rent, I had bought the business manager a drink at the bar before the performance. He had invited me into his office during the second interval, and I had still been there when the performance ended.

Eventually, I reached Lawford Road. I managed to let myself in and crawled upstairs on my hands and knees. I flopped on the wooden chair by my desk and groaned.

Orwell came in, fully dressed.

'Look here . . .' he said.

He said more than that. I looked at him stupidly, sometimes

seeing him and sometimes not, hearing his thin, expostulating voice, going on and on.

'Sorry, Eric,' I said, 'if I disturbed you.'

But the voice did not stop.

'. . . Bit thick, you know . . . This time of night . . . Wake the whole street . . . I can put up with a lot . . . A bit of considera-tion . . . After all . . .'

Exemplary sentiments, but somehow not quite to the point.

'Eric,' I said, 'do shut up and go away.'

'. . . Time of night . . . Put up with a lot . . . Bit thick . . . The neighbours . . . I do think. . .'

I had wanted, if I could find just that little bit of strength, to roll my mattress down and lie on it. Orwell was standing in the way, nattering. The man sounded as though he might go on all night.

'Eric,' I said, 'go away. If you don't go away, I shall hit you.'

'. . . Whole street,' said Orwell. 'Really I do think. . .'

I sighed with misery, raised myself from my chair, tottered, feebly swinging a bandaged fist, towards Orwell and came to, perhaps ten minutes later, sitting on the floor in a pool of blood. This seemed to have come out of my nose, which was sore.

On hands and knees again, I crawled to the kitchen and washed my nose at the sink. I looked for a cloth to wipe the blood off the floor of my room, then decided that this was beyond my strength and that I would sleep in Michael Sayers' room.

There were no sheets on Michael's bed. I took off my jacket, shoes and trousers, pulled the blankets over me and closed my eyes. My head swam. I heard Eric come out of the back room and tip-toe along the passage. The door opened a little and closed again. A key turned.

I lay flat on my back, eyes open. This was too much. I had felt no particular resentment at being knocked out. In the state I was in, it had been unnecessary, but no doubt Eric had panicked. This locking in, however, I felt justified in resenting.

I got out of bed, and to my surprise my legs did not give way under me. I went to the door and banged on it.

'Open this door,' I called. 'Eric, open this bloody door.'

There was no sound of movement.

'Right!'

I felt strong again. I heaved my shoulder into the door. It squealed, but did not give. I kicked at the door with the flat of my foot. This hurt, but I felt one of the lower panels give. I kicked again, and it cracked. Again. My foot went through.

Then there was rapid movement. The key turned in the lock. The door opened. The light came on. There stood Orwell, armed with his shooting-stick. With this he pushed me back, poking the aluminium point into my stomach.

I pushed it aside, and sprang at him. He fetched me a dreadful crack across the legs and then raised the shooting-stick over his head. I looked at his face. Through my private mist I saw in it a curious blend of fear and sadistic exaltation. I moved sideways, caught up Michael's chair. I had it raised sufficiently to receive on it the first crash of the descending metal-fitted stick.

Then there were two other figures in the room, and Orwell had gone. The tram-driver on the floor below and the plumber on the floor below that took me downstairs. The tram-driver's wife was making tea. They put me in a chair and started fussing over me.

'We never did think much of that Mr Blair,' said the tram-driver's wife. 'Keeps us awake till three and four o'clock in the morning he does sometimes with his typing.'

'I do type myself,' I said, animated by a passion for justice.

'Yes, but not over where we sleep.'

In the morning, I went as usual to Mabel's in Hampstead Garden Suburb. I told her and her companion how, earlier in the day, Eric had called out to me while I was in the kitchen, had called me by my surname, had interviewed me like a district commissioner and, of course, had said I must go.

'Heavens!' they said. 'Keeping it up the morning after! Oh, the silly ass!'

I, too, thought it took some understanding. I supposed Eric must have been saving it up. He must be one of those people who couldn't address you directly without first whipping themselves up into a fury. I *had* got a bit behind with the rent, I admitted. And perhaps I didn't really do my share of the washing-up. . . .

'George Orwell' was coming down to give one of the morning lectures [at an *Adelphi* summer school] (using this name for serious things now, it seemed, not merely for his pot-boiling novels). Middleton Murry and I both independently had the idea that I ought to be Orwell's chairman. He duly came, and I was. After his lecture, the two of us withdrew to the Shepherd and Dog. We talked a great deal, but I do not think Spain was mentioned (it was four months later when Orwell went to Spain). The marriage had taken place two months before, on 9 June. Eric and Eileen would live at the village shop in Wallington, near

Baldock, Hertfordshire.... No reference was made to the rather spectacular set-to eight months ago. Inwardly, I recalled it without discomfort, though also without feeling that I should ever understand what it had all been about. The humorous after-thoughts and the residual puzzlement would be, if not exactly mutual, yet compatible. Orwell and I settled down to the position of old friends. The ideal frequency with which we should hence-forward meet would be every few months. . . .

In November, Richard Rees, who had returned from ambulance-driving with Julian Bell on the Madrid front and was living in Upper Park Road, had the American thinker and novelist, Waldo Frank, in tow. On 2 December he gave a small party to which Orwell, having now finished *Homage to Catalonia*, came.

A dated appearance of Orwell in Lisburne Road was on 17 January 1938. He came unexpectedly and stayed to supper. After supper, he and I went out drinking and ended up in a Soho base-ment from which we returned between one and two o'clock in the morning. While my wife and I, a yard or two away, huddled together on the narrow divan, Orwell slept in the 'coffin' [a truckle bed]. An hour or so later, pyjamaless, he had to get up for the usual reason. My wife remembers waking to see, in the dim light from a street lamp, against the shiny, dark-green painted walls, the tall bony figure of our guest padding, naked but for his little moustache, out of the room and presently back again.

My own clearest memory of that night is of confidences at the bar-counter. Orwell had concluded (whether by any systematic means and with medical confirmation, I do not know) that he was biologically sterile. He badly wanted children and was miserable about it. Then he became involved with a tart, and I had to rescue him. That was an exceptionally sunny January. It is noted that on the afternoon of the 17th I had walked in Ken Wood and seen my first jay.

I went to Wallington on 15 February, travelling by a Green Line 'bus which reached Baldock at a quarter past four. This was a Tuesday. The Stores was not a pretty cottage, and the village seemed desolate. There were two goats in a stinking shed at the back, and the Blairs rented a strip of ground, across the road at the front and above road-level, in which they grew vege-tables and in which Eric and I dug together. He and Eileen behaved with conspicuous affection, fondling each other and sit-ting, if not on each other's knees, at any rate in the same arm-chair. The following winter, Eric went to Morocco, and Jack Common, former assistant editor of *The Adelphi*, borrowed the cottage at Wallington.

'A Fugitive from the Camp of Victory'

Sir Richard Rees (1900–70), editor, painter and critic, published some of Orwell's earlier essays and reviews when he edited *The Adelphi* from 1930–6. He greatly admired and helped Orwell, and was a constant friend until Orwell's death, visiting him on Jura and even putting capital into the farm at Barnhill. The caricature of him in Orwell's *Keep the Aspidistra Flying* as Ravelston the dilettante, rich publisher with a social conscience and a liking for good food is not generous – even if it was perhaps not consciously based on Rees. Orwell made Rees his joint literary executor with Sonia, his second wife. When Rees wrote about Orwell he tended a little to remake him in his own image, 'almost a saint'.

The first of these extracts is from the last chapter of Rees's book *George Orwell: A Fugitive from the Camp of Victory* (Secker and Warburg, London, 1961) and the second extract is a transcript from an interview in connection with Melvyn Bragg's BBC *Omnibus* programme of 1970.

It is unsatisfactory, at least for biographical purposes, to have a memory that records general situations, moods and states of mind, but not concrete facts. Thus it was possible for me to know Orwell for twenty years and yet to remember very few definite facts about him. I know from records, not memory, that I probably first met him in 1930, when he was twenty-seven and I was three years older. I was then working with Middleton Murry on *The Adelphi*, which was a quarterly at the time; and in the March-May issue we published a review of Lewis Mumford's *Herman Melville* by E. A. Blair. After that, reviews, articles and, occasionally, poems by him appeared fairly often, usually signed Eric Blair until 1935. In April 1931, we published *The Spike*, which later formed part of *Down and Out in Paris and London*. I remember talking with him in a New Oxford Street tea-shop near our Bloomsbury office. He made a pleasant impression and I did not guess that he was having a struggle to live, though he struck me as rather lacking in vitality. It came out that we had been at the same school, Eton, though the difference in our ages had prevented our knowing one another. I do not remember if it also came out that he had been there on a scholarship, but if it did he must certainly have been embarrassed and I equally certainly was unaware of his embarrassment.

A word of explanation may be necessary here. There are about one thousand boys at Eton, of whom about seventy are 'King's Scholars' and live in the College proper. The remainder are called 'Oppidans' and live in houses supervised by housemasters. The Scholars pay lower fees than the Oppidans and in class and chapel they wear academic gowns over their black Eton suits. These are the only differences, except of course that the Scholars are as a rule cleverer and work harder than the average Oppidan – which would tend – or did in my day, to make them unpopular with the unintellectual majority. But I don't think that any *social* snobbery was involved. Aristocratic parents whose boys were clever enough to win scholarships quite often sent them to College. And, moreover, the disapproval of the majority was extended also to any Oppidan who showed much interest in the lessons. But Eton is a tolerant school, and the disapproval was only mild. On account of the gowns they wore, the Scholars were known as 'tugs' (from *toga*). So far from being despised, I should say that by the more intelligent and serious-minded Oppidans they were rather admired.

But this evidently had not been Orwell's feeling. One day in 1948, when I had known him for eighteen years, I incautiously used the word 'tug' and although he was too polite to say anything he winced as if I had trodden on his tenderest corn. That a famous middle-aged writer should have retained such a deep trace of boyhood sensitiveness and suffering seems remarkable.

Between 1930 and 1935, if my memory is accurate, Orwell lived mainly in or near London, and his first job was at the school in the western outer suburbs which he pillories in *The Clergyman's Daughter*. . . . But the poem *On a Ruined Farm Near the His Master's Voice Gramophone Factory* (*Adelphi*, April 1934) was certainly suggested by the landscape around the detested school:

The acid smoke has soured the fields,
And browned the few and windworn flowers –

Nevertheless, Orwell undoubtedly knew how to keep his bitterness to himself. During the five years when, on the evidence of his novels, his mood was so black and his circumstances so penurious, he was always a friendly, considerate and amiable companion. If one had been asked to describe him one would have said first of all that he gave the impression of absolute reliability and of lacking completely the jealous, pushful, intriguing, self-centred mentality which is so common among young ambitious literary men. He was obviously intelligent and able, but did not seem especially original or gifted. His novels seem to me better today than I thought them when they appeared in 1934, 1935, and 1936. In those days 'experimental' and surrealist prose was fashionable, and Orwell's writing seemed rather stodgy and old-fashioned. He himself, indeed, seemed rather old-fashioned.

The Adelphi did not encourage surrealist prose but it did publish a good many of the new intellectual Leftist poets whose verses Cyril Connolly parodied so well:

M is for Marx
and Movement and Masses
and Massing of Arses
and Clashing of Classes.

Compared with these excited young men Orwell seemed quite tame, and this in spite of the fact that one knew he had really lived among the proletariat instead of merely writing poems about it; and in spite of incidents like the following. He came to my flat one day and asked if he might change his clothes. Having left his respectable suit in the bedroom, he went off again dressed more or less in rags. He wanted, he said, to know about prison from the inside and he hoped that if he were picked up drunk and disorderly in the East End he might manage to achieve this. Next day he reappeared very crestfallen. He had duly got drunk and been taken to a police station. But once there he had received a fatherly talk, spent the night in a cell and been let out next morning with a cup of tea and some good advice.

I have said that Orwell seemed rather old-fashioned, and the truth is that in many ways he *was* old-fashioned. He once said to me, apropos of nothing, so far as I can remember: 'I hope you love your family?' I may be wrong in thinking there had been nothing to lead up to this remark, but in any case I knew him well enough to be able to interpret it. He was thinking of the Oedipus complex, the fear of castration by the father or absorption by the possessive mother and all the other psychological bogeys that have inspired so much of modern art and literature, and he was repudiating them. Rashly perhaps, because he was not always completely successful in loving his own family. He was estranged from his father for a number of years, and I can understand that the elder Mr Blair may have felt that he had reasonable grounds for complaint. A retired Indian civil servant cannot be expected to enjoy seeing his son become a voluntary down-and-out. But they were reconciled before his father's death as Orwell told me with deep satisfaction, adding that he himself had closed his father's eyes in the traditional way by placing pennies upon the eyelids. He further added that after the funeral he had been embarrassed to know what to do with the pennies. 'In the end I walked down to the sea and threw them in. Do you think some people would have put them back in their pocket?'

The only direct reference I ever heard him make to psycho-analysis was when he said: 'A psychoanalyst would need to be cleverer than his patients.' Upon which I made the obvious comment that there are many different *kinds* of cleverness, and he replied: 'I mean cleverer in regard to the matters under discussion.' And there was nothing more to be got out of him. But once again his thought is easy to interpret, and it goes to the root of the matter. The relation of father confessor and penitent in religion is governed by a tradition which transcends their personal characteristics and makes any question of their relative 'cleverness' irrelevant. But it seems to require considerable assurance on the part of a psychoanalyst to rely upon his own skill in using a modern technique in order to enlighten other people upon the workings of the psyche, or soul. Orwell's thought, in fact, is closely related to that of Lise in *The Brothers Karamazov* when she is plotting with Alyosha to persuade Captain Snegiryov to accept some money while at the same time restoring his self-respect. 'Aren't we showing contempt for him,' she says, 'for that poor man – in analysing his soul like this, as it were from above, eh? In deciding so certainly that he will take the money?' Beneath Orwell's bluntness and hostility to psychologis-ing there was a delicacy of feeling, which a great many confi-dently subtle psychological artists conspicuously lack. (Note, for example, in *Homage to Catalonia*, his concern about the boy who was wrongly accused of stealing.)

When I passed through Barcelona in April 1937, just before the street fighting and the liquidation of the POUM (see p. 146), I called on Orwell's wife, Eileen, at the POUM office, where she was working, and found her in what struck me as a very strange mental state. She seemed absent-minded, preoccupied and dazed. As Orwell was at the front I assumed that it was worry about him that was responsible for her curious manner. But when she began talking about the risk, for me, of being seen in the street with her, that explanation no longer seemed to fit. In reality, of course, as I realised afterwards, she was the first person in whom I had witnessed the effects of living under a political terror.

What made this so hard to believe was the fact that one associated the Blairs with their cosy little village shop at Wallington and with his parents' quiet home in provincial Southwold. The fact that they had suddenly transplanted themselves to the front line of militant working-class resistance against Fascism, thereby also exposing themselves to a Communist reign of terror, brought home to one the realities of twentieth-century European politics in a way that all the demonstrations and meetings and book clubs and intellectual Marxist poems entirely failed to do.

I went to the Mediterranean in 1943 and did not see Orwell again until after his wife's death and the publication of *Animal Farm*. His financial situation had improved, but not his health; and I have since heard that both he and Eileen had underfed themselves during the war, in order to share their rations with people whose need they judged to be greater than their own. So in 1946, as a widower with an adopted baby to look after he seemed, in spite of his comparative financial affluence, to be living a more difficult and uncomfortable life than ever; and when he told me he intended in future to spend the summers in a farmhouse on a Hebridean island I ought to have foreseen that he would contrive to find the most uninhabitable house in the British Isles. His letter inviting me to stay concluded with the ominous words: 'It's quite an easy journey really, except that you have to walk the last eight miles.'

The house was at the extreme north end of the island of Jura, and about twenty-five miles from its only port and its only shop. The first seventeen miles of road were difficult and the last eight virtually impossible for motor traffic. It was also accessible by sea, if you could control a small boat with an out-board engine in a channel some four miles wide and swept by heavy Atlantic tides. Milk was obtainable from the only neighbour, about two miles away. The next nearest house was eight miles. Orwell and his sister and the baby seemed very happy, and he had ambitious plans for fruit trees and vegetables. For a strong man in perfect health it would have been a good place for a semi-camping holiday; and it had indeed been Orwell's original intention to spend the winters in London. But very soon his health began to make travelling difficult and he stayed there winters as well as summers, except for occasional unavoidable visits to a sanatorium near Glasgow.

As the last eight miles of road were gradually improved it became possible, sometimes, to drive to the nearest village, which was in fact only a big house and some cottages with no post office and no shop. But the road was never more than a moorland track at best, overgrown with rushes and liable to be washed away in bad weather and, being built on boggy soil, the stones with which the holes were patched soon sank in and had to be replaced. At night the chances were at least even of getting a wheel stuck in one of the boggy open drains which bordered it. After a doctor had told me that Orwell was liable to a haemorrhage if subjected to rough or violent movement I developed a strong reluctance to driving him on this road. 'Civilisation is Communication' and Orwell had chosen to live in a place where civilisation was liable at any moment to collapse. But it was here that he wrote *Nineteen Eighty-Four* and during his increasingly rare spells of good health he was certainly happy – working in the garden, fishing for mackerel from a boat, being bullied by his adopted son. He felt that he was at last putting down roots. But in reality it was obvious that he had chosen a too rocky soil.

And that was typical of him. I remember his comment when I told him of an experience of mine in the early 1920s. In those days the Communist Party enjoyed very little prestige in England and was still affiliated to the Labour Party. One day I was at a Labour club in north London and someone said: 'You must meet our Communist poet.' I was then introduced to a dishevelled-looking man whose name, to my astonishment, I recognised as that of a distinguished member of the Symbolist group. When I told Orwell about this many years later he said: 'Ah, but in those days, you see, it *didn't pay* to be a Communist; and it's a pretty safe rule to say about anything that as long as it doesn't pay it's all right.' Justice, in other words, is always with the weaker side, and you know which is the weaker side because it does not pay to join it. But he certainly sometimes carried the principle to absurd lengths, and this aspect of him was wittily described by Mr V. S. Pritchett in an account of how Orwell once advised him that he ought to keep goats. The chief point being, so Mr Pritchett gathered, that it would put him to a lot of trouble and he would be certain to lose a lot of money; and

Orwell got quite carried away with enthusiasm as he expounded the 'alluring disadvantages' of the scheme.

In the same way, again, I fear that the near-impossibility of making a tolerably comfortable life there was a positive inducement to Orwell to settle in the remotest corner of the island of Jura.

Anyway, as the months went by, his bad days, when he had to keep to his bed, became more frequent, and finally after three years the day came, in January 1949, when I drove him for the last time over the terrible moorland road on the first stage of the long journey to a sanatorium in Gloucestershire. He had finished *Nineteen Eighty-Four* and was very weak, though mentally as active as ever and full of ideas for future work – a novel, and essays on Conrad, Gissing and Evelyn Waugh. In the year of life that remained to him he was to marry again and make plans to go to Switzerland; but he died just before the day fixed for the journey.

One of the last long conversations I had with him was in the train travelling to Gloucestershire, and in the course of it he revealed two quaint pieces of ignorance. From Glasgow the train runs south for about a hundred miles before reaching the English border at Carlisle, but as soon as we were clear of the Glasgow suburbs Orwell remarked: 'The weather seems to be just the same in England', and I discovered he thought England began immediately south of Glasgow. At first he couldn't understand my surprise, but he became more interested when I gave the matter a literary slant by pointing out that the part of Scotland whose existence he ignored includes the birthplace of Carlyle, the Burns country and the Walter Scott country. A little later we were discussing cross-country railway journeys and he wondered if it is possible for the trains of one railway system or company to run on the tracks of another. I told him it was frequently done, but did not investigate this piece of ignorance. Whether he thought the gauges might be different or that the lines of the various railways never joined one another, I do not know. But it seemed odd that he could live in England for nearly fifty years without noticing that its railways, like those of most other countries, not merely use one another's tracks but also frequently use the same stations.

It seems odd, too, that having known one of the most interesting men of his time for a period of twenty years, so many of one's memories should be of trivial conversations like this. But for some reason the memory of them is quaintly endearing.

It is difficult to imagine that anyone who knew Orwell can have any memories of him that are not endearing. One of the chief memories that I retain of this strenuous and self-martyrising man is the atmosphere of cosiness which he often managed to diffuse. After one of the frequent disastrous expeditions in Jura – returning on foot, for example, at midnight in a misty drizzle having left the truck containing drums of indispensable lamp-oil bogged down somewhere in the hills – one would find that he had come down from his sick-room, stoked up the kitchen fire and made preparations for supper, not merely with efficiency but with a comforting, hospitable, Dickensian glow.

Life on the isle of Jura revealed clearly another not un-expected characteristic, namely, his enthusiasm for heroic and desperate remedies. The district was supposed to be infested by adders and Orwell greatly relished the idea – though I can imagine no one who would be more reluctant to apply it – of the cigar cure for snake bites. This consisted, according to him, in lighting a cigar and then stubbing it out against the wound. I also remember an occasion when his sister dislocated her arm in jumping over a wall. Orwell rushed back to the house and called to me: 'You've done first aid, haven't you? Avril's put her arm out. You'll be able to get it back? You just have to jerk it sharply upwards, isn't that it?' The remedy did not work, perhaps because I didn't summon up enough sharpness (Orwell made no attempt to summon up any) and we had to drive the twenty-five miles to the doctor, who was also unsuccessful. So we drove back again and took to the sea, and the arm was finally re-set on the mainland, about twelve hours after the accident occurred.

Orwell was sardonic about the gradual relaxation of war-time restrictions. He professed that he had never believed that the black-out regulations would be withdrawn. Having once got us all neatly blacked out at night with no chinks of light showing, surely 'They' would never allow us to show lighted windows again. He said, too, that he had not thrown away his ration book and clothing coupons because the apparent abolition of rationing must be some sort of trap. And when socialists told him that under socialism there would be no such feeling of being at the mercy of unpredictable and irresponsible powers, he commented: 'I notice people always say "*under* socialism". They look forward to being on top – with all the others underneath, being told what is good for them.'

Although entirely without personal malice, he was capable

sometimes of surprisingly penetrating personal criticisms; and yet I could never feel that he was at all a reliable judge of character. Or it may be that he kept his shrewdness for what he considered important matters and was simply careless about his own personal interests. At any rate, although he had a lynx eye for humbug and inconsistency in politics and art he seemed often to be unaware when he was being taken advantage of in private life. And he was, or appeared to be, somewhat obtuse about what was going on inside the minds of those nearest to him. But this may have been one of nature's protective devices. For a man with such a gentle heart and so much intelligence and such a tender conscience, life would have been impossible if he had been as sensitive in personal relations as so many cold-hearted egoists are capable of being.

One is tempted to close on that note, but it would be a little too simple. Not that there is anything false in describing Orwell as gentle and unselfish and easy-going in personal relationships. But neither the character he showed in private life nor even the character one may deduce from his books can fully explain his unique quality both as a writer and as a man. Obviously, no full explanation of a man is ever possible. But Orwell did once make a remark to me which seems to give a clue to the obscurer part of his character. Speaking of the First World War, he said that his generation must be marked for ever by the humiliation of not having taken part in it. He had, of course, been too young to take part. But the fact that several million men, some of them not much older than himself, had been through an ordeal which he had not shared was apparently intolerable to him.

This is an example of his exaggerated sense of honour carried to the point of Promethean arrogance. It explains his ruthlessness towards himself and perhaps also his occasional inconsiderateness towards others. And yet it would not be easy to think of many victims of his inconsiderateness, apart from his wife and anyone else who was concerned to counteract his disregard of his own health and safety. But everything in this life has to be paid for and sometimes – although this was not my own experience in the case of Orwell – the price of associating with a man of exceptional disinterestedness and courage is a high one. If the raw material of heroism consists partly of a sort of refined and sublimated egoism, it is to be expected that the progress through life of a man of superior character will leave behind it a more disturbing backwash than the sluggish progress of the average man.

EXTRACT FROM THE BBC *OMNIBUS* PROGRAMME

Did you foresee that Orwell's reputation and fame would grow so high and so fast?

Well no, I should say I certainly didn't, not at all. But there is just a slight doubt in my mind, because of something that Rayner Heppenstall has recalled. Rayner suggests that I did foresee something rather special in Orwell's future. According to Rayner, I once said, 'Of course, the thing about Eric Blair is that he likes to think of himself as an unpopular highbrow writer, but he's obviously really doomed for popular success.'

Do you think that going to Wigan, to the north, to write The Road to Wigan Pier, *was a crucially important time in Orwell's life?*

Well it's very hard to say in what way it was. I think it must have been because there was such an extraordinary change both in his writing and also in his attitude after he'd been to the north and written that book. It was almost as if there'd been a kind of fire smouldering in him all his life which suddenly broke into flame at that time. But I can't understand it or explain exactly what happened; I just don't know. But I quite agree there was an enormous change. And in a way a change almost in his character. Because I would certainly say that before then I wouldn't have expected him to feel strongly about patriotism. There's no question that for Orwell Englishness, or Britishness, if there is such a word, was of high value, and that he set enormous value on the fact of being British or English. But I'm not at all trying to suggest that that was his thing . . . in the way that you might say that patriotism was General de Gaulle's thing. Orwell had something other and better than that. And there was certainly nothing idolatrous or chauvinistic or jingoistic in Orwell's patriotism. But still, it was extremely strong. And also I think Orwell tended to be rather sketchy and rather naive in lots of domestic political matters. I think his patriotism gave him an extraordinary kind of hard-headed, almost Machiavellian sort of commonsense in questions of international power politics.

Do you think that after he went to Wigan his idea about society and people changed?

Well in a way I would almost say that before he went to Wigan he didn't seem to have much idea about society or about people. . . he had a kind of Bohemian Anarchist attitude. I mean he didn't appear to have thought very much about it.

What would you say Orwell's ambition was?

Well up to about 1935 or 1936 I've no doubt that his ambition was to be a good novelist. His very conscious ambition was to be a good novelist. He preferred perhaps to be a good poet but I think he was too modest to think that was likely. After 1936 he'd made up his mind that it was impossible in modern circumstances to follow a completely literary career. And he practically ceased to be a novelist. It's true that he wrote what I think is his best novel some years afterwards, in 1939, *Coming Up for Air,* but apart from that, what did he really do? He became a very interesting political essayist and critic. And then he wrote two world-famous bestsellers which were really not so much novels but fables with a political moral. . . . I think he was a very good writer indeed. But I think he had something else, something other than literary genius, which made him a very remarkable man. And it's extremely hard to describe what that something else was without falling into exactly the attitude that Orwell most detested; that of the comfortable armchair idealist who criticises people less comfortable than himself for their materialism and love of pleasure. And I can't think of anyone who was a more consistent and persistent and deadly critic of that kind of humbug than Orwell was. I remember for instance when Marshal Pétain attributed the fall of France to the love of pleasure of the French people, Orwell immediately asked how much pleasure there was in the life of an ordinary French peasant or French working man compared to Pétain's own life. As in one of his essays he says, 'The damned impertinence of these politicians, priests, literary men and whatnot, who lecture the working-class socialist in his materialism.' He puts materialism in quotes, so-called materialism. How right the working classes are in their so-called materialism, how right they are to realise that the belly comes before the soul, not in the scale of values but in point of time! Well now, at the risk of being oneself a damned impertinent whatnot, one can and must observe that it's only in the point of time and not in the scale of values that Orwell puts the belly before the soul. And furthermore when he comes to make a list of the needs of the belly, that must be fulfilled before the question of the soul can arise, his list is a really very ascetic one. He lists the minimum demands of socialism in the same essay in this way: 'Enough to eat, freedom from the haunting terror of unemployment, the knowledge that your children will get a fair chance, a bath once a day, clean linen reasonably often, a roof that doesn't leak, and short enough working hours to leave you with a little energy when the day is done!' He doesn't say whether he means a hot bath or a cold bath; I hope he means a hot bath.

But even so it's not a list of very exorbitant demands. And I think one would have to conclude that Orwell himself really was essentially a sort of ascetic. And a moralist although he wouldn't have liked to be described that way.

And I would go further and say that I think that all Orwell's life, all his adult life anyway, he was really driven and obsessed by a kind of mania of the same sort that you find in a Tolstoy or Dostoevsky or in a Kierkegaard. But of course in Orwell it didn't take a religious form. It couldn't; his beliefs were not such that it could have taken a religious form. But nevertheless – it obviously was an obsession about some kind of value. And I wouldn't hesitate to say that this value was conceived by him as relating to the human soul. He does in fact use the word 'soul' a good deal more often than might be thought, though to use that word might suggest that Orwell believed in immortality and a whole lot of other things that he didn't believe in. And it seems to me he came nearer to describing the things that drove him all his life in one of his poems when he refers to it in an almost impersonal way as the crystal spirit.

I think probably the best way to try and make clear what he probably meant by that is to look at his last and most famous book, *Nineteen Eighty-Four.* . . .

How would you describe Orwell's behaviour in personal relationships?
Well, as I've said several times before in differing contexts, I would say, cosy, easy to get on with, dependable, reliable. But if you asked me was he highly sensitive in the psychological sense in personal relationships, I should say he didn't appear to be. I don't think he really *wasn't*; he didn't *appear* to be. He was never inconsiderate, but it could be said he was rather unaware of other people. But I think that as in the case of other people I've known who have had a strong idealistic drive in life, that it wasn't to do with any failure to understand other people very well. I think he probably did. But a person that is so permanently occupied with some idealistic urge in life that's driving him on, that possesses him, tends not to have very much time for personal relationships.

The Brother-in-Law Strikes Back

Humphrey Dakin (1896–1970) married Marjorie, Eric's older sister. He was a civil servant in the National Savings Committee and he and his wife lived in Leeds where Orwell, after his return from Burma, would visit them occasionally to get some writing done and to be looked after by his sister. Humphrey seemed to resent this and there was tension between the two men. Humphrey plainly viewed him as a work-shy drop-out, though Marjorie continued to help her brother.

This is taken from a transcript of an interview in connection with Melvyn Bragg's BBC *Omnibus* programme of 1970, but it was not broadcast.

What did you make of Orwell during the period 1935–6?
Well, I was glad to see him. I can't say that I liked him very much. He was rather aloof, but I certainly didn't dislike him. He used to stay for a week, two or three weeks, and then move on somewhere else.
Was he full of his political opinions?
Not with us, no, we used to have lively conversations about all sorts of things but very, very seldom on political matters. I didn't know that he was a political bird at that time.
Had you read any of the books?
Oh yes of course, yes . . . I didn't like his early novels at all. He was terrifically industrious; he was determined to be a writer. And I myself and his sister Marjorie, we didn't think that he was likely to be a great success. *Down and Out in Paris and London* I thought was readable, very readable, interesting. Slightly phoney because I don't think he was down and out, he could always have gone home to Southwold or come to stay with any number of friends if he'd liked. But his novels I just didn't like. And *Burmese Days* I thought was definitely unnecessarily spiteful.
You use words like spiteful and phoney. Was this in him as a man?
Well the last thing that you could call Eric was a phoney. If I use the word phoney about him it was quite wrong; he was transparently sincere and believed everything that he did and talked about. I thought it was a bit wet at the time if you follow me. He was looking for dirt and squalor and that sort of thing and he found it. . . . It was a mystery to me. I think that he was naturally not of a sanguine temperament, and I think that that was due

probably to chronic ill health which he'd had ever since he was a little boy.

You had known him since he was six. Was he always –

Oh yes. Yes, our gang of kids knocked him about in Henley; he was about the youngest member and he was an absolute nuisance. He was a little fat boy and he was always whining. And sneaking, telling tales and so on. Very, very different from his subsequent character when he grew up. But he was not a very nice little boy and looked on the black side of life a bit, and I think he carried along that aspect of it through most of his life.

He stayed with you while assembling Wigan Pier. *Did he talk about it?*

Oh yes. I used to pull his leg there. You see . . . he was living with us when he actually came to Barnsley and then went on to Wigan, and I told him he'd find what he was looking for. It was there all right, the kind of thing that he wanted to see, the sink of life if you know what I mean.

Do you mean he started with a prejudice?

I thought so. I may be wrong. But even in those days, you know, in the 1930s, the unemployment and so on, life was definitely grim, you couldn't laugh everything off. But nevertheless, in these sorts of places like Wigan and Barnsley there was quite a lot of cheerfulness for those who could find it and see it. Even these rows and rows of squalid little houses, they look awful from the outside but in point of fact they were always warm and there were good fires and they were kept remarkably clean and tidy.

You must have been surprised to read the details in Wigan Pier.

No, it didn't come to me as a surprise at all. And it's quite accurate. What he describes is accurate. But it's only half, it's the depressing half. He didn't go to any of the football matches where they were enjoying themselves, he didn't go much to pubs or anything of that kind; I don't think he participated a great deal in anything other than the social life of a very narrow description.

Was he a man who did enjoy himself much?

I think in his own way he did. But he didn't appear to be enjoying it. I myself was, and always have been, a pub man. I'm quite at home in pubs. And preferably working-class pubs and artisan clubs . . . where one can always get a game of dominoes. And so I'm at home in pubs. But Eric wasn't until getting on towards the end of his life . . . .

When he came to you, he was lonely, unsuccessful. What did you think would happen to him?

I can't say. I thought that he'd fade out in some way . . . . He really didn't look after himself properly, his clothes were thin and threadbare, he wore enormous mufflers round his neck, and so on. But he wasn't a very well man.

Are you surprised by the grown reputation?

Yes. I knew he'd get somewhere with his writing because he was a tremendous worker. I've never known anybody that worked as hard as Eric did. As soon as he'd had his meal and we'd had a bit of a chat on this, that and the other, he'd disappear to his room and you'd hear his typewriter going right through the night apparently. Enormous worker, you can't put in all that amount of work and not get somewhere. Do something. I thought his essays and his various miscellaneous writings were good and very interesting. But I didn't think he'd get anywhere as a novelist. . . . I think if I had been able to write – sadly enough I can't – I could have told him what Wigan Pier was like before he went there.

Was he a socialist?

No. I often wondered what the clue to Eric's character was, but rather diffidently I put forward the theory that he disliked his fellow man. He had a contempt for his fellow man. Intellectually. He forced himself to think of his fellow man with compassion. And put on an excellent act, you know, with being a friend of the poor. But I think that he hated poverty, he was partly ashamed and partly angry about having to put up with being so hard up. He was the last man in the world who would ever scrounge or do anything like that, or indeed do anything dishonourable. But I think that he wanted money. In order to lead a more pleasant life and get away from poverty as it was for him in those days. I think in the period that we're talking about in the thirties he was bitterly ashamed of being poor. He wanted money, to lead a more pleasant life. He used to say that his tastes were very simple and he didn't mind living with very poor people; I think he did; I don't think he liked it. I think he had many of the characteristics of an aristocrat who'd seen better days or something of that kind, you know. But I may be quite wrong. Of course he was a sick man. He never really had good health.

Going to Wigan had changed him as a writer?

Oh no, I don't think that was the turning point. I think that *Wigan Pier* comes into the same category as his early books, novels and so on. No, I think what changed Eric completely was the Spanish War . . . I remember being somewhat critical of the whole adventure myself at the time. But he went and he learnt a lot. And he came back a changed man. He used to say sometimes that he wished that he'd been in the war, the 1914–18 war. I think he was almost hurt that he'd missed that experience; so perhaps the Spanish War filled in a gap in his experience. But I think he was a different man after the Spanish War. I don't think that *Wigan Pier* had got anything to do with it.

With the Wigan Miners

Joe 'Jerry' Kennan (dates unknown) was an activist in the Independent Labour Party and a coal miner, though unemployed when Orwell visited him. He found Orwell lodgings with John and Lily Anderton, whom Orwell called 'H' in his so-called Road to Wigan Pier Diary which was, in fact, a first draft of *The Road to Wigan Pier*. Orwell says that the house was overcrowded and none too clean, but Jerry Kennan's family when I interviewed them in 1977 were adamant that it was 'spotlessly clean', chosen for that reason: and that Orwell left it for the tripe shop in order to find somewhere worse. Some would see a streak of masochism in this; perhaps, but the main reason lay in the fact that *The Road to Wigan Pier* was a polemical book: 'clean and decent' would not shock the consciences of Orwell's readers. Orwell believed that everyone saw dirt as both symbol and reality of imposed poverty. Many people in Wigan to this day are critical of Orwell for giving the town a bad name and claim that most unemployed people, especially the miners, kept their houses spotless; some of the men even claim to have helped around the house. Yet they are very appreciative of his description of mining.

Jerry Kennan showed Orwell round a lot, yet when *The Road to Wigan Pier* was published he had to join the queue for the book in the Public Library: Orwell did not send out copies to those who had helped him. Kennan mistook intimacy for friendship, forgetting that Orwell was a journalist.

The interview is taken from a BBC *Omnibus* television programme made in 1970 and the interviewer is Melvyn Bragg.

How did you first meet Orwell?
There was a knock at the door one Saturday afternoon. We were just having tea. I opened the door and there was this tall fella with a pair of flannel bags on, a fawn jacket, and a mac. And he

told me that he had two letters, one from Middleton Murry who was a pacifist author, and the other from a Frank Mead who later became editor of Labour's *Northern Voice*. . . . So I asked Orwell in, he came in, and he had tea with us. Later, after tea, we went down to Market Square where there was always, every Saturday and Sunday, a series of political meetings. There was the ILP, there was the Communist Party, there was the National Unemployed Workers Movement and there were also various religious bodies. There was always at that time seven or eight meetings going on in the Market Square. I introduced him to some of the lads connected with the Unemployed Workers Movement. I'm not positive who found him the actual lodgings. . . .

Did he find what he wanted in Wigan?

He told me that he'd been a colonel in the Burmese Military Police, he'd been educated at Eton, he'd never been in an industrial area in his life, and I distinctly recall him saying, that prior to his journey up north here, he had never seen a large factory chimney or a colliery chimney smoking.

Do you think all these changed his view of politics?

As far as his politics were concerned, he was a fella of a cynical character, seemed to be looking and delving for a philosophy. He certainly expressed dissatisfaction with British Imperialism as he had seen it. And he wanted to find out the mood and the thoughts of workers. Particularly miners or unemployed workers. And to see the effects of the means test and Anomalies Act which was having such a devastating effect on life in places like Wigan.

You took him down the pit?

Yes, I made the arrangements. I was working with the electricity department, Wigan Corporation. And we had just electrified that pit. Well, we rigged him out in a helmet and a lamp and trammelling down the main road which, of course, I could comfortably stand up in, but the way he took the roof bent a number of girders! We hadn't gone more than 300 yards when Orwell just didn't duck his head quick enough. It didn't knock the helmet off; it knocked him down. He was flat out. Then we revived him, got him round, and we travelled the best part of three-quarters of a mile, bent absolutely double. I had to be bent. There had been an 'eavy fall in what they call the ravine mine, and we couldn't get through. And this made a longer detour to the working face. And the working face was, I think, 26 inches. And by the time we landed there, Orwell was unquestionably exhausted.

And I remember him lying down on the coal on the floor and I said to him, 'It's a so-and-so good job they don't want you down here for to write a book about mining.' I said, 'The roof would bury you. . . .' Well, we did get back, but there were three occasions altogether in which he was completely out. And we came back and went into a public house the end of Chapel Lane; it's now been destroyed and the Ministry of Insurance is there. We had a drink or two and I left Orwell. He went to his lodgings which was a few yards away, perhaps 25 yards from there in Darlington Street. And Monday night when I came home from work, the wife will recall, she said, 'Have you seen anything of Orwell?' I said, 'No.' Tuesday night when I came home, she said, 'Have you seen him?' I said, 'No.' She says, 'Don't you think you have to go and look for him?' I said, 'I'll wait another day.' Wednesday night I came home from work, I haven't seen him. And the wife was just putting her coat on to go to a meeting of the Cloth Guild, when there was a knock at the door. This was Wednesday night. Something about 7.30. Believe me, Orwell was not much taller than me on the Wednesday night. Three days after being down the pits. He was as stiff as a grunt. He said he'd stayed in bed the whole of the time and he'd spend an hour or two here that night. And that was where I wrote him quite a lot of the notes on this house and quite a lot of other things in connection with the town. I found out the statistics for him. It was something like 36,000 of an insurable population, and there was well over 10,000 totally unemployed. And a good proportion of them had exhausted their benefits. . . .

What did you think of him living in a tripe shop?

It's indescribable. There were a table, and the *Manchester Evening Chronicle* was the evening newspaper then. And believe me, there's no table cloth. They would put one *Evening Chronicle* on and then the next day another went on the top of it. And I should think I've seen it where there must have been a thickness of ten or twelve *Evening Chronicles* put on.

Were you surprised that a man like Orwell would want to live there?

Well he certainly didn't like living there, but he said he was gonna be hard, he wanted to see things and learn things really at their worst. And there were one or two regular lodgers, two elderly people were there, but most of the other people used to stay a night there, or two nights. There were newspaper canvassers, they were flooding the area at that time. *Daily Dispatch*, the *News Chronicle*, the *Daily Mail*, the *Express* and quite a number of those people stayed there.

How did these people regard Orwell? Did they take him seriously?
Well no. Some did and some didn't. There were several of the boys really on the left, who very much doubted Orwell's sincerity. Because he was very cynical and he certainly never expressed any thanks for anything that was done for him. For instance, he had one full meal, several snacks on other occasions. But he never showed any appreciation of hospitality. Or anything like that. He was kind of up in the air and a snob in some ways, and was trying to come down to earth and find what things was really like. And I wouldn't say by any means he was a convinced socialist, although he was convinced that drastic changes was required.

Did you yourself admire him?
I did in some respects. And in some ways I didn't like his cynicism. He was a real cynic. And the last time I saw anything of him was in London. I think it was in August '36 when he joined the section of the International Brigade [*sic*]. And I know I reminded him of the book then, but I never got anywhere with him. Well I think anyone who you showed round for some weeks was gonna write a book, would have seen that you at least had an autographed copy, wouldn't you? And I thought, well what a peculiar type. Wasn't the money I was thinking about or anything like that. But I'm not surprised at anything he did.

What did you make of Wigan Pier *when you read it?*
Victor Gollancz wrote a tremendous foreword to it, you know. And I don't think he was entirely in agreement with it. But I think the book had a great effect on plenty of people, middle class and upper class. I know I bought several of the books. I ran a bookstall at the time. Wife and I and one or two others. We sold quite a number. And I know that people all in responsible positions, clergymen, doctors, wholesale business people who I got to read the book, it had a profound effect on them. There was no question. And his description of the means tests and the Anomalies Act certainly made quite a number of people in Wigan, as it must have done in many other parts of Britain, really appreciate and recognise something had to be done.

Finally what did you think of the book?
Well I thought the book was a fair book. I don't think it exaggerated the situation at all. And I think it gives a clear picture of what conditions was like in industrial areas in 1936.

A Visit to Liverpool

May Deiner (dates unknown) and her husband John ran a Liverpool branch of the *Adelphi* circle. They knew Middleton Murry
and Richard Rees, one of whom had given Orwell a letter of introduction to the Deiners. It seems that Orwell had already decided
that he wanted to visit Liverpool but the timing and length of his
visit, which does not figure in *The Road to Wigan Pier*, was determined by his virtual collapse after his gruelling day down the pits
(described in the last extract). The Deiners had a comfortable
house and when, after four or five days, he had recovered, they
drove him around Liverpool in their car. The George Garrett, to
whom they introduced him, was an unemployed seaman who
wrote short stories under the pseudonym of 'Matt Lowe'. Orwell
enquired while in Liverpool about the possibilities of working his
way back to London by sea, which proved impossible (otherwise
there might have been a chapter of *The Road to Wigan Pier* about
seamen's conditions).

The interviewer is Melvyn Bragg for his BBC *Omnibus* television programme of 1970.

*When Orwell came to see you in 1936 do you remember what he was
like then?*
Well, he came very early morning; he'd come on the workmen's
train, you see, from Wigan. He stood at the door and it was a
horrible morning in February, all frosty and fog, no overcoat, no
hat, no bag, and a threadbare coat. Standing there and shivering,
he was actually shivering from head to foot. Well, he collapsed,
well not quite collapsed, but as near as made no matter, so my
husband and I, we got him to bed, as quickly as we could, and he
was really very ill. But he wouldn't have a doctor. So we did the
best we could in those circumstances, gave him hot lemon. Anyway, he got better later on. When he was better George Garrett
came. Well George Orwell was very interested in Garrett
because he was just the kind of man actually he would want to
meet at that time. Because he was a dock labourer, and he'd
been out of work, oh about seven or eight years. They got on very
well together because George Garrett was able to give Orwell all
his experience of being – well, first of all a stoker in the bowels of
ships, although he hadn't been employed for about, oh seven or
eight years I should think, and George Garrett said that he was
unemployable because of his Communist views. Whether it was

true or not I don't know; but anyway George Orwell was very interested and Garrett was equally interested because Garrett himself had written quite a number of things, short stories, and articles. I don't think actually that George Orwell knew that Garrett was the man who'd written under the name of Matt Lowe though he was very interested in what he had to say. . . . When he got better, they talked, they talked oh, far into the night, and Stanley and I, we just sat and listened; they talked politics, they talked of the depressed areas, they also talked of Orwell, where he was staying in Wigan, and of course by this time Orwell, he was getting pretty – you know, it was about as much as he could stand, he'd been down the mines and the conditions were awful there. So anyway he wanted to see the slums in Liverpool. At that time we had a very early Austin 7 and Garrett and I got in and George Orwell, he – well he was jack-knifed in the back, knees up . . . We went round all the slums of Liverpool and there was a considerable amount of slum property in Liverpool. And then Orwell wanted to see the docks and dockland. Well of course Garrett was very familiar with this, being part of it, and we went round all these slums and the dock-yards, and one thing Garrett took us to was, they were taking on some men for the day. In those days, of course, it was all casual labour at the docks. And they were picking men out, there was a boat in, and there was a man there, I think he was called the gaffer, I don't quite remember, and he came out. There were about 200 or 250 men, all waiting to be taken on, hoping for jobs. This man came round and touched them on the shoulder, 'and you and you and you', and took them on. Then they went inside the gates and the others, of course, they were very dejected, they just all had to go away. Well, this moved Orwell very much, and Garrett himself, although he was used to it, he was a very emotional man and so both of them were utterly miserable about this.

Well, then afterwards we went over to Port Sunlight. We went through the tunnel. And we saw the houses there, small houses but they were the first sort of council house there was; it was a garden city . . . And of course after being round all the slums, these were quite an event after that.

But when Orwell came to your house, you'd been in contact with him before?

Yes, at the Middleton Murrys, but he didn't leave any impression at all. It's surprising really, seeing the great man that he is. But he didn't leave any vivid impression; only his height of course.

He was a very withdrawn man. That was all that we remembered of him. So we'd almost forgotten him and then some while after, I think it was some months after, Richard Rees wrote to us saying that Orwell was writing this book on the unemployed and the miners, and could we help in any way, either by letting him meet people who would be valuable to him, or even using our home as a base, because of course we were easy travelling distance to Wigan. And so we said that was all right; we were delighted of course. We'd read his books by then, well the two of them that were published then, and we were delighted. . . . He was terribly involved in what he did; there was no sort of fake about him at all. And this you felt in everything he said and did. Of course there were a lot of writers about at the time who weren't like that. So you did notice the difference, you noticed that he was this type of man.

When Wigan Pier came out, what did you think of it?

It seemed to me a very important book; it seemed to me that the question of the unemployed and all the distressed areas was terribly well portrayed, and you felt that really he'd done all in his power to get himself into this situation in order to be able to – you really felt that he'd become one of them as far as is possible for anybody with such a different background. . . . It was in everybody's mind at this time; I mean this was the burning question of the day. People were only just beginning to be aware of the depression and the unemployment and all the misery of it; you see, before it had just been accepted. And he really pointed out, it was the thing that had to be remedied. . . .

He was such a real man; I think that covered it. We didn't feel any embarrassment at all with him. Just that he hadn't much to say unless he was talking about his books or about the things that interested him, about the depression; he hadn't much of a personal nature, you see. And yet you felt the warmth there; you felt the concern if you like. So there was no embarrassment.

On a Street Corner in Wigan

Sydney Smith (b. 1909), now a bookshop proprietor in Wigan, remembers talking to Orwell in 1936 when he was a young man. He is here interviewed by Nigel Williams. He gives a different address for the tripe shop where Orwell lodged (having condemned Jerry Kennan's house as too clean to be typical) than either the one I give in *George Orwell: A Life* (see pages 282 and 612) or Jeremy Seabrook's in *New Society* (20 Jan. 1977). I still believe that it was 22 Darlington Street since the names of the owners or their lodgers found in the electoral role are euphonious with the pseudonyms used by Orwell. But local memory supports Mr Smith. The dispute will continue until the Town Council establish a committee of enquiry to determine which tripe shop was described by Orwell and to mark the spot with a plaque.

Mr Smith, these are the streets near where Orwell stayed when he came to Wigan. Have they changed much?
They've not changed one bit – they're every bit as clean today as they were then.
Whereabouts were you at that time in 1936 when he came?
I was living at number 21 Sovereign Road and that is the corner of where my friends, including my younger brother, and I first met Orwell. Well the only time I really met him in conversation was when Orwell came and we thought at that time he was quizzing, in the sense that there was a means test operating – very severe – and people who were unemployed were doing jobs on the side. Fortunately, from our point of view, my brother and myself and the two or three friends with us, we all worked in shops, so the unemployment was not so severe for us as it was with the industry.
So can you tell us about that meeting? You were standing on the street corner?
Standing on the street corner as young men will. We were very keen cyclists in those days and we probably were planning to have a ride to wherever, when this gentleman – tall, thin, in a rather unkempt mac and a dirty trilby hat – came and asked us what were our jobs and, as he spoke the language different to us in the north, we became suspicious immediately that this man was quizzing whether we were working, or drawing dole and working, and we were rather a bit averse to this. We weren't keen on carrying on the conversation.
You thought he was a social security snooper?
Well the social security didn't come into it – it was means test, that was the name of the game. The persons who were employed and became unemployed, they had thirteen weeks unemployment pay, commonly known as the dole, and after that they had

to go in front of an enquiry and if they qualified they got a little bit more, and if they didn't qualify, they didn't get anything.

Can you tell us how Orwell looked? He was an extraordinary looking man wasn't he?

Orwell was tall with . . . when you say how did he look, all I can describe him is as a tall fellow with a very nice accent, with a dirty mac and a rather unkempt trilby. That's all I can say about his appearance.

And what sort of questions was he asking you?

He was asking what we did for a living and also had we had experience of unemployment, which I had earlier, in earlier years, but now I was working in the bookshop, the book stall in the arcade, which my mother had bought me.

He was very much an officer and a gentleman wasn't he? Is that the way he struck you?

Well, yes, I would think he was superior class, if you like to put it in that way, while we think we're just, we must be honest, we're working class; and this chap came along dressed more like working class but with an accent more higher class. . . .

Can you tell us about the lodgings where Orwell stayed – that's quite a famous shop isn't it?

Oh yes, the lodgings where he stayed. The landlord who was the tenant of the shop was a fellow about 5 feet 2 inches or 3 inches in height – very square built. He was an ex-miner and, of course, in the depression days people resorted to all sorts of things to get a living and he opened this corner shop at thirty-five Sovereign Road to eke out a living. He sold everything from tripe to household commodities, the lot. And, of course, to augment the income besides he took in lodgers at number thirty-three, which was adjacent to the shop at number thirty-five.

One of the most famous things in the book is Orwell's description of the tripe in the shop window.

Well, yes, I would say that was quite right, tripe was a cheap form of food wasn't it? You couldn't afford meat in those days, tripe was the next best thing you could afford and there I would say that Orwell's description of the shop was accurate, I don't think that was the correct image of Wigan, not by any means. Wigan people are rather proud and they were clean and those that could work worked hard and being unemployed was a kind of stigma on their pride. I knew from my place in the town centre, people walking about and on some occasions, on the cold days, they used to go into Woolworths, really to get a warm. This is perfectly true and since an article appeared in the *Sunday Times* a number of people have come to me and said how well they remembered those incidents.

Jack Common's Recollections

Jack Common (1903–68), author of novels about his working-class childhood on Tyneside (*Kiddar's Luck* and *The Ampersand*), met Orwell in 1930 when he was working for *The Adelphi*. They became good friends. He borrowed Orwell's cottage in Wallington, when Orwell was abroad during 1938–9.

'Orwell at Wallington' is a manuscript found among his papers and written some time in the late 1950s.

My friendship with Eric began in disappointment and grew under mutual suspicion. When I explain that this 'Eric' is the one that later called himself 'George Orwell' you'll appreciate that mutual suspicion was the right climate to meet him in. We got on fairly merrily by this method of regularly turning over one another's statements to look for the bug underneath, integrity undamaged by intellectual contact being a minimum demand of Orwellian intercourse. But first the disappointment.

The thirties began for me with the reorganisation of *The Adelphi* magazine, and a job pushing circulation at the hard-times rate of two pounds a week. This I hoped would be a latch-lifter into the world of writers. Fair enough, I did meet *Adelphi* contributors and others in the Bloomsbury Street office after my return from beating the bounds of circulation. One name that interested me was that of 'E. A. Blair'. He wrote no-nonsense reviews and vivid pieces that looked like sections from a coming book. In addition he had a legend. He was a rebel, he was a tramp, he belonged to the underworld of poverty. A man to look out for then, a man to meet.

He was sitting in Katherine Mansfield's arm-chair one dusky afternoon talking to [Sir] Richard Rees and Max Plowman, the editors. Like that, at that low level at which one took in first the scrub of hair and curiously-ravaged face, he looked the real thing, outcast, gifted pauper, kicker against authority, perhaps near-criminal. But he rose to acknowledge the introduction and shake hands. Manners showed through. A sheep in wolf's cloth-ing, I thought, taking in his height and stance, accent and cool built-in superiority, the public school presence. What he said in subsequent conversation that day I do not remember – perhaps because of the let-down in how he said it.

Our next encounter was just before Christmas. I happened to be alone in the office but I offered the traditional Bloomsbury hospitality of the cup of tea and cigarette before the twelve flaming asbestos columns of the gas fire. I think we probably began by making a mutual moan about the nonsense of Christmas. Anyway it is certain that he was tempted to launch out with one of the statements he loved to use for shock value and which made him appear like an *enfant terrible* in decay. He wanted to spend Christmas in gaol; therefore he thought of starting a bonfire in Trafalgar Square.

Now this was just the public-school-undergrad sort of fancy that irritated me then because it mocked the real destitution I and my folks had known. Was Eric just a phoney then? Or anyway an amateur pauper? Hinting at that last, I put the professional case against wasting a possible prison sentence on frivolity, advising him to go in for theft instead – after all it might succeed, then he could have a genuine Merry Christmas where he liked.

It was his turn to be suspicious of me. How come that a poorly-educated, hard-up, working-class dialect-speaker such as me came to be employed by a literary-philosophical Bloomsbury magazine? While out of work, I explained, I wrote various pieces including one sent to John Middleton Murry, founder of *The Adelphi*; that led to a meeting, the promise of a job some day.

Eric nodded. He was putting me down as a vagary of Murry's romantic idealism and cranky enthusiasm, I felt. So I asked how he came to write for *The Adelphi*. When in Burma he was a sub-scriber, being interested in the debates of the intellectuals. But he was not a loyal supporter of the Murry crusades. Often the magazine disgusted him. Then he used to prop it up against a tree and fire his rifle at it. (I wanted him to put this in the birth-day symposium but he didn't.)

This story, a careless confiding as it was, warmed my imagina-tion towards the man. We parted that day, me to dearest wife and he to dungeon, much better known to each other, the more so for not having been taken in.

We got that Christmas over safely (no arrest of E. A. Blair reported), and entered Year One of the thirties. Eric had jobs, school-teaching at Southall was one, and was writing hard. He made few appearances at the office. Once he had with him a Hawk Moth caterpillar – 'a Privet Hawk Moth,' he said when we failed to name it. He was wrong I found out a couple of years later (a Poplar Hawk, it was) when I'd taken to living in the country. But at the time, I was impressed by the perception of another side to him, Eton, Burma, now English countryside.

This was when his book *Down and Out* was going the rounds of imperceptive publishers, a time of anxiety for the writer struggling with *Burmese Days*. I remember running into him at Max Plowman's place in Hampstead. He was staying almost next door with Mrs Fierz, a keen Murry follower, and this was a bit of luck for him. After he had abandoned an assault on publishers to buy *Down and Out*, she asked if she might make a last attempt. He agreed. She sent the manuscript to Gollancz, which was the sort of vulgar, enterprising liberal-minded publisher which made Eric squirm but acceptable, even obligatory, to George Orwell, a name that now came into notice for the first time.

When I saw it I asked him why he wanted to bury Eric. He has given several replies to this question to different questioners and probably it was unanswerable, or could have been answered only if he'd been a much greater writer than he was. To me his reason was that the publication of *Down and Out* might have distressed relatives had they known he was tramping the roads, putting up at 'spikes'. As to the name itself, he did not borrow it but compiled it, seeking for something that sounded solidly English. That seemed to me very true. The rootless, non-dialect speakers of the public school élite are apt to over-value nationality, just as exiles do. It did not surprise me once I'd considered it that Scots-descended, Anglo-Indian, Etonian Eric Blair would like to be accepted as English. The trouble about 'George Orwell', I remarked, could be that it is so English that some Englishmen are bound to be already wearing it. He'd thought of that. They'd have no legal redress, he said. All the same, it must be hard lines on some harmless young choirmaster or writer of boys' adventure stories to see his name headlined in connection with a scurrilous work about able-bodied paupers or Communist commiswaiters. If I came upon such a one I promised to let Eric know. Twenty years later, too late unfortunately, I found out that the real George Orwell of all these years was a Hampshire antiquary, well-known to a small circle.

After *Down and Out* the false George Orwell was well and truly launched as a novelist. That is, he was always well reviewed and could count on a faithful readership likely to grow. The danger was, this being the thirties, that they might come to seem irrelevant. It was typical of the way things were going that *The Adelphi*, formerly a monthly ivory tower sheltering or gathering together the devotees of truth-beauty, beauty-truth in writing, was now a political lighthouse in which doughty polemicists argued about which way to direct the beam. At that same old blooming asbestos gas-fire where Eric Blair airily described himself over a cup of tea as a Tory Anarchist and nobody objected to such a harmless description, now Marxist and Fascist and acidulated Liberal fought wickedly to establish a derogatory meaning to each other's phrases and cigarettes were sucked to death in short, sharp puffs.

Partly for peace's sake, partly for economy, Rees, now sole editor, with myself as assistant, moved the office to a room in his Chelsea flat. Orwell occasionally called in. His talk was about his struggle to get his books written, discoveries made in back streets, particularly bits of phoney folklore, such as the one about the threepenny bit in *Keep the Aspidistra Flying*. He made no violent change of political conviction, but somehow one gathered he now approved of socialism on moral grounds.

Of course, his success as a novelist was relative and limited. By working fast he could just make enough to live, three or four pounds a week that is. Like many another before and since he looked for some small non-intellectual occupation that would supplement the income slightly, take the pressure off and incidentally perhaps pay another bonus by giving him new experiences to write about. After I had not seen him for some time, I had a letter from him addressed to the Hertfordshire cottage I was now commuting from. He wanted advice. Having himself rented a Hertfordshire cottage, eleven miles north of me, he had the idea of reviving its one-time role as village stores. I had not long given up my own experiment in writer's income bolstering, a confectioner-tobacconist place in Chelsea, so might I advise him on how to obtain stocks, a licence to sell tobacco, etc?

Even in those days of carlessness among writers and other proletarians, eleven miles was not all that far away (I walked to his place once), so my reply was an invitation to a meal. He promised to bike over next Sunday morning.

As our cottage might be hard to find, I walked out to the brow of the hill north of the church to await the visitor's coming. He had Datchworth's oaken spire, today shooting up to a sky of silk and summer, to aim at. I leaned against a three-armed signpost which read To Knebworth, Woolmer Green; To Datchworth

Green; To Bragbury End. From that last direction, and very much downhill, there presently appeared a solitary cyclist, a tall man on a tall bike. He could have got off and walked at the worst gradient. Not he. This Don Quixote weaved and wandered this side, that side, defeating windmills of gravity till he grew tall on the hillbrow and tall too was that Rosinante of a bicycle, an ancient Triumph that could have belonged to his father.

Fellow-countrymen, men of Herts, we made greetings. It was odd, a new vision, seeing him in these country circumstances. He might have been a seedy Empire-builder, the reality of some character read about in boys' adventure stories, a broken-down ex-officer. Whatever it was I saw that morning, I am sure I had a fuller appreciation of my friend Eric. For the moment it was drowned in talk, country-dweller's talk first. He had far more interest than I'd expected in my efforts to make a garden out of bare meadow. He was negotiating, he said, for a bit of rough land opposite his cottage; he could run hens there and sell the eggs in his village stores. We continued this pleasant chat down to the pub.

The landlord, a cheerful drunkard ex-Navy rating, called him 'sir' tentatively, expecting me to correct him if this was one of the lads, despite his gentility. But I did not – no particular reason. Years later I realised that no pub ever knew my friend as 'Eric', let alone 'George'.

A Meeting with Henry Miller

Alfred Perlès (b. 1900), an American and friend and companion of Henry Miller the novelist, wrote this fascinating account of an odd encounter in Paris. Orwell had reviewed Miller's *Black Spring* and written to him about his admiration for *Tropic of Cancer*. In his great essay of 1939, 'Inside the Whale', he symbolised Miller as the artist who must be defended for his art, even though he was grossly irresponsible in his social attitudes. This is from Perlès' memoir, *My Friend Henry Miller* (Neville Spearman, London, 1955).

The political situation was fast worsening. The League of Nations had succumbed, unable to survive the combined shocks of the Sino-Japanese conflict and Mussolini's attack on Abyssinia. Hitler was firmly entrenched in Germany and the victims of Nazi oppression were mass-emigrating to Europe and the Americas – those who weren't in the concentration camps, that is. In Spain the civil war was raging with unabated fury: dress rehearsal for World War II. It was the heyday of totalitarianism, the seeming end of democracy. The war clouds were gathering.

One morning a tallish emaciated Englishman walked into Miller's studio and introduced himself as George Orwell. The meeting between the two writers didn't quite come off as one might have expected it to. On the face of it they should have had a lot in common, both having been through the mill, both having been 'down and out' in Paris and elsewhere. But what a difference between them in their outlook on life! It was almost the difference between East and West. Miller, in his semi-Oriental detachment, accepted life, all the joys and all the miseries of life, as one accepts rain or sunshine. Orwell's detachment was less innate than inflicted upon him by the force of circumstances, as it were. Miller was vulnerable and anarchic, expecting nothing from the world at large. Orwell was tough, resilient and politically minded, ever striving in his way to improve the world. Miller was a citizen of the universe and no more proud of it than a green olive is of being green or a black one of being black. Orwell, a typical Englishman, sceptical and disillusioned though he was, still had faith in political dogmas, economic doctrines, in the improvement of the masses through change of government and social reforms. Liberty and Justice, which for Miller were personal attributes to be acquired only by constant individual self-improvement, were in Orwell's opinion the appendage of democracy. Both were peace-loving men but, whereas Miller manifested his love of peace by refusing to fight for *any* cause, Orwell had no reluctance to engage in war, if the cause were, in his opinion, a just one.

'You admit somewhere in your letter that you have never been fond of war, though at present reconciled to it,' Miller wrote to me during the last war in a long letter which was later published under the title *Murder the Murderer*. 'The truth is that nobody is really fond of war, not even the military-minded. And yet, throughout the short history of the human race, there have been only a few breathing spells of peace. What are we to conclude from this seeming paradox? My own conclusion is the simple, obvious one that, though fearing war, men have never truly and ardently desired peace. I do earnestly desire peace, and what intelligence I have tells me that peace is not attained by fighting but by acting peaceably.' . . .

These lines were not written until June 1944, but the words he employed when Orwell came to enlist his sympathy for the Spanish republican cause were more or less the same, namely that liberty – a spiritual value – cannot be gained by war, any more than a mere military victory can enforce the justice of a cause, any cause. Miller did not try, of course, to win Orwell over to his way of thinking or even to dissuade him from going to Spain. Every man must do what he thinks is right, even if what he thinks right is wrong, was his conviction.

During the course of his visit that afternoon, as I learned later, Orwell had confided to Miller that his experience while serving in the police in India [sic] had left an indelible mark upon him. The suffering he had witnessed and which he had unwillingly aided and abetted, so to speak, had been a source of unremitting preoccupation ever since. It was to wipe out an unwarrantable feeling of guilt that he deliberately invited the deprivations and humiliations so graphically and poignantly described in *Down and Out in Paris and London*.

Miller of course not only understood Orwell's desire for self-flagellation, being himself a notorious self-flagellant, but he also felt a great sympathy for him in his predicament. But why, having undergone all that he had, why, he wondered, did Orwell choose to punish himself still further? Miller would not have spoken in this vein to an ordinary volunteer whose idealism required the test of action. In Orwell, however, who he felt had already atoned for any guilt, real or imaginary, he sensed an individual who was of more use to humanity alive than dead.

To this Orwell made the classic reply that in such momentous situations, where the rights and the very existence of a whole people are at stake, there could be no thought of avoiding self-sacrifice. He spoke his convictions so earnestly and humbly that Miller desisted from further argument and promptly gave him his blessings.

'There's just one thing,' said Miller, raising his glass in a final gesture of assent. 'I can't let you go to war in this beautiful Savile Row suit of yours. Here, let me present you with this corduroy jacket, it's just what you need. It isn't bulletproof but at least it'll keep you warm. Take it, if you like, as my contribution to the Spanish republican cause.'

Orwell vehemently denied that he wore a Savile Row suit (it actually came from the Charing Cross Road) but accepted

Miller's gift in the spirit in which it was offered. Henry discreetly refrained from adding that Orwell would have been welcome to the jacket even had he chosen to fight for the opposite side.

With the ILP in Spain

Robert ('Bob') Edwards (b. 1906), Labour and Co-op. MP since 1955, was in command of the Independent Labour Party's contingent of volunteers on the Catalan Front near Huesca. The ILP were to the left of the Labour Party but bitterly opposed, though many of them were Marxists, to the Communist Party. In Spain they fought alongside the POUM (the United Workers Marxist Party) who were Marxists but anti-Communists. The POUM were commonly called Trotskyites but strictly speaking were not. Their leader Andrés Nin (killed by the Communists in 1937) had been Trotsky's personal secretary in Russia but had broken from him because of his dictatorial behaviour and ignorance of Spanish conditions. Orwell, impatient to be in the war, went out on his own ahead of the ILP contingent and fought with the POUM alongside Anarchist contingents until transferring to the ILP company when they arrived, though he remained in the same section of the line.

The POUM and the ILP were hated by the Communists, first called Trotskyite and then 'Fascist collaborators', principally because they had been the first to translate and publish reports coming out of Russia which were critical of Stalin's state trials of the old Bolsheviks. When Bob Edwards went home for a political rally but could not or did not return, the men of the ILP company elected Orwell (who fought as Eric Blair) as their leader.

The first two paragraphs are from an introduction to the Folio Society's edition of *Homage to Catalonia* (1970) and the succeeding paragraphs are from a transcript of a BBC recording of 14 April 1960 made by Rayner Heppenstall.

He came striding towards me – all 6 foot 3 of him – dressed in a grotesque mixture of clothing – corduroy riding breeches, khaki puttees and huge boots caked with mud, a yellow pigskin jerkin, a chocolate-coloured balaclava helmet with a knitted khaki scarf of immeasurable length wrapped round and round his neck and face up to his ears, an old-fashioned German rifle over his shoulder and two hand-grenades hanging from his belt. Running to keep pace, one on each side of him, similarly equipped, were two small youths of the militia, whilst farther behind was a shaggy mongrel dog with the letters POUM painted on its side.

The youth of the militia protested violently when they heard that they were about to lose George Orwell for, despite the weary and frustrating hours he had spent trying to train them into a disciplined force with regular guard duties and rifle practice, they all idolised him. This sector of the front had previously been taken from the Fascists after violent action but was now about one and a half miles from the nearest Fascist post, and there was a temporary lull. Thus Orwell eagerly agreed to the transfer because, as he informed me, he had yet to make his first contact with the opposing Fascist forces. . . .

TRANSCRIPT OF THE BBC PROGRAMME MADE BY RAYNER HEPPEN-
STALL

We captured two of Franco's soldiers. We discovered that they were conscripts from the Italian Army. They tried to persuade us that they were not out on patrol – they were actually cutting down firewood, and Orwell's instantaneous reaction was, 'Now where did you leave the axe?', because on our front we didn't even have an axe.

He had a phobia about rats. We got used to them. They used to gnaw at our boots during the night, but George just couldn't get used to the presence of rats and one day, late in the evening, he caused us great embarrassment which resulted in the loss of some very valuable material and equipment. A particularly adventurous rat had annoyed George for some time and he got out his gun and shot it. But the explosion in the confines of his dug-out vibrated – it seemed throughout the whole front – and then the whole front and both sides went into action. The artillery started, we threw patrols out, machine-gun nests were set going and after it all, our valuable cookhouse had been destroyed and two buses that had brought up our reserves.

Our positions in the Aragon mountains were so strong on both sides that the war was stationary – the only action being between large patrols. In one of three skirmishes, a particularly close friend of Orwell's was badly wounded. We tried as best we could with our little equipment to stop the blood from the wound, but were not very successful, so Orwell and I decided to take his friend to the nearest village which was Alcubierre where we had a little hospital. We strapped Orwell's friend to a donkey and led the donkey out into the darkness. We were new to this territory, but we both agreed that, if we followed the valley just behind our lines, we were bound to arrive in the village where the little hospital was situated. As dawn was breaking we reached the village and were marching, leading the donkey up the only road, being saluted by little groups of patrols on either side of the road. As we got into the market square of the village, to our astonishment we found the gold and red flag of Franco flying there. We turned the donkey round, stepped out as fast as we could, but with as much dignity as was possible under those conditions. Patrols were still saluting us and we got back to our lines. Our friend seemed a lot better, due to either fright or natural causes, and the blood had actually stopped flowing.

In the early part of the Spanish War, they imposed a system of complete social equality. Everybody in Spain received ten pesetas a day. Every child got ten pesetas a day, a mother, a widow, a worker, a general in the Army, a captain and the rank-and-file Militia man. Orwell was greatly impressed by the fact that the Spaniards had cleaned up Barcelona and had completely abolished prostitution and bullfighting. And one thing I know which impressed him greatly was the beautiful, artistic, political posters of many colours which had taken the place of the vulgar commercial advertising. He was very, very distressed when he returned to Barcelona from the front to discover that all these social advances had been halted and they were back to the old system of inequality in payments; and the black market, that hadn't existed when he joined the Militia, was reintroduced.

In the Spanish Trenches

Stafford Cottman (b. 1918) was the youngest member of the ILP contingent who fought alongside the POUM in Catalonia. He was with Orwell almost the entire time and they escaped together at the end when the Communists began a purge of the Anarchists and the independent Marxists such as the POUM. He at first inclined, as Orwell did, more to the Communist view of how the war should be fought, and wanted to be transferred to the Communist – led International Brigade on the Madrid front where there was constant action; but both Orwell and Cottman changed their minds after the May riots in Barcelona.

He is interviewed on the site of the old battle lines by Nigel Williams for the 1984 BBC TV *Arena* programme, *Orwell Remembered.*

Stafford, how long is it since you were last here?
In La Granja, forty-six, forty-seven years.
Has it changed much?
Yes, it has. There is much more greenery about than when I last saw it. . . . We used to sleep in this part of it. I remember quite well if you were on guard early in the morning George Orwell would often be writing . . . in spite of his preoccupation with writing, he was always very practical in matters that concerned soldiers, such as guns. I think he was honestly the only one that really felt the lack of oil for the guns, you know. Whereas the rest of us said, 'Oh well, no oil, too bad.' And with foodstuff too; where we accepted the fact that there wasn't very much, when he knew that there were things like potatoes about, well, he thought let's get 'em. He was very practical. Of course it was in a sort of no-man's-land and his officers, like Bob Edwards and Georges Kopp, didn't think it was worth it and involved more danger than was necessary. But he used to get 'em all the same. Similarly with fire. He would go out and look for firewood until they used to make a joke about it. But he was one of the most practical men, funnily enough, in the whole outfit.
How old were you then?
I was seventeen, eighteen.
So did he drill the men?
Not very much. He didn't seem to be particularly keen on the drill side, he was then more concerned with being able to change the bolt of a rifle, being able to oil it, and making sure that the ammunition clip was well oiled. He thought a lot of the Mexican clips. He reckoned they were more efficient. At my tender years I couldn't tell much difference. The people more concerned with drilling were young Spaniards. They really wanted to be drilled. And they've asked, even gone up and asked people, 'Can you find someone to drill us,' you know, which is extraordinary really. And I remember that they thought that anyone from Europe, France, England, Germany, were much better military fighters than themselves because they'd been used to a history of wars and had all the military equipment and they said anybody

with that background must be better than them. And Orwell made the point that no Englishman would ever make a remark like that, even if he believed it; you know, you must be better than the next man.

Was he unapproachable, apart from the rest of the unit?

No, not at all. No, he'd more than likely give you a nod, a wave, a grunt you know, your turn sort of thing. No, I never remember him in any way as being discouraging or hard to get along with, as we would say now. He tended always to encourage, and even in Barcelona when he had the injury and Eileen naturally looked after him and to some extent screened him from a lot of questions, he would always say, 'Yes, I'd like to see . . .' whoever it was. He was, we forget, a schoolteacher and this gave him an air of authority, which is given to some people. And it shows up a lot, I think, in any sort of thing requiring uniform. Even with his funny brown hat and long trenchcoat he had this dignity. And because you knew that he would be the man most likely to put you right, you went to him. He was a natural teacher in that sense.

Did you feel like an army of occupation?

I never felt that. I was probably not sensitive enough. You know, we were here and that's it. I really didn't see anything that would suggest, you know, an army of occupation or any unnecessary ill manners or arrogance. Orwell was probably more sensitive about some things. Probably a few things happened that made him think that we could have behaved a little better than we did. And no doubt people could. . . .

Stafford, you were saying that in the mornings you'd catch Orwell writing. Did he ever talk about what he was writing?

No, I don't recall him ever talking about what he was writing. But he did talk about what he had read or what he was currently reading. And for some odd reason I remember one of the books he was reading, a strange thing really because it's an eighteenth, nineteenth-century thing, a book called *Hard Cash* by Charles Reade. And the point that he made about the book was that it showed how people then used their money to dispose of relatives who were in their way by bribing other people to certify them as insane. He was equally outraged by the injustice of that as the injustices that were happening at the time.

You mean he had a capacity to get really angry about things?

Yes, he did, yes, very much so. And it wasn't simulated anger. It tended to mount as he spoke. And he didn't overdo it but, you know, he could get very ironic and acid, if you like, which I believe some people that knew him during his schoolteaching days have some evidence of.

Did he get on with the other people in the unit, all the other English contingent?

Most of them, yes. I would say that he was the most popular man in the contingent generally. There were about three or four people who didn't like him. I think, because of a sort of wrongly applied class prejudice. The little group I'm thinking of didn't give him credit for having a sympathy and affinity with working people. They would comment on his accent, or the fact that he'd been disdainful over some subject or another. So really I don't think that the fault was his. There was this . . . I call it inverted snobbery. Personally I think that deeds are more important than origins. And I'm sure he recognised that. I remember him saying, never judge people by their accent. A man cannot help the way he speaks.

You ended up in Spain because of your politics obviously. . . .

Oh yes. I went to a socialist Sunday school in Barking and I got as indoctrinated as any Catholic kid except I got Keir Hardie, Karl Marx, William Morris and we were taught socialist principles almost parrot fashion. Such as 'observe and think in order to discover the truth'; 'never deceive yourself or others.' We recited such things and, you know, we believed them. And when the Spanish thing broke out, the injustice to the Spanish workers was so emphasised that this is why a lot of youngsters, particularly from English universities and, of course, all over the world, volunteered to come over. I was so keen that I volunteered for the International Brigade and the ILP contingent and this interested George Orwell, because he was in exactly the same position. He would have gone to Madrid if he hadn't found it quicker to get to the front here. And he thought you could work your way up to the front, you know, promotion sort of style. His insistence on wanting to join the International Brigade upset Bob Edwards a bit. He said that Orwell was allowing his duties or career as a writer to get in the way and he wanted to go to the International Brigade because it was better copy and better material. This was Bob's suggestion, which I don't think was so at all. I'm sure he wanted to get there because he believed in what he was doing. He felt that the war was a bit, you know, stagnant here. Bit like the Second World War where things didn't happen and everybody said we must start a second front. Well there was one around the Madrid area and I'm sure he wanted to join it and really get stuck in. And I thought that this was a bit unreasonable of Bob, you know. But I think again, this is sort of inverted snobbery, class prejudice. Orwell was here to do his best, in the war, as a soldier. It's true that he came here as a writer and journalist in the first place but from what I could see of it that was a sort of second part-time thing. His soldiering was the main thing.

Did you talk politics much with him, Stafford?

Yes, we did. Particularly concerning why did I not see things so clearly as to want to go on one side or the other, that is to say, the International Brigade or the POUM. Of course my position was I'll take whichever came up. I think he was disturbed by the fact that there was insufficient military activity here. And I thought the same thing, to some extent; that if we could be better used in the Madrid area then we ought to be used.

How long were you actually here at La Granja?

Two months perhaps. I'm not quite sure. Talking about getting upset, the thing he was upset about was the way that local Spaniards treated the horses. They really did flog 'em. And steam used to be coming off them and sometimes the poor things had collapsed. And he even said that in countries where the Catholic influence was strong, there was always a history of bad treatment to animals.

Can you tell us about Orwell and the Catholic Church?

Yes. His attitude to the Catholic Church was extremely critical. I think he distrusted them, particularly because at that stage they always identified with the oppressors rather than the oppressed. He seemed to understand that very clearly. Probably because he found no support from them in his own very well-recorded endeavours to identify and understand the oppressed.

This church behind us, had it been damaged by the local population?

Yes, it had. Inside there were signs of the altar having been battered. The altar cloth had been torn across and was left lying on the floor. There were very crude slogans written in human excreta on the walls. It was obvious that at some stage this desecration had occurred. We found it strange that nobody cleared it up. But then I don't think, in retrospect, we could be critical about that because we made no attempt to clear it up either.

Did that shock Orwell, did that shock his sense of the proprieties, his conservative nature?

He regretted it . . . but he understood it.

This is the difference between him and Auden who said that it was the damage done to churches in Spain that finally turned Auden off socialism.

Oh that's right. Applied to the background of war it was a very incidental chapter. There was evidence that they were used as armouries and that weapons had been concealed in them and that therefore they were liable to come under attack. And certainly I have since seen newsreels during that period where people were being ushered out of churches with boxes of ammunition and things like that around them.

We are now just outside Huesca. And it must have been about here that the red line which divided the Republican forces from the Fascist forces over in Huesca came. Of course it wasn't a straight line. It crossed over and varied from time to time and therefore at night in the dark if you didn't keep particular track of the place you'd just left you could easily find yourself on the wrong side of the line.

Did that ever happen to you?

No, this didn't happen to me because my comrades, in particular Orwell, made sure that I had a junior role. And I'm quite grateful to them for that, even though at the time I did tend to resent it.

What kind of action did you see then, Stafford?

Well, the main action I saw was sporadic fighting on the front here, which was chiefly aimed at us by snipers. And several times Spaniards were hit and they would fall from the sandbags and I have memories of them, you know, haemorrhaging and the blood coming out of their mouths and going down into the sand. And instinctively one wanted to go to them but we were always discouraged until they were looked after by the medical orderly and the stretcher bearers.

One of the things he talks about in Homage to Catalonia *is the difficulties sometimes of firing. He was talking about training his gun on somebody who is holding up his trousers.*

Yes, that's right. And he was human enough to recognise not an enemy but a human being and he writes to the effect that he couldn't possibly kill a man who was pulling up his trousers. But other times he got moving dots – which were people – in his sights and he had no hesitation at all in firing at them. I think this is something which is peculiar to almost all, particularly modern, wars. When you see your enemy as a human being he ceases to be an enemy. Probably the best examples are bombing raids. I'm sure that if those of us that released bombs over targets with obvious tragic results to people below were asked to land our aeroplanes and take cudgels and go round the houses and batter these people, we wouldn't do it. So it's sort of corruption; distance lends not so much enchantment but the reverse. Distance dehumanises human beings. This was borne out quite well in the Orson Welles' film *The Third Man* of the man on the big wheel when he says, 'Look at those dots down there. Does it matter really if a few thousand of them cease to exist?'

Stafford, you lived through the same war as Orwell out here in Spain. Do you think his description of it glamorises the war? Do you think it dehumanises it . . .?

No, I don't think it does. I think it's viewed and described very sensitively. He never trivialised suffering. I can't remember a single time when he even suggested that it didn't matter. No, I think the reverse. That because he lived in a world where tyranny would prevail if you didn't resist, he saw the necessity for resisting. But he was also careful not to glorify or sanctify it.

Was it a well-organised war from your point of view?

No. But then it would have been a miracle if it had been anything else. I'm not much of a Marxist student but one of the maxims often quoted is that revolutions are won when the ruling class are divided and the working class are united. Well I've come to the conclusion that the working class will never be united because we are divided more and more by an increasing variety of dogmas, of which there were some embodied at the time that Orwell and the ILP contingent with the POUM were out here. No, it was disorganised and this very much worried us. It's interesting, for example, that all the delays and divisions had an adverse effect on the morale of the International Brigade. So much so that they sent Walter Tapsall to investigate. That's another story, but it does show that the divisions had a bad effect, particularly on the International side. And I would imagine that it would be even more so on the part of the Spaniards.

Also the equipment you used. You were saying that many of the casualties were self-inflicted. Was that correct?

Yes, that's right. The equipment really was archaic and disastrous. Most of us had long German Mausers, dated about 1890. The internal riflings which give the rifle its velocity, or the bullet the velocity leaving the rifle, if these aren't really well engineered the gun loses its precision. People like George Orwell could look through and they'd start cursing and saying 'Look at the damned thing, it's a danger.' As far as I was concerned the inside just looked like a whirly thing going back. No, the equipment was a disaster. I think Orwell says somewhere in *Homage to Catalonia* that the best ammunition was German, the

Mexican was quite good, but mostly it didn't have the precision that it should have had, particularly these odd ones. Many times he said to people, 'Well look, I wouldn't fire this one unless you have to. Try and get another one.' And certainly there was evidence of a number of self-inflicted wounds, quite accidental, where in shouldering it the bolt blew. Apparently if this happens to you the wound tends to be blackened and burnt, rather than if you're hit by an enemy bullet where it tends to be smoother and cleaner. So the equipment was pretty much a disaster. Which in some ways increased our resentment because the Fascists had the advantage of much more modern Italian and German equipment.

To sum up, Stafford, it was a pretty quiet war. Orwell calls it a comic opera war at one point.

Yes that's right, at one point. And he even says that our defences were so bad that any dozen Boy Scouts armed with airguns or two dozen Girl Guides with catapults could have penetrated our defences. He was laying on the heavy irony a bit then which, I think, he often does amusingly.

Stafford, can I ask you now. Was it here at Alcubierre that you first saw George Orwell?

Yes, that's right, it was here. Early one morning when my Spanish friends here were dishing up the very tasty early morning coffee, *café con leche*, and it was very early in the morning, Bob Williams and George Orwell came up with their mugs and got their ration and we were introduced to the two new Englishmen. George had a very ragged woolly hat on and a long trenchcoat.

And can you tell me about the propaganda exercise of the Red troops.

Yes, it was mutual really. But there were large megaphones and we used to ask or plead that the Fascists should desert and come over to us. We tried all sorts of things and said what nice food we'd got and how much better off we were than they were. Even, I understand, to the extent of becoming so lyrical as to say, 'You should taste our lovely buttered toast.' And of course we'd had no buttered toast for a long time. And that was one side. Perhaps the other side of it was the insults that were hurled at 'em, like Fascists are male *connes*, which in a brief translation means nancy boys. And I shouldn't think we would get many people to desert to us on that score. We were more likely to win on the buttered toast one.

Escaping from Spain

Fenner Brockway (b. 1888), now Lord Brockway, recalls a brief
meeting as he crossed the Spanish frontier in 1936 when, as
General Secretary of the ILP, alarmed by reports of Communist
purges, he sought to protest to the Spanish Government and to
bring home his members. In May 1936 the Spanish Government
tried to assert direct control on Barcelona which was mainly in
the hands of the Anarchists supported by the POUM. This led
to street fighting in which Orwell was involved. The result
appeared to be inconclusive. Orwell returned to the front, was
wounded, but when he returned to convalesce at Barcelona the
following month, he ran right into the purge of the POUM and
the Anarchist leadership instigated by the Communist Party.

This is an extract from Lord Brockway's autobiography, *Inside
the Left* (Allen & Unwin, London 1942).

On 3 May 1937, the Government decided to occupy the telephone building and to disarm the workers; the CNT [a trades
union federation] staff resisted, and within an hour the workers
of Barcelona, from one end of the city to the other, were on
strike and were throwing up barricades in the streets. Although
the city, except for its 'Whitehall' area, was practically all in the
hands of the workers, the struggle was called off by the CNT
leaders after four days. The rank-and-file responded to their
advice to end the struggle, not because of any sense of immediate
weakness, but because of fear of divided forces in the face of
Franco and knowledge that large Government forces were
marching on the city from Valencia. Responsibility for this
Barcelona 'rising' was immediately ascribed by the Communists
to the POUM, and so the Liberal, Social Democratic and Communist journalists in Barcelona told the world. In truth, the
POUM only participated when the resistance began, and then
ordered its members not to fire a shot unless attacked. When the
spirit of the struggle died down the 'Communist' representatives
in the Madrid Government got their Social Democratic and
Liberal colleagues to outlaw the POUM and to authorise the
imprisonment of its leaders. . . .

Meanwhile, John McNair's presence in Spain had become
untenable. After narrowly escaping arrest he crossed the frontier
with Eric Blair (George Orwell, the author) and Stafford Cottman
(a boy of eighteen with the heart of a giant). As McNair was con-

triving to leave Spain, I was contriving to enter it. . . . My departure was hurried by two reports. The Press Association phoned me that John McNair had been arrested in Barcelona and a telegram came from Paris stating that the POUM leaders were in immediate danger and begging me to join a delegation of deputies which was ready to start. I took the next plane from Croydon. My last visit to the airport had been to bid farewell to Gorkin on his deportation; now I was leaving the same airport in an effort to save his life. In Paris I had an impressive reception from three German comrades, two Italians, one Spanish and four French – but I found that there was no delegation ready. 'Tomorrow it will be ready to go,' I was assured, so I spent the day getting the necessary papers to cross into Spain. In the evening when I met the French Committee I despaired; there was not only no deputation waiting, its personnel was undecided. But one reassuring thing happened; McNair telephoned from the frontier village of Cerbère that he and his companions had reached France safely.

I decided to travel the next night to Perpignan to meet them and to wait there for the French deputation which, I was promised, would follow two nights later.

I met McNair, young Cottman, and Eric and Eileen Blair. Eric had missed death at the front by the fraction of an inch, a bullet just scraping his windpipe, and his voice was thin and husky. He was staying at a nearby village on the coast for a few days' holiday. I only saw him for a few hours, but I liked and respected him at once. He was transparently sincere, concerned only about getting at the truth of things. His *Homage to Catalonia* expresses his character as I sensed it; the beauty of its writing and the careful striving to be exactly accurate; artist and scientist together. John and Stafford were travelling on to Paris and I had to make the most of the opportunity to get a detailed report and to collect tips about my best procedure in Spain. He was a little nervous about my visit: the Communist secret police were powerful and remorseless in hunting down friends of the POUM. His worst news was support for the rumour that Nin had been assassinated: he said everyone in Spain accepted its truth.

Bullet in the Neck

Georges Kopp (1902–51) was a Belgian engineer, socialist and soldier of fortune, who was Orwell's battalion commander in Spain. He became friendly with both George and Eileen who had followed her husband to Spain. When Orwell was wounded and permanent loss of voice was feared, Kopp wrote this letter, at Eileen's request, to her brother, an eminent surgeon, as neither he nor Eileen were fully confident in the local doctors. Kopp was imprisoned by the Communists in Barcelona and Orwell relates in *Homage to Catalonia* how he tried to get Kopp's release. When Kopp escaped from Spain, he joined the French Foreign Legion, before again escaping, this time to England where he married Eileen's half-sister. He eventually bought a farm at Biggar in Scotland.

Barcelona, 31 May 1937

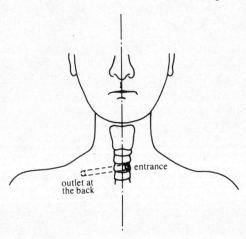

Eric was wounded on the 20 May at 5 a.m. The bullet entered the neck just under the larynx, slightly at the left side of its vertical axis and went out at the dorsal right side of the neck's base. It was a normal 7 mm bore, copper-plated Spanish Mauser bullet, shot from a distance of some 175 yards. At this range, it still had a velocity of some 600 feet per second and a cauterising temperature. Under the impact, Eric fell on his back. After dressing his wound at a first aid post some half a mile from the actual line, he was transferred to Barbastro and then to the hospital of Lerida, where I saw him with Eileen some forty hours after him having been wounded.

Eric's general state was some sort of excellent; the temperature (taken in the left armpit) had never reached 37°C. Eric complained about his right arm aching from the shoulder down to the tip of the middle finger along a humer-cubital line and about a pain, according to himself, severe but not unbearable, in the left side somewhere between the ultimate rib and the spleen. His voice was hoarse and feeble, but covering all the practical purposes of conversational speech. Breathing absolutely regular. Sense of humour untouched.

At the hospital in Lerida, Eric only received an external treatment of his wound. After a couple of days, the dressing of the entrance wound could be dispensed with. He remained at this hospital, under care of Dr Farré, up to 27 May when he was transferred to Tarragona.

Dr Farré told me on 22 May that no essential organ had been touched by some sort of unexplainable luck; he admitted that the pain in the arm might be produced by abrasions of one of the arm's main nerves and that the pain in the left side was probably due to hitting the ground when falling from his tremendous height. He told me that there was nothing to fear about the basic wound.

We had Eric ordered to be evacuated from Tarragona to Barcelona and went to fetch him on 29 May; we found him with a semi-complete aphasia and a slight fever. The pain in the left side had disappeared in due course. The one in the arm (supposed of nervous origin) subsisted unchanged. The doctor at Tarragona's hospital had told Eric on that very morning that his larynx was 'broken' and that he would never recover a normal voice. In fact, Eric was able to utter any articulate sound but feebly and with the characteristic, grinding noise of the brakes of a model T, very antiquated, Ford; his speech was inaudible outside a range of two yards.

Eric reached the sanatorium Maurin in Barcelona on 29 May at 10 p.m., having travelled sixty miles in a saloon-car without any special accommodation. His temperature reached at 11 p.m. 37·8°C (in left armpit); he received an aspirin and went immediately to bed, without any meal.

On Sunday, 30th, his voice had improved considerably, his temperature was normal in the morning and his appetite restored. He was able to walk about the place and its park without any exhaustion. I saw him from 11 a.m. to 6 p.m. and found his voice and spirits continuously improving during this period. Eileen was with her husband all the time and states his comportment was absolutely peace-timely.

Today, 30th, [31st?] Eric travelled by tram and tube, on his own initiative, down to the centre of Barcelona, where I met him at 11.45 a.m. He explained his escapade by the want of cocktails and decent lunch which were duly produced by Eileen's tender care (with help of a barman and several waiters).

Eric's temperature had remained normal, the pain in the left side had not reappeared and the pain in the right arm was rather reduced. His voice, according to himself, had improved since yesterday, but Eileen and I don't share this impression, without thinking it was worse. I explain this apparent contradiction by the fact that to reach his present quality of speech costs him less effort than yesterday.

I arranged to have Eric thoroughly examined tomorrow morning by Professor Grau of Barcelona's University and for a subsequent treatment either by some professor, or by another prominent specialist of this town.

I propose to add to this 'bulletin' Professor Grau's opinion with the narrative of the manipulations he will perform on my friend's throat.

Professor Grau examined Eric today, 1 June, at 9.30 a.m. at the Hospital General de Cataluña. His diagnostic is: 'incomplete semi-paralysis of the larynx due to abrasions of the right side larynx dilating nerve.' He confirmed Dr Farré's statement that no essential organ had been touched; the bullet went right through, between the trachea and the carotid.

Professor Grau said that electrotherapy was the only thing to be recommended just now and some sort of promises to restore Eric's voice in a long, indefinite, but reasonable time. He took Eric to Dr Barraquer, specialist in electric treatments of nervous disturbances and began by having a private talk of some twelve minutes with his colleague. It is not known if they spoke of Eric's wound or of some other topic. When Eric, Eileen and myself were ushered in Dr Barraquer's study, Professor Grau explained the case just as if he had never spoken of it before and wanted his friend to investigate any possible nervous lesions outside of the purely laryngic zone.

Dr Barraquer's additional diagnostic was: 'abrasions of the first right-side spinal rachidean nerve' which accounts for the pain in the arm. Dr Barraquer also advocated electrotherapy for both of the nervous lesions and it was agreed upon Eric coming twice a week (on Wednesday and Friday) to have an electrical treatment and once a week (on Fridays) to let Professor Grau look into his throat and hear him saying 'aaaaaah' whilst his tongue is maintained stretched out at full length by the Professor.

Both of the doctors concerned with the case are decent, efficient and fully civilised people, with a lot of similar cases having passed before them since war began; the machinery and installations of the General Catalonian Hospital is complete and modern; most of the nurses are brunettes.

Of course, the doctors have not given any definite opinion upon the duration of the treatment and I felt I could not possibly put any questions about it before they can prove the effect of electrotherapy on Eric's nerves. I think that in any case, it would be advisable to let the treatment go at least two weeks and then ask the medical people 'what about having it continued in England?'

I advocate you writing to Dr Barraquer (who speaks fairly good English) a 'colleague's letter' in the reply to which you may be told something more than we, mere mortals, are admitted to hear. Then you would be able to form a reasonable opinion about the case and send Eileen definite instructions which I am sure she will follow without any reluctance, so high is her admiration for your professional capacities.

With the hope I shall some day have the opportunity of sharing this feeling not only from faith but on experimented evidence, I remain
Yours sincerely
Georges Kopp

Eileen Blair

Lettice Cooper (b. 1897), novelist and biographer, got to know Eileen, Orwell's first wife, during the war when they worked together at the Ministry of Food. The character of 'Ann' in her novel of 1947, *Black Bethlehem*, is plainly based on Eileen. They were good friends; indeed Eileen wrote to her shortly before her fatal operation, admitting its seriousness and true nature, something it seems she had not told her husband (the question of whether or not he ever really knew she had cancer is discussed in my *George Orwell: A Life*).

This memoir was prepared by Miss Cooper for the Orwell Archive at the request of Ian Angus in 1964 when he was editing *The Collected Essays*.

George first saw her at a party at which she was 'rather drunk and behaving my worst, very rowdy'. He said to somebody here that he was going to marry that girl. After their wedding there was a lunch in a pub; George's mother and sister took Eileen upstairs and told her that they were very, very sorry for her, she was taking on something. She knew but didn't mind. I think she must then have been about twenty-six or seven, but I can't remember the date of the marriage. Before that, Eileen was working as secretary to her brother, who was a surgeon. He was killed at Dunkirk; this was a blow from which I think Eileen never entirely recovered.

She and George went for their honeymoon to a cottage at Wallington in Herts, which they seem to have rented for a long time as they still had it in 1944 when they lent it to us for several weekends. A nice old cottage in a remote, pretty village. This was always their retreat. But it was frequently lent to other people, or else nominally let to people who could not afford to pay rent. Anything that Eileen or George possessed was liable to be lent or given to anybody in need.

The only story I heard about their honeymoon was that somebody had given them a special pot of marmalade, and Eileen put the pot on the table. George objected solemnly that the marmalade should have been decanted into a jam dish. Eileen said that they hadn't got one. George said that they must get one, jam and marmalade should always go in a jam dish. This amused Eileen very much as George had warned her that they were going to live like the working class, but she discovered that there were a lot of gentilities that George set great store by. She shared his political views, but much less solemnly. I don't know much about their pre-war life, I heard about various adventures in Spain where, of course, Eileen went with him and which she seemed to have enjoyed very much.

When I met her, she arrived at the Ministry of Food in Portman Square to take the place, looking after the 'Kitchen Front' Broadcasts, just vacated by Pamela Frankau, who had gone into the ATS. I can see Eileen very vividly now, the first time I met her. Small with blue eyes and nearly black hair, pretty with very pretty hands and feet and a body beautifully poised on her legs. Good but shabby and unbrushed clothes, generally black. She generally walked as if she wasn't thinking where she was going, as indeed she seldom was. Often in the lunch hour I used to meet her, if we hadn't been lunching together, drifting along Baker Street or Wigmore Street, deep in thought. She had the kind of mind that was always grinding. She was interested in most things, but especially in people. George was not in the least interested in people except in large political masses. He seldom wrote about them and knew nothing at all about them. He was in many ways a very ingenuous man, but with an immense charm that was very difficult to define. He was surrounded by adorers, male and female, and at that time anyhow he stalked through them without noticing them very much, so that they used to turn to Eileen for sympathy. Somebody was always ringing up and saying, 'Have I annoyed George?', 'What is the matter?', 'George wouldn't speak to me', when George had just not happened to be thinking about them at all.

No one of us is entirely without jealousy or rancour, but Eileen seemed to be as free from them as anybody I have ever known and she had an inexhaustible capacity for being interested in other people's affairs. She and George were always hard up, always bombed out, always in difficulties, but always helping somebody else, and never really ruffled by their difficulties. Their housekeeping was spasmodic; if Eileen was ill as she often was and asked George to go out and buy a cauliflower, George went to the nearest greengrocer and said, 'Have you a cauliflower?' If they hadn't he came home; it never entered his head to go on to another shop or buy a cabbage instead. I saw that somebody wrote that George had starved Eileen during the war by giving away all their rations. I can only say that all the time I knew her, she was not starving, we used to range far and wide round the Ministry looking for the most palatable war-time lunch, and discuss very carefully if we met during the morning where we should go that day, and which were their best dishes. Eileen didn't like the potato salad and vitamin dishes which we had to try and put over; she liked meat, eggs, cheese, wine. When I went to the flat in Islington after she left the Ministry, we had meals as good as were possible in war time; she liked cooking . . . the meals were always late, you would go to dinner at seven and get it about nine. But it was all right when you did get it. They certainly did give rations away. I remember once that Eileen brought me a pound of sugar for my Wardens Post where we were kept very short of supplies and needed much more than the allowance of tea and sugar when we were up all night. Eileen said, 'I told George I was going to take you a pound of sugar for your Post and he said, "Why?" I was surprised, because he never minds as a rule and I said, "We've got plenty, you don't mind, do you?" He said, "Good God, I didn't mean that, I meant why didn't you give them all we'd got?"'

George had certain fixed ideas about his friends and one was that anybody he liked always drank beer and wouldn't drink lager. We often used to have a drink in a pub at the end of the day and whenever I asked for lager or light ale I always got the darkest kind of beer if George was ordering. I protested and Eileen said, 'It's no use, once you are established as a friend of his, you become the kind of person who wouldn't drink lager or light ale if you could have dark ale, and nothing will shake him.' As indeed it never did whatever I asked for.

I can't remember how many flats they were bombed out of, but I know that when I first knew them they were living in Maida Vale, then I think that was bombed and they went to a flat in a block, I remember Eileen telling me that she had been coming downstairs when a bomb dropped nearby. There was an elderly woman in the block who was terrified, and she was crouching down in the hall trembling; Eileen saw George kneeling by her with his hand on her head, patting her and 'looking like Christ'. He had sympathy for human beings in situations he could understand. He just never knew anything about the complications of their thought and feelings. Both he and Eileen were among the most fearless people I met, though she hated the 'doodle-bugs' (flying bombs). She said that George once said in bed at night, 'I always know when one is coming right over us because I feel your heart beating faster against me.'

Although humane, George was completely selfish, I think from the same unawareness of what anybody else was feeling. Of course, the marriage didn't always go smoothly. I don't think George was the kind of person who likes being married all the time. But that he could have found anybody who would have fitted in with him better over a term of years I doubt.

They had the same ideas about how to live. Eileen was very delicate. She was constantly being tested for TB but the tests were always negative. She needed a good deal of care and George was incapable of giving it, but I believe that if she had lived, their marriage, with interruptions and diversions, would have lasted all the time in the background, especially as they were both so devoted to the child.

George was mad to adopt a baby, since they had not had one. Eileen was nervous for fear she should not be able to love an adopted child enough. It meant giving up her own work in the Ministry of Food where she was very happy and where she had a life of her own, not as George's wife, but she would not deny him the wish of his heart. . . . George's great wish was that the baby should have a white perambulator with gold lines on and should go to Eton. Eileen became at once devoted to the child [Richard], and George was transfigured with tenderness. I do hope that some of the photographs of him with the baby are still about, for they show such open, loving feeling in George's face that it was moving to look at them.

Eileen's sister-in-law, Gwen O'Shaughnessy, owned a house near Newcastle; she had a little boy of her own about five and an adopted girl of two. She herself was a doctor working in Greenwich. She sent the two children with her nurse to this house away from the flying bombs. Eileen joined them there with Richard, I think early in 1945 when George went abroad. She had been ill, there was some question of a hysterectomy, and the doctors said she must get out of London and rest. I left the Ministry in March, and just after I came out, Eileen came up to London and came there to look for me, but collapsed, and had to go to a specialist who found a growth. She was only up for one night and I was out somewhere; she never got in touch with me but went back to Northumberland, and the next I heard of her was the one letter I kept, which, being forwarded from the Ministry only reached me on the day she died. If I had known about the serious operation and that she was going into Newcastle alone, by bus, to have it, with no one there, I should have gone up to her, but I heard too late.

She was keenly alive to George's work and seemed to me a very good critic of it. He read it all aloud to her. I think certainly he read *Animal Farm* every evening when she went home, and she used to come in and tell us next morning how it was getting on, she knew at once that it was a winner.

Eileen, called Emily in the Ministry for some reason that I've forgotten, was good at her job, which consisted of getting the scripts arranged and Kitchen Front interviewing would-be speakers of whom there were a large circle who used to visit us weekly in the hope of getting jobs, and who vigorously tried to impress us with their personalities. 'Oh,' Eileen groaned once, 'I hope I don't have to see any more women of great vitality this week!'

She always gave you the impression that she wasn't getting any work done, and that nothing would be finished in time, but it always was, although we spent a good third of our time in Selfridges' snack bar across the road, talking. Several of our senior officers tried to prevent this, but they never managed to.

An Anecdote of the Blitz

Sir Victor (V.S.) Pritchett (b. 1900) is a great admirer of Orwell's writing and was a personal acquaintance. He had reviewed *The Lion and the Unicorn*, hailing Orwell as being in the great English tradition of polemical pamphleteers, and had broadcast a talk about him in the early days of the Third Programme in a series, *Living Writers*. In that talk he coined a famous phrase, 'I might best describe him as a writer who has gone native in his own country', and he went on to say, 'He belongs to no group, he joins no side; if he dallies with the idea, he turns out to be a liability to his party. He is entirely on his own. But not flamboyantly, not theatrically, not, for example, like Shaw or Cunningham Graham. George Orwell is rashly, almost bleakly, almost colourlessly and uncomfortably on his own. One forgets where he is wrong, because of his remarkable honesty.' (From Gilbert Philips, ed., *Living Writers* (Sylvan Press, London, 1947).)

This passage is from *Cab at the Door and Midnight Oil* (Penguin, Harmondsworth, 1979). Later we print his obituary of Orwell (p. 275).

Once Louis MacNeice and I wandered down the streets in St John's Wood and tried, unsuccessfully, to carry away a stone lion from the garden of a destroyed house. The thing was too heavy. But in the raid I was describing, our fears were allayed by John Betjeman, who kept us laughing by assuring a child's teddy bear that he and the bear were all right because they had been to confession, whereas the rest of us, as non-Christians, would certainly be in hell any moment. After a couple of hours the raid was over and then I discovered how terrified I had been: I could not speak clearly because one end of my upper lip had risen up and was stuck to my right nostril. I was not a man who could keep a stiff upper lip. I must have been looking like a rabbit.

There is another note about an evening with George Orwell, who, in the melancholy way of one who had been trained for duty when he was young and was inured to suffering, rather liked the war, for he saw it as a fight against the governing class as well as a fight against the Nazis. I went to a flat he had taken at the top of an apartment block; the beauty of the place (to him) was that one could more easily get out on to the roof to put out fire bombs if one lived on the top floor. His health had been ruined by the wound he had got in Spain and he had the strange lonely detachment and fevered half-laughing energy of the sick.

Koestler on his Friend

Arthur Koestler (1905–83), novelist, journalist, critic and philosopher, had covered the Spanish Civil War for the *News Chronicle* between 1936 and 1937, and was imprisoned by General Franco. After his release he served in the French Foreign Legion for a year and then the British Pioneer Corps when he first met Orwell. He had read Orwell's *Homage to Catalonia* and Orwell later reviewed Koestler's *Spanish Testament*. They became close friends. Orwell was obviously greatly impressed with *Darkness at Noon* and Koestler saw Orwell as the ideal representative of an Englishman – so much so that when Eileen died, he urged Orwell to marry his (Koestler's) wife's twin sister; however Koestler could not have his own way in everything and the marriage did not take place.

The first extract is from an interview with Ian Angus in 1964, which was made while collecting material for the Orwell Archive, and the second from Rayner Heppenstall's BBC programme on Orwell of 1960.

George and I were the only anti-Stalinists who could get printed. We felt we were persecuted by the *New Statesman* etc., and what appalled us was not just the refusal to print what we had written, but the systematic suppression of fact so that people simply did not know what was going on. Sources of truthful information were the privately circulated news sheets, like Stephen King-Hall's *Newsletter*. But people like Beaverbrook suppressed a great deal. I remember the 'Beaver' saying how we all liked 'Uncle Joe' and therefore mustn't say too much against him.

I remember George writing a most savage, unrelievedly critical review in *Tribune* of my play *Twilight Bar* which had just been published [reviewed on 30 November 1945] and the day the review appeared in *Tribune* or the day after George came down to stay with us [Arthur Koestler and Mamaine] in North Wales. I met him and asked him why he couldn't have softened the review just a little and George said that it didn't occur to him to. On driving George down to the station George said in the car (presumably this was at the end of the weekend) that yes, perhaps, it had been a bit too severe and that he should have softened the review slightly in some way. . . .

I remember arranging to meet George for dinner in the Hungarian Csarda restaurant in Soho and George came wearing a shirt with a collar which was not just frayed but so torn that people gasped at seeing someone enter the restaurant dressed like that. . . .

In 1945 George sold me his set of the *Encyclopaedia Britannica* for five pounds [minus 1 volume which Avril had. She eventually sent it to Koestler]. George bought himself a new set.

A group of us used to meet twice or three times a week in the Elysée. The group consisted of David Martin who had been in the Canadian Air Force, Julian Symons, Malcolm Muggeridge, Tosco Fyvel and Orwell. It was in this restaurant that George said about a moussaka (which was a bit of awful Greek cooking, as opposed to the good sort of Greek cooking) that 'in all London there wasn't anywhere else that you could get food like that'. George had no taste in food.

I first met George between December 1940 and April 1941 when I went into the Pioneer Corps. We talked about doing a book for Orwell's Searchlight book series. I came out of the Army in 1942 and shared a house in Drayton Gardens with Cyril Connolly and Peter Quennell. We three, David Astor and George were all very friendly. . . .

One evening in 1946 or 1947 on my way to dinner at Connolly's I called on George in his dismal place in Canonbury Square and found George very depressed. I asked him if he had got a girl. George said no and I said I knew of someone who was at a bit of a loose end and would be at Cyril's for dinner. George came along to Cyril's for dinner and found Sonia there – Sonia was wearing a costume with square cut shoulders to the jacket and military looking buttons. . . .

I remember George saying how lovely it was to be in a hot bath and dream of the tortures one is inflicting (in fantasy) on one's enemies.

The torture scenes in *Nineteen Eighty-Four*, especially the electric shocks, were a recreation of the pains George felt in his chest. George was not impotent. Witness the scene in *Nineteen Eighty-Four* where Winston meets Julia in the country. No impotent person would imagine a situation like that.

George was very indulgent of young Richard. I remember young Richard clambering all over me and fouling me and George gently and ineffectually upbraiding the child.

TRANSCRIPT OF THE BBC PROGRAMME MADE BY RAYNER HEPPEN-STALL

He was ruthless towards himself. He had to fight that lung disease from childhood. If he had given in to his friends who wanted him to go to a Swiss sanatorium or something, he may have lived a few years longer, but I think *Nineteen Eighty-Four* and *Animal Farm* would not have been written. He was a rebel against his own biological condition and he was a rebel against social conditions; the two were very closely linked together. I remember once he wrote a review of a very bad book of mine in which he said: 'The chink in Koestler's armour is his hedonism.' Now I don't think that hedonism in itself, if it is only an additional thing to a basic pursuit in one's life, is to be condemned, but George did condemn it.

He was unkind to himself, and he was unkind to his friends. The closer they were to him the more unkind he was to them and his enormous warmth only came out in an impersonal way in his books. The closer somebody was to him, the more he felt entitled to treat that friend like he treated himself. . . .

As a writer, he was a sort of missing link between Swift and Kafka. The cabbage smells, the tripe in *Wigan Pier* – I mean it's quite obviously the hatred of Gulliver for the smell of the Houynmhms [sic] – however you pronounce it – after the clean horses, vegetarian horses. . . .

He fights an enemy and the body is an enemy, the sweat of the body, the smell of the body, everything about myself then becomes loathsome, infected, putrid, and intimacy becomes loathsome. A natural continuation in sort of revolutionary terms of Swift is Kafka, but I have to qualify that. Because Swift never had any positive faith in humanity – he only saw the absurd: nor had Kafka. But George did. That passage which he wrote about the crowd in the big towns with their knobbly faces, their bad teeth and gentle manners. The queues outside the labour exchanges, the old maids biking to Holy Communion, through the mists of the autumn morning. There his warmth was allowed to come out, towards the anonymous.

George was a rebel. A revolutionary makes compromises to hang on to power; a rebel is a rebel, he is against; and he was against everything which stank in society, everything which was tripe and cabbage and decay and putrefaction, in himself and in society, and there was no compromise.

The most difficult thing for a writer to describe is physical pain. You can describe a broken heart, but try to describe a toothache. You remember the torture scene in *Nineteen Eighty-Four* when the rats are being let loose. That was not morbid or anything, that was only a man who lived on familiar terms with physical pain, and he knew that if he is submitted to the acid test of physical torture he would collapse. And for George social injustice was a physical pain; it smelt, it hurt like a tooth, like a gangrene – there was an identification between the biological and the social which you have in Kafka. It was, of course, totally unswallowable for the evasive English critics, who just don't want to get too close to reality anywhere, so everybody came down on that rat scene, where the man betrays his girl and says, 'Let the rats eat the girl's eyes, not mine.' That was a technique, that was contemporaneity, that was what we were living through – in Russia and in Germany, when the old Bolsheviks accused themselves of having always been British agents from the first moment, from the inception of the Revolution and in Germany. So the critics can object, by saying that it isn't art. Every junior editor of a publishing firm will tell you now, 'Look, you feel strongly about that, but cut it out – it isn't art.'

I don't think George ever knew what makes other people tick, because what made him tick was very different from what made most other people tick. This uncompromisingness which is such a cliché was such a reality with him that he couldn't see what makes others tick.

'That Curiously Crucified Expression'

John Morris (b. 1895), traveller, anthropologist and author, was head of the BBC Far Eastern Service from 1943 to 1952 and Controller of the Third Programme from 1952 to 1958. He worked in the same department as Orwell, in adjacent rooms, from February to October 1943. They plainly did not hit it off.

John Morris wrote this under the title 'Some Are More Equal than Others' for *Penguin New Writing*, Number 40, September 1950.

George Orwell always reminded me of one of those figures on the front of Chartres Cathedral; there was a sort of pinched Gothic quality about his tall thin frame. He laughed often, but in repose his lined face suggested the grey asceticism of a medieval saint carved in stone and very weathered. I first met him in February 1943 when I joined the BBC Eastern Service, as it then was, of which he had already been a member for some time. We were both talks producers and I saw a good deal of him nearly every day until he resigned to become literary editor of *Tribune*. His most striking features were his luxuriant and unruly hair and the strange expression in his eyes, a combination of benevolence and fanaticism; it was as though he saw more (as indeed he did) than the ordinary mortal, and pitied him for his lack of understanding. Although he wrote so well, he was a poor and halting speaker; even in private conversation he expressed himself badly and would often fumble for the right word. His weekly broadcast talks were beautifully written, but he delivered them in a dull and monotonous voice. I was often with him in the studio and it was painful to hear such good material wasted: like many other brilliant writers, he never really understood the subtle differences between the written and the spoken word, or, if he did, could not be bothered with them.

To say that we occupied adjacent rooms would be to give a false impression of the conditions in which we worked at 200 Oxford Street. Before the war this building formed a part of the premises of a big department store, and its vast high rooms, each occupying one whole floor, had been hastily converted into the necessary number of small offices by the building of lath and plaster walls which, because of the need for economy, only extended to a height of some seven feet from the floor. The result of this arrangement was that we worked against a background noise of conversation, dictation, clattering typewriters and, owing to the shortage of studios, even the rehearsal of talks and features in various oriental languages.

It was difficult and at times impossible to carry on a telephone conversation, and my earliest recollection of Orwell is of him standing, with that curiously crucified expression which seemed never to leave his face, in the aperture (there was no door) which separated his room from mine. 'For God's sake shut up,' he would say in his rather harshly petulant voice, and then return to his telephoning. Sometimes he would come back a little later; he would never apologise for his outburst, but, as though to hint that he bore no ill-will, would offer me one of the horrible cigarettes which he himself made from a particularly pungent and acrid shag. I would take a puff or two and then, because it started a paroxysm of coughing, would stub out the beastly thing. This would always cause Orwell to smile in a rather contemptuous manner. Nothing was ever said but I think we both knew that my inability to enjoy his filthy cigarettes was symbolic; it represented other things which made any sort of intimacy between us quite impossible.

There was also William Empson who, by the time I arrived, had become Orwell's most and perhaps his only intimate friend in the department. . . . When I joined the BBC Empson was in charge of our Chinese programmes; and since I had been brought in for the express purpose of starting up a service to Japan he, quite unfairly I think, regarded me as some sort of enemy; because I made no secret of the fact that I had enjoyed my time in Japan and had acquired a number of lasting friendships (which still endure), I must therefore be against the Chinese. . . . When I afterwards became head of the Eastern Service my personal relations with Empson were to become even more difficult, and the intimate friendship between him and Orwell undoubtedly affected the latter's attitude to me.

Besides this, there was another difficulty, and it was perhaps the most significant of all; my background had been very similar to Orwell's own. I had even spent some years in government service in India, but, unlike Orwell, it had in no way turned me against my own class, and certainly I had no feelings of shame about it. Like him, I had resigned at a fairly early age, but for quite other reasons. . . .

I have never felt the slightest shame that I happen not to have sprung from the working classes; nor, I should add, do I take any pride in the fact that, so far as I know, none of my forebears has

been a labourer. This question of class is obviously of no importance; certainly it ought not to trouble anybody of even moderate
intelligence, yet in recent years, in certain literary circles, it
seems to have become a matter of pride to be able to display at
least some sort of working-class origin. . . . Nothing could have
turned Orwell into a working-class man; yet I believe nothing
gave him more pleasure than to be mistaken for one.

I remember, soon after we first became acquainted, going
down to tea with him in the BBC canteen. The place as usual
was crowded and after collecting our cups from the queue we sat
down at an already occupied table. Orwell immediately poured
his tea into the saucer and began to drink it with a loud, sucking
noise. He said nothing, but looked at me with a slightly defiant
expression when I continued to drink my own tea in the normal
fashion. The two doorkeepers who were also occupying our table
looked somewhat scandalised, and after a few minutes got up
and left.

There was another occasion when I went with Orwell to a pub.
I suppose most people have their oddities, and one of mine is an
intense dislike of the English public house. I do not like their
atmosphere and their sordid ugliness distresses me; also I am
terrified that some garrulous stranger will address me as, on the
rare occasions I enter these places, generally seems to happen.
However, anyone who wanted to get to know Orwell had to do so
on his terms and none other. He asked me what I would have to
drink and I replied, reasonably, I thought, with the one word
'Beer.' He looked at me with the sort of horrified expression one
might reasonably expect to see on the face of a parson whose ears
had been suddenly assailed by a stream of obscenities, and I
wondered what offence I had so obviously committed. But he did
not say anything; he simply turned to the barmaid. 'A pint of
bitter please,' he said, 'and a glass of beer for my friend.' The
last part of the sentence he pronounced with a sort of contempt,
but it did not at all produce the effect he had apparently
intended, for the barmaid immediately handed up the two drinks
for which he had asked. I was so mystified by all this that later
on, after we had left, I asked him to explain. 'You gave yourself
away badly,' he said; 'a working-class person would never ask for
"a glass of beer".' 'I don't happen to be a working-class person,'
I said. 'No,' he replied; 'but there's no need to boast about it.'

I believe Orwell was a man of deep feelings, but he had an
almost Oriental capacity for hiding his emotions. His first wife,
who was working in the Ministry of Food at the time, died very

suddenly during the war. I myself am not very good at managing human relations and I made what was undoubtedly a clumsy attempt to express my sympathy. 'Yes,' he said in reply, 'it is most inconvenient. I don't know how I shall be able to look after the child.' This child, at that time a small baby, had been only recently adopted. I suppose the desire for paternity is a perfectly normal one, but in Orwell's case it seemed to have been exaggerated to an almost pathological extent. I do not think he had any particular fondness for children as such, but he desired above all things to be the father of one. It was only after he knew this was impossible that he and his wife decided to adopt a son. He seemed devoted to this child and in order to provide it with fresh milk, which was difficult to obtain in sufficient quantity at that time, spent many of his few leisure hours in looking after a couple of goats which were housed in his back-yard.

I must now recount briefly a very painful incident, which occurred in the winter of 1943. I had been for many years an intimate friend of the late L. H. Myers, who was a great admirer of Orwell's work. Myers also had been educated at Eton, and while he shared Orwell's dislike of and contempt for social privilege he retained his own fondness for good food and clean linen. Myers was a comparatively wealthy man, and while he always lived in comfort, he was extremely hospitable and generous and did a great deal, usually anonymously, to help poor and struggling writers. Earlier than most, he had recognised Orwell's great talent, and a little before the war, learning that Orwell was both desperately poor and already stricken with tuberculosis, he enabled him to spend the winter months in North Africa. The two had met on a few formal occasions, but they were not close friends, and at the time Orwell was, I believe, unaware that it was Myers who had made it possible for him to escape from the English winter. At the beginning of the war Myers gave up his flat and went to live at Marlow, but he often came up to London and would sometimes spend a week-end with me. He knew, of course, that Orwell and I were working together, and as he had rather lost touch with him he asked me if I would get him to come along to the flat one evening. Orwell refused an invitation to dine with us but said he would come along about nine o'clock. He arrived soon after, dressed, as I always remember him, in a pair of rather dirty and shabby corduroy trousers and an aged tweed coat patched and bound with pieces of leather; his shirt, as usual, seemed to be several sizes too large in the neck, and his shoes had obviously not been polished for days. As soon as I brought Orwell into the sitting room I sensed that it was not going to be a comfortable evening. 'I suppose you two have been dining at Boulestin's,' he said, by way of greeting. As a matter of fact we had dined there, as we usually did. It was one of Myers' concessions to his former life which he refused to abandon. I sometimes used to twit him about spending so much money on food in wartime, but he always laughingly excused himself by saying that it was not really extravagant because it so happened that he was one of the directors of the restaurant, and his bills there were merely paper transactions!

I left the two of them alone while I went into the kitchen to make some coffee, imagining that they would find plenty to talk about. But no sound came from the living room, and when I returned Orwell was staring silently into the fire and Myers, normally the easiest and most delightful of conversationalists, was looking strangely ill at ease, like a schoolboy summoned to his headmaster's study. I tried desperately to get the conversation going again, but it was no good and soon I too became tongue-tied. We sat on for a little and then, making some lame excuse, Orwell got up and left. Myers himself died in the following spring and the two never again met. He was deeply hurt by what appeared to be Orwell's indifference towards him. I had thought at the time that the latter's conduct had been prompted, perhaps subconsciously, by the knowledge (which he had by then acquired) that it was Myers who had been his anonymous benefactor; one half of him resented the help that had come from a man who was rich, the other, the half of his nature which he seemed to me always trying to suppress, felt only gratitude. I think he felt it would have been unnecessarily ungracious to refuse my invitation – to admit that he would prefer not to meet Myers again – but when it came to the point and the two were face to face the resentful side of his character came to the fore. I still think this explanation partly accounts for his strange conduct, but it is only recently, since his death, that I have come fully to understand it. It was Cyril Connolly, who was perhaps Orwell's most intimate friend (they were at both preparatory school and Eton together), who provided the clue. 'I was a stage rebel,' he has said; 'Orwell a true one.' This is a personal comparison, but it seems to me valid for the whole of Orwell's generation.

I can understand now that from his point of view Myers, although a serious artist, was more of a stage rebel than most. At this period he was much attracted to the Communist theory, but he was never, so far as I know, a member of the party, and I am sure that had he lived he would, like so many other intellectuals of his generation, have rejected Communism. But even at the height of his enthusiasm he continued to live, as far as it was possible in wartime, in civilised comfort: he liked to have good books, pictures and old furniture about him, and it would never have occurred to him to offer his guests anything less than the best food and drink. It was this that Orwell, in his perverse way, despised, although he himself was I think quite sincere in believing that a man's private life should be organised in accordance with his political convictions. What he never realised was that, live as he might, he never could have become absorbed into the working class; his preoccupation (so evident in his earlier novels) with the sordid details of lower-class domestic life was a romantic fiction.

After that unfortunate evening, although I continued to see Orwell almost daily, our relationship became purely formal. He never referred to it, but the following morning, when I saw him in the office, he addressed me, as he had not done for many months, by my surname, and on those terms we remained until he left. I never expected to hear from him again and I was greatly surprised when later he asked me if I would do some reviewing for *Tribune*, of which he had become literary editor. It was the more surprising because Orwell was well aware that I was opposed to the socialist policy for which his paper stood. I agreed, however, to work for him; but after he had published some four or five of my articles, and happening one day to meet him in the street, I took advantage of the occasion to remind him that I had not been paid. 'Oh,' he said, smiling rather sardonically, 'we don't pay for reviews, you know; it's all for the Cause!' It was the last time I saw him. I wish I could have known him better, for I greatly admire his work, but we seemed always to irritate each other. When we were alone together he always tried to behave in an aggressively working-class manner, and the effect of that was to make me talk like an unrepentant reactionary. But I am sure the fault was mostly mine.

William Empson and Orwell at the BBC

Sir William Empson (b. 1906), poet, scholar and critic, worked in the same BBC department as Orwell, the Eastern Service, between 1941 and 1943. He returned to Peking National University in 1947 and later became Professor of English Literature at Sheffield University. He is best known for his *Seven types of Ambiguity*. He and his wife Hetta got to know Orwell and he was a fairly frequent visitor to their home.

Empson is not correct in saying that Orwell began to write *Animal Farm* while at the BBC, nor that he ever made 'the debunking pronouncement' that 'the working classes smell'. In *The Road to Wigan Pier* Orwell said that he was brought up to believe that they smell.

Sir William wrote this for Miriam Gross's excellent anthology, *The World of George Orwell* (Weidenfeld and Nicolson, London 1971).

On the day when a stranger offered me his hand and said 'I am George Orwell', we were both students at the start of a six-week course in what was called the Liars' School of the BBC: my future wife was also a student there, and it seems to me now a time of great happiness. He must have been writing *Animal Farm* while employed by the Corporation, but he never discussed work in progress, and had resigned some time before it was published. We remained friends afterwards, and sometimes had dinner together; but practically speaking, as I went back to China soon after the war, the Indian Editor of the BBC Eastern Service was the only Orwell I knew.

It is interesting to consider why he was there, a question which would not occur to us at the time. My future wife and I, come to think of it, represented the two main types of student at the 1941 session (the School was a yearly event). I had served an apprenticeship, working for a year on the big daily Digest of foreign broadcasts, and towards the end writing earnest memos recommending myself as a propagandist to the Far East (the Digest staff acted as a kind of pool for the propaganda expansion); whereas Hetta, like many other high-minded people at the time, had been dubious about working directly for the Government until Hitler attacked Russia, though it had been all right to drive lorries or ambulances through the London blitz. Orwell was the only student who jeered at those who expressed pleasure at having recently acquired the powerful ally. One might expect this to have annoyed people, and maybe it would have done but for another recent event, slightly earlier; the Battle of Britain had been won, so that we were no longer afraid, in a furtive and astonished manner, of losing the war, as we had been for a year, since the fall of France. (There was a night when the figures of German aircraft shot down over Britain, chalked up on a black-board in the sub-editors' room of the Digest, rose so high that no one's bet was anywhere near, and the sweepstake had to be given to charity. Maybe the figures were wrong, but they were decisive for many people, and Hitler decided the same way.) During that year before I met him, Orwell, though quietly growing food in the country, had been to do with an official scheme planning resist-ance after a successful German invasion. Survivors of the Spanish War were being taken seriously, by some elements of the British Army, as advisers on how to organise a *maquis*. I did not ask about this, but realised that he would love teaching the British Army how ignorant it was. Still, he would not do even that for mere pleasure, and now the immediate occasion for it had stopped. He would have liked to be a war correspondent, but his health stood in the way. 'I hold what half the men in this country would give their balls to have,' he was accustomed to remark, 'a yellow ticket' (or whatever colour it was, meaning that he could not be conscripted), 'but I don't want it.' In writing this I paused and searched my memory, feeling that another bright phrase should come next; but no, he did not sustain his rhetoric, though he would use a phrase intending it to glitter. He was indignant at being told he was too ill to go abroad. 'The impu-dence of it, when they know perfectly well I'm too ill to stay here. Probably save my life to go to North Africa. But if it didn't, they might have to give the widow something, d'you see.' No doubt he would have enjoyed being a war correspondent. But radio propa-ganda to India might offer a more important role. If Hitler broke right through Russia to the Persian Gulf, and India joined Japan, the Axis might win after all. And then again, if Churchill won, he might prevent the liberation of India. As it happened, Orwell was Indian Editor at the time when these major questions became settled, though he could not have been sure they were settled when he resigned. He always regarded his work in a high manner, not to say a self-important one, as many of us were prone to do.

It was lucky for me that George thought I was all right, as I admired him and wanted his friendship, and he might easily have decided I was not. I had come back from China voluntarily for the war, and no doubt this made me sufficiently unlike the types he was denouncing. 'I don't know people like that,' he was soon remarking about Kingsley Martin, who (it seemed) had printed a picture in the *New Statesman* of how much gold would make a US dollar, so as to help rats to rat. George, I thought, sounded a bit like what one had read of Lord Curzon, another isolated ailing and public-spirited Etonian who had cultivated a funny accent. I had returned feeling that the defeat of Hitler was of immense importance, to be sure, but also feeling reasonably confident that I would be allowed an interesting war by being let into the propaganda machine; and, then again, I was protected by my obscurity, unlike the poet Auden who, I still think, was right in refusing to become the laureate of Churchill. For that matter, my Chinese university had simply assumed that I would require indefinite wartime leave (the Chinese were already regarding our war as a part of their war); it would have been embarrassing to act otherwise. Having practically remained on my tram-lines, I felt it was a rather undeserved bonus to be approved by Orwell. But we never cleared this point up either; he was not a man who asked personal questions.

When the two editors were settled in, which took another year or so of the gradual expansion (I rather think we each had a brief period as Burmese Editor, but it was I who held the office during the fall of Burma), they worked among many others on the open space of a whole floor of an Oxford Street shop, in offices separated by partitions about nine feet high; one of these lay between us, so that I could hear parts of his interview with the Indian propagandists whom he was vetting or briefing – or rather I could hear the bits which he said in a special tone of voice, as a rule one standard sentence. At first the visitor would do most of the talking, with George increasing his proportion gradually; no doubt he had to lure the visitor into providing an entry for the tremendous remark which one learned to expect towards the end of the interview. 'The FACK that you're black,' he would say, in a leisurely but somehow exasperated manner, immensely carrying, and all the more officer-class for being souped up into his formalised Cockney, 'and that I'm white, has *nudding whatever to do wiv it*.' I never once heard an Indian say 'But I'm not black', though they must all have wanted to. This no doubt was a decisive part of the technique; if he had used the phrase to actual Negroes, from an official position, they would be likely to object, and he would have to stop; but the Indians, who of course chatted to a variety of people in the basement canteen, were clearly in no mood to complain. They thought he was a holy saint, or at least that he must be very high-minded and remote from the world. Nobody ever mentioned, to my knowledge, that this dread sentence was being pronounced; I never even mentioned it privately to George. In his writing, of course, he often uses shock tactics, but I actually did feel a bit shocked to hear them put into practice. (Naturally the Chinese Department had an entirely different lay-out, having to handle so different a situation.)

One can see, however, that the tactics might have an important function. George was intensely devoted to the liberation of India (though the discovery that his Number Two was working for an independent Pakistan came as a great shock) – so much so that he felt Hitler's war would be worth while if it spelt the end of the British Raj, as it was likely to do if properly handled; but the 'advanced' Indians who imagined they would secure this result by helping Hitler to win were (he was convinced) disastrously deluded. Actually, most of the Englishmen you could have found for the job would have held these opinions (though Churchill insisted that he himself did not), but to political thinkers from the subject countries the English attitude was incredible; and it could only be made credible by someone who was plainly not mealy-mouthed. George would be uniquely good at this rather odd line of work. However, for all his skill, he found himself having to allow broadcasts to go out to India, from speakers too important to offend, which he thought likely to do more harm than good; well then, the great organisation should accept the advice of an editor, and simply tell the engineers to switch off the power. The man would be thanked and paid as usual, and could be told later if necessary that there had been an unfortunate technical hitch. He seemed genuinely indignant when complaining that the BBC had refused; surely we could not expect to defeat Goebbels, if we were so luxuriously honest as all that. (The stories about Milton when he was a propaganda chief amount to saying that he behaved as George wanted to do, very charitably in a way, so I won't believe that they are merely libels, as is always assumed by critics with no propaganda experience.) The Liars' School, I should perhaps explain, had only dealt with lies in passing, and only under the form of warning us against the methods of the enemy. I chiefly remember two young disc jockeys who put on a very saucy turn with two gramophones and two copies of a record by Churchill; the familiar voice was made

to leave out all the negatives, ending with 'we will (hic) sur-
render'. Towards the end of his time with the BBC, Orwell
brought out a volume of specimens of the political reflections by
Indians which he had provided for India, with part of a speech by
Hitler as a contrast; and at this late hour he was really pleased to
discover that Hitler too was receiving his due royalties, forwarded to him by the Royalty Department through neutral
Sweden. The modern world, it now occurs to me, is liable not to
realise how high-minded the whole affair was; George and the
Corporation were both leaning over backwards, though in rather
different directions.

'The working classes smell' was one of his famous debunkng
pronouncements, printed in italics if I remember; and this was a
settled enough assumption in his mind to make him feel that only
tramps and other down-and-outs were genuinely working class.
It was a serious weakness in his political judgement, otherwise
very good, and it clearly resulted from deep internal revulsions. I
judged it to be connected with his firmly expressed distaste for
homosexuality: at that time, or when we were both a bit younger,
many young gentlemen who loved the Workers did it practically,
and would explain to you that the ruling classes, owing to their
vices and their neuroses, were the ones who stank. You may
think I should have confronted George with someone who said
this, but it would have been worse than useless. For the truth is
that he himself stank, and evidently knew it – well, his (first) wife
talked to mine about it quite frankly, and she would be unlikely
to treat her husband to a frozen silence on the matter. It was the
rotting lungs that you could smell, not at once but increasingly as
the evening wore on, in a confined room; a sweetish smell of
decay. Maybe I will be told that this does not happen, and indeed
I have never met it in other TB patients. But then, Orwell told
me more than once that he hadn't got TB; he had an allied lung
disease; and as he made no bones about the threat of death I
expect some doctor had really told him this. Most other doctors
would call his disease merely a variety of TB, while agreeing that
the condition of the lungs was unusual. Bodily disgust, or rather a
fear that a good man may at any moment be driven into some evil
action by an unbearable amount of it, is deeply embedded in his
best writing; and at the time I thought all this was easy to explain
– he just hated his own smell. But surely, he wouldn't be likely to
live many years with his lungs in so extreme a condition. Much
more likely, when he was putting himself through the experience
of being down-and-out, or among down-and-outs, he smelt

quite all right. It would be like what they say to children pulling faces, 'you'll grow like that'; and, in a way, it would suit his expectations, as the later writing became more and more confidently grim.

Whether because of this backgrond of suffering or from his very active experience of life, he had a great power to make you feel ashamed of yourself, or, if your moral resistance held firm, to feel sorry that poor George felt ashamed of you. My wife and I ran into this at a quite unexpected point. At that time the Government, or Churchill himself probably, had put into action a scheme for keeping up the birth-rate during the war by making it in various ways convenient to have babies for mothers going out to work; government nurseries were available after the first month, I think, and there were extra eggs and other goodies on the rations, clearly a reward for Mum, or even Dad, since they could not be digested by baby. We took advantage of this plan to have two children; it seems rather athletic, looking back, as one or other parent had to retrieve them from the nursery as soon as the official worktime stopped, and the arrangements in case of illness were left to be improvised. I was saying to George one evening after dinner what a pleasure it was to co-operate with so enlightened a plan when, to my horror, I saw the familiar look of settled loathing come over his face. Rich swine boasting over our privileges, that was what we had become; 'but it's *true*, George,' I cried out piteously, already knowing that nothing would alter his mind. True, that is, that these arrangements had been designed for the whole population, and did apply to all factory workers. He did not refer to the subject again, but at the time his disapproval was absolute.

And yet, as so often when one brushes up an old anecdote, I am not sure now that I did not get him wrong. Not long after that his wife died, and he resigned his job. They had adopted a child, which needed attention during the day, and so did the two goats, living in his garden to supply the child with proper milk. Writing articles for *Tribune* was all right, because he could do that at home, but he could no longer spend most of the day at an office. This looks as if he thought the Government arrangements inadequate rather than too luxurious, but perhaps he was objecting to something else in what I had said altogether. Also it looks as if he was not quite so devoted to his high duties as I had presumed (in writing this, I felt so baffled to understand why he had resigned that I asked John Morris, who was our boss at the time; but now I feel sure that George had told us what he told John

Morris). He can hardly have decided that the problems of India had been solved, but they had become less explosive, and I daresay these goats were partly a polite excuse; he might well feel, as well as wanting a change, that the postwar election would be decisively important and was beginning to loom up, so that writing internal propaganda for Labour in *Tribune* was the most important duty now before him. Also he had at last found a publisher for *Animal Farm*.

The experience of being Indian Editor continued to work on him, and the early parts of *Nineteen Eighty-Four* were evidently conceived as farce about it, so that one expects the book to be gay. Many people get the impression that the author merely chose, for some extraneous personal reason, to make the later parts as horrible as he could. But one cannot understand either book without realising that he considered having to write them as a torture for himself; it was horrible to think of the evil men, stinking Tories, who would *gain* by his telling the truth, let alone jeer about it triumphantly. But tell it he must, he could do no other. Awful, though, for instance, to think of Hetta reading *Animal Farm*; 'it is like cutting off the baby's arm,' he said. (So far as I could tell, she did not feel any of the distress he feared, because she did not believe him.) 'Anyway *Animal Farm* won't mean much in Burma,' he said to me one day with timid hope, 'because they won't know what it is about; they haven't got mixed farming there, like the English mixed farming.' A year or two later, when I passed that area on my way back to China, every detail of English mixed farming was being explained to the Burmese on a comic strip of a vernacular newspaper, solely in order that they might relish to the full the delicious anti-Russian propaganda of Orwell. And though he was rather anti-aesthetic, indeed one might sometimes think Philistine on purpose, he was inclined to retreat into an aesthetic position when the book first came out. With all the reviews ablaze he stayed cross about the reception of the book, so that we said: 'What more do you want, George? It's knocked them all right back. They all say it's terrific.' 'Grudging swine, they are,' he muttered at last, when coaxed and stroked into saying what was the matter; 'not one of them said it's a beautiful book.'

David Astor and *The Observer*

David Astor (b. 1912), former proprietor and editor of *The Observer*, had Orwell recommended to him in 1942 by Cyril Connolly, and after some false starts, Orwell reviewed regularly for *The Observer* until his last illness. They became good friends. Astor admired Orwell greatly, recognised his talent and integrity even before *Animal Farm* appeared, and was indirectly responsible for Orwell finding a house to rent on Jura. He gave Orwell friendly and practical help in his last illness.

Astor is here talking with Bernard Crick for the 1984 BBC *Arena* programme *Orwell Remembered*.

Mr Astor, back in 1942 when you were in the army, the son of the proprietor of The Observer, *probably knowing that you were going to become editor, you spared a bit of time to try and liven it up; and you got Orwell to write leaders on the leader page. What led you to go to a quite unknown writer?*

Yes, well I wasn't really trying to lighten anything. I was trying to find substantial writers. He was known to me from his *Horizon* essays and I also read *The Lion and the Unicorn* which I think is a marvellous piece of political writing. I actually heard of him through Cyril Connolly and I met him through his introduction. As soon as I did meet him I liked him enormously. I'd liked all that I'd read of him, but he was not at all a well-known name. He was more of an essayist and was doing something in the BBC, but he wasn't an established figure.

Where did you first meet him and in what circumstances?

I met him in a restaurant near Portland Place. He was working at the BBC at that time, broadcasting to India. We met in this restaurant and he was somebody who, as soon as you met, got right down to business. He talked very easily as if he'd known you all his life and was extremely easy to approach.

Some people found him very tight and very difficult to talk to.

I found him very easy, very easy indeed. In fact I was amazed how easily we did talk – as if we'd known each other for years. But he didn't waste much time with small talk; he'd make a few little jokes about the BBC and working for it, but that was about all. We got right down to talking business. I really think one realised at once that he and his writings were the same thing, which is not at all usual with writers. Very often you'd meet a writer, having read his work, and you'd get quite a surprise when you discovered what he was like.

Yes. And the writing of the essays comes across. But you were trying to use him originally for political leaders on the front page.

No, it wasn't only leaders, it was essays that appeared at the foot of the leader page. I was collecting a little team to contribute to this, but they were all writing serious articles about the war. *The Observer* had advertisements on the front page at that time. This was only changed to putting news on the front page later. And the essays that were contributed by my people that I introduced to the paper, appeared at the foot of the leader page. There was a little feature called Forum, which was a title indicating free speech, and I tried to get people who would say something substantial. And Orwell certainly did. He wrote a marvellous piece on India.

Did you sense any tension at that time? Because after all he'd written The Lion and the Unicorn, *he called himself a revolutionary socialist, he said the war could only have been won if there was a thoroughgoing socialism. He thought this was arising, he evidently thought the Home Guard was going to be the Catalan militia. There were you, a journalist, but also part of a liberal newspaper not exactly identified with revolutionary socialism at that time or any other. Was it difficult?*

He wasn't going on the lines you're talking about all the time by any means. These were things that he only hinted at. Because he was quite ready to imagine that there would be some sort of invasion in this country, when goodness knows what would have happened. I think he was putting together his Spanish experiences with what he thought might occur, but he wasn't particularly a military thinker. He was intensely interested in the war, in how it could be prosecuted. But he didn't approach me as if he now wanted to advance some revolutionary doctrines. He wanted to do things like work for the independence of India during the war, because he thought that a war against oppression and racialism must include a change in the British attitude towards India, or a speeding up of the self-government of India. And that was one of his themes.

Oh yes, concerning that he would have been completely at one with The Observer. *He then moved into the book reviews and the literary section didn't he?*

He wanted to do that. He was always more interested in writing think articles of a wide kind; he wasn't really a political journalist in the normal sense. He was more a political thinker who wrote in newspapers occasionally.

I think the last review he ever wrote was for The Observer *and he was one of your star reviewers from 1944 onwards. He didn't write articles; whether he would have felt it politically difficult or he liked you so much that it would have been embarrassing. . .*

Well you are right, his political position was to the left of *The Observer*'s. He aligned himself more or less with Aneurin Bevan. And that's why he wrote in *Tribune*.

He became literary editor didn't he? While he was reviewing for your-selves?

That's right. But his relationship to *The Observer* was in fact happy, not at all a difficult one. I mean he did have one little rule which was whenever he was asked to write for any particular publication he'd always make his first contribution one that he thought they might wish to reject – to see whether he was going to be allowed his head to write what he wished. He did that to us and he did it to *Tribune*. He wrote an article for *Tribune*, I think it was about gardening, and the cultivation of roses or something, which they would think a great waste of time.

But you think generally he felt no constraint as a left-wing socialist writing for The Observer?

No, I think he knew exactly the position that *The Observer* was in, which was incidentally one of transition. It was in movement; Garvin had it in a certain conservative position, Ivor Brown moved it into a liberal position; and I think when my time came along I pushed it a little further to the left than that, roughly the Social Democrat position; and he wouldn't have written for us at all if he hadn't felt at home. On the other hand, as I've said, he told me that whenever he wrote for any paper – and I know that he did it for *Tribune* as well as for us – he'd put in an article which he thought they would wish to reject, just to test them as to their willingness to let him have his head.

Then came the period when he began his really regular – once a fort-night I think – writing on the literary pages.

Well my memory isn't good on how that was, but I think he wrote for the paper a lot when Ivor Brown was editor, which was the latter part of the war and the year immediately after the war. And Ivor Brown liked him very much. But he didn't like it, for instance, when Orwell wrote an article on H. G. Wells, taking him to pieces in certain respects, and this produced a violent letter back from Wells to Ivor Brown. But Ivor was perfectly willing to take Orwell's pieces.

Was it your idea that he should report on Germany in 1945?

No, it was his wish. He wanted to go into Germany with the first troops that went in because he was aware that, although he'd written a lot about dictatorships, he'd never been in a country that was under a dictatorship. And he thought, because he had never been to the Soviet Union and he didn't go to Italy or Franco's Spain, and he'd never been to Germany – under Hitler – he wanted to go and breathe the atmosphere and see how it was. He'd never done any reporting and he asked me to back his request to go as a war correspondent, but in fact the news editor was delighted to send him. He went to somewhere near Strasbourg. . . . I don't think he felt he saw anything particularly useful.

I thought the despatches from Paris on the immediate liberation were by far the best, because, of course, he knew French, he knew France. He was always a little bit of a Frenchman in that way; but Germany, no, he didn't get to grips with. And, of course, his wife died and . . . it was a telegram from The Observer *I think which first alerted him to this and he came hurrying home. What was Eileen like?*

I liked her very much. Well the funny thing is she was very like him . . . they'd become similar, particularly in their voice and way of speaking. You know, long-married people sometimes do. But she certainly had . . . I assume *she* adapted to *him*. But she was a very nice woman indeed and very lively and energetic. Came from a medical family . . . and I think her attitude to George was a very good one. They were like partners. There was a good bit of harmony on general things as well as their marital relationship.

And she followed him to Spain and egged him on with the rest of his enterprises. What was their life-style like? You visited their flat once or twice?

I think it was the basement of a house in the Belsize area of Hampstead; there was a ground floor and basement. And he had his carpenter's shop in the basement and he really worked away there, he liked working with his hands. And he also kept chickens in the garden. At that time you were allowed to, you wouldn't be today. And he enjoyed doing all that, running this little farming economy. But their living rooms were very simple and agreeable; nothing very striking one way or the other, but I'd say just a touch of elegance. You know Orwell once said that when asked what he liked he said he liked solid objects and useless information.

Did you get any feeling that they were both very ill and both really seriously neglecting themselves?

Well, I do now, looking back with hindsight, you see, but at the time I didn't. I mean they both of them were obviously working extremely hard. She had a job so they both went out to work and they managed their house when they came back in the evening. And if I remember how they looked, they were thinnish and strained; but they were very unselfpitying, they weren't people who talked about their health and would never treat themselves as overworked. I think neither of them believed in taking a lot of trouble about their personal well-being. They seemed to view that with a certain indifference.

Yes. He deliberately went to live in London to be at the crisis of the bombing; but quite early on was saying he wanted to get out of London into the country. You were actually instrumental, weren't you, in finding him somewhere to go? I think he was very vague where he wanted to go, just as long as it was off the telephone and far from London.

Well that's true. I did put him in touch with Jura and indeed this particular part of Jura, which is the northern extremity, the loneliest part, because I knew it from going for holidays to that island for many years. But the place he went to is just the most remote place you could find almost in the British Isles. I never imagined that he'd stay there. I only suggested that he go there for a short holiday because he obviously needed a holiday. He had been working very hard and under rather trying conditions. When I mentioned it I at first thought he wouldn't go at all, but you couldn't go to the Continent you see. If you wanted to get away somewhere you had to go somewhere remote in these islands.

Foresight and hindsight, it's very difficult, but do you remember feeling any worry at the time that that wasn't the place for a tubercular man to go? Did you know that he was tubercular?

No, I didn't. He never mentioned that. All I knew was he'd been to Morocco for his health, and he talked a bit about that, but I never remember him using the term tubercular.

No, he told all his friends he was a bit bronchial or something of that kind. He did know he had tuberculosis because he'd been in a sanatorium, you see, before the war.

No, I didn't know that. But I think he would have taken the risk anyhow, you know, because when he got there it must have been like a blinding flash of recognition, discovering that the place suited him, because he did settle there extremely happily and very few people could possibly have lived in that house. You see, there was only one other house in the neighbourhood, and that was quite a way off. And those two houses were some ten miles from the next nearest house, and the road between was not a road, it was a track. And he had no means of travelling, he had no vehicle. And the post came twice a week and didn't come all the way up to where they were, they had to go to meet it. He didn't go himself, somebody in the neighbouring family went.

He did have vehicles but none of them were much use. He bought a lorry off an old Spanish War friend, Georges Kopp. You sent him a horse at one stage.

Well he wanted to have a horse, which might have been the best thing. But he certainly lived there to start with with no way of travelling at all. The easiest way to travel from there is by boat across to the mainland, but it's a very tricky passage and I'm glad he didn't try to do it.

I wouldn't have thought that the climate as such would necessarily be a specially bad one for a tubercular person.

I just don't know enough about tuberculosis to know whether that's so or not. But it's hard to believe that the degree of dampness that there is in most houses up there would be helpful to him. His house was a well-built one and it wasn't particularly uncomfortable; it was a farmhouse that had been deserted for quite some years. But I mean, with hindsight, yes certainly it was the wrong place to go. He should have been in a drier place, a more comfortable house and near to a doctor.

When his tuberculosis got worse and he had to leave Jura for Hairmyres Sanatorium, you visited him there didn't you?

Yes, I did, several times. He was going through an extremely bad time. Because the treatment was very painful. I know it included putting a tube down his throat. He had to have his head right back. And he was terribly thin. He had a funny relationship with the doctor because the doctor didn't quite know who he was and had very different political opinions from George's. He was quite amused to hear the doctor's opinion but he didn't enter into a discussion with him. I sometimes felt that that episode in the hospital and all that he went through must have been, or could have been, the background to the torture scenes in *Nineteen Eighty-Four*. That he was going through something extremely unpleasant by rather polite, friendly people who he felt were sorry for him.

He was the first actual patient to have streptomycin. You had something to do with obtaining that?

I managed to get it sent over from America, through connections of mine over there, but it came too late, by quite a long chalk too late.

He was allergic to it, in fact. His fingernails and hair began to drop out and it affected his liver so that he got symptoms of jaundice, it was

189

really very terrible. But it saved the life of two women in the same ward, so it did some good.

I didn't realise the two other women were helped by it, which is good to know, but I imagined that he'd had tuberculosis for so long and that his lungs were in such a condition that it was pretty hard even for streptomycin to have much effect.

You had flowers waiting for him when he finally went to University College Hospital. Did you think he was dying then or. . . .?

I don't remember that I sent him flowers but I certainly wouldn't have thought he was dying. I'd been to see him in the other place he went to in Gloucestershire. I saw him down there, too, where he was living more or less out of doors . . . it was a relic of the old tubercular treatment of being in the sun and fresh air. But when he went to University College, well, I knew he was pretty bad.

That was a Freudian slip actually on my part. You sent him fruit and flowers.

Did I?

Flowers sounds like death doesn't it?

Yes it certainly does. But no, I can imagine I sent him fruit, and I called in on him fairly regularly on my way home from the office and had lots of little chats with him. And he asked me whether I thought that one could die if one had a book in one's mind, ready to be written. Which was a question I couldn't answer of course. But he brought up the question of death.

Oh that's curious because D. H. Lawrence is said to have told his friends towards his end that you couldn't die while you still had a book in you and of course he died of tuberculosis; and it was by coincidence the same consultant, Andrew Morland.

Someone could very well have told him of this.

But he himself appeared to think that he was fighting for life, he wasn't resigned to death in any way?

Oh not at all, not at all, no. He was certainly fighting for life . . . I can't believe he would have got married if he'd been really expecting it.

You had to do a last and strange favour didn't you, David? He left a surprising instruction in his will. He wanted to be buried according to the rites of the Church of England. You found the graveyard; it was just near your estate or belonged to someone you knew.

Yes, well it was really luck that the vicar of that village was an admirer of George, and he talked the parish council into giving him a plot you see. It's normally very difficult to get buried if you aren't a member of the parish.

There's a rose bush on the tomb, or are there two rose bushes?
He asked – I can't remember where or how, it certainly wasn't
directly, that roses should be planted beside his grave. He was
extremely fond of roses and of flowers altogether.
*David, could I ask you generally, because you knew him well and for
quite a period of time, what do you think was his lasting achievement?*
Well I think his work is going to stand, and I'm amazed to find
how all, not merely his few well-known books, but all his essays
and even some of his journalism, read extremely well today. It's
all done with a great deal of thought and a great deal of integrity.
Also courage. He took on big subjects and wrote about them very
simply and very bravely and with this enormous good sense.
Even when he was advancing an improbable view, he managed to
use his own enormous good sense to put it across in a way that it
did not seem an outrageous view. I think some of his literary
assessments are like this. He assessed all sorts of well-known
figures of this century and the last, doing so differently from the
accepted view of them. And I think his literary criticism, his
critical essays, will stand. I also think that he has made a contribution to thinking, as to how we see our time. I think a lot of it
was not entirely popular and is already being forgotten. I mean
for instance he was a great person for trying to see things as they
are and not through the glass of some orthodoxy, some 'ism'; he
wanted you to look around with your own eyes. And people find
that very difficult. For instance, his views on pacifism. A lot of
his friends were pacifists but he thought it was an untenable view
because it meant either you gave no value to your society or you
relied on somebody else to protect it for you. And although he
was a very unmilitary character, he was anti-pacifism.

He certainly was a great individualist, but I found him very
easy to get on with, I really did. I think perhaps because I liked
him very much and I liked his way of thinking. But I also found
he was not a touchy person and he was not a complicator. He
would be quite straightforward with what he wanted and what he
would do, and I think it is true that he was enormously an individualist, even though he's had this great success with his last
two books. Most of his life he was working quite on his own, not
related to any particular party or to any firm or to any college. He
was really self-directed as to what he wrote, what he chose to
write about. And he was getting a minimum response from the
reading public. He was virtually unknown. And this didn't deter
him, he could go on like this, with this wonderful independence
and this wonderful dignity as a human being. 'Above all unto

thyself be true' is somehow what you felt with Orwell, he was doing what was right, what he wanted to do, but he was extremely unaggressive in pushing his views and he met dis-agreement very lightly and well. He was the least quarrelsome of people. And yet he was a real hero of combat. But he was really fighting nonsense, illusions, misunderstandings of things – and he was devoted to literature. I mean devoted to understanding writers of the past and of today and of writing about them. But all this was inner-directed, it was his wish to do it. And in fact for a long while I'd say he was writing against the grain. For instance, in the matter of his patriotism. You see, all the people of his political complexion had more or less abandoned patriotism, but he wouldn't. He thought it was right; it was a defensive patriot-ism, not an aggressive one, but he kept that going without over-emphasising it or exaggerating it. He would simply say, 'That's how I am.' I remember Cyril Connolly saying of Orwell, 'amongst us', meaning the sort of left-wing literary people of his day, he said, 'his distinction was that he discovered the English.' All the rest of them were inclined to admire foreign writers of one sort or another. . . . But there was nothing chauvinistic about him, he wasn't saying Britain is better.

You once called him an anti-totalitarian of the left, but at the end of the day, looking back at it, do you think there was a tension between his libertarianism and his socialism?

Oh yes, I think there was. I think he realised that countries that were calling themselves socialist were not libertarian.

No, I meant more inherent, theoretical contradictions. Can a man be a socialist as he was and a libertarian as well?

Well I haven't seen anything in his writing which says that he felt that was an impossibility. I remember him saying once something very characteristic which was that he thought ordinary people, quite ordinary proletarians, had been more independent and free in the middle part of the nineteenth century in the United States than ever before or since in the history of man. And this fasci-nated him, what life had been like there. But this is very much the libertarian's idea of freedom.

His Second, Lasting Publisher

Fredric Warburg (1898–1980) began publishing Orwell's non-fiction after Victor Gollancz turned down his *Homage to Catalonia*, for fear of offending the Communist Party. Gollancz still kept his rights to Orwell's fiction for a time but then relinquished those to Warburg after he turned down *Animal Farm*.

Warburg wrote about Orwell in his two autobiographical volumes, *An Occupation for Gentlemen* (Hutchinson, London 1959) and *All Authors Are Equal* (Hutchinson, London 1973).

His vivid testimony both in these books and in this interview makes up in liveliness and energy what it lacks in accuracy: he trusted his own memory utterly and never checked anything. Orwell did not go to Spain to write a book or through any publisher, and only wrote to and met Warburg after returning. Warburg was not offered *Animal Farm* until three other more famous houses had rejected it, nor was it written over two or three years, but was in fact quickly written in under four months. His views on Orwell's alleged lack of socialism mirror his own confusions – as an increasingly conservative publisher of left-wing books. He does not mention the novels that Orwell wrote for Gollancz. Cranham Sanatorium was in Gloucestershire not Somerset, a small point; but the idea of travelling on mules on Jura is urban fantasy. Yet he knew Orwell well and recognised his stature by beginning to reprint all his books in Orwell's lifetime.

This is taken from transcripts prepared for Melvyn Bragg's BBC TV *Omnibus* programme of 1970.

Did you read Wigan Pier?
Indeed. More than once.
What did you think of it?
Well I thought it was one of the most contradictory books I'd ever read. It was obviously intended to be basically a book in defence of socialism, but it had a good slam at practically every type of socialist. And it had, of course, nothing positive to say about socialism. Indeed I remember Orwell saying at one stage of the book that he hoped one day he might become a socialist proper, and be accepted as a member of the working class. Which according to him, meant sinking down into a slightly uniform mass of good-hearted proletarians.
So he didn't come out of the northern experience as a socialist.

No, I don't think he was ever a socialist, although he would have described himself as a socialist. After all, socialism is supposed to be a creed in favour of progress and efficiency. And one of the things that Orwell has a most eloquent passage about in *The Road to Wigan Pier*, is what a menace to everything progress is, so that you use always an artificial material instead of something like wood or stone and all the rest of it, you use some plastic or something like that. He didn't like progress; he preferred the old ways, the traditional ways, which is surely not the road of socialism. *When you read* Wigan Pier, *did you think you'd like to publish this writer?*

Well I'm not sure that I read *The Road to Wigan Pier* until later. I hadn't read a great deal of Orwell at the time he came to me.

How did you become his publisher?

I think the circumstances were absolutely crucial. Because before he came to me he'd been with an extremely efficient and lively publisher [Gollancz] who'd published already, I don't know, four, five, six books for him. So why should he have changed? Well, of course, he changed for the reasons I've already mentioned, that he was not really a socialist, and he was far from being a Communist. Now when *The Road to Wigan Pier* was published, it was recognised by Gollancz's Left Book Club, of which it became a choice, as a book that was certainly anti-Communist. Whether or not it was anti-socialist is an open question perhaps, but it was certainly anti-Communist. Now Gollancz's membership of the Readers' Book Club, which ran about 40,000 people, was basically Communist and fellow traveller. So when Gollancz had to publish this book, he had a very awkward problem to solve. How could he publish a book which, brilliant as it was, was all the same violently anti-Communist and in some sense anti-socialist? He solved this in a very neat manner, by putting out the ordinary hardcover edition as he'd [Orwell] written it, but the paperback edition, in the famous orange covers which was the Left Book Club edition, contained a preface by Gollancz himself saying that Orwell was in fact acting as devil's advocate against socialism, though omitting to mention that Orwell was not only a devil's advocate but believed the views of the devil's advocate. Orwell of course didn't like this preface, which he didn't know about, I think, until afterwards. The next thing he wanted to do was to go to Spain on the Republican side, and obviously not as a Communist, but he knew quite well that Gollancz wouldn't send him. And so he had to find a new publisher. Well, Orwell was a member of the Independent Labour Party, the ILP, of which the marvellous James Maxton was the leader. And the secretary of the Independent Labour Party was Fenner Brockway whom I knew quite well. And Fenner Brockway had a number of members who were writers, Ethel Mannin, Jennie Lee, many others, and Orwell, who were finding it difficult to get published. Because they certainly were anti-Conservative but they were also certainly anti-Communist. So what the hell could they do? And these writers, Fenner Brockway thought, would be well suited to come on my list, which was small and very unsuccessful. I was a brand-new publisher then, feeble in the extreme, and so he introduced several of them to me, and I published several of them. . . . One of them was Orwell. So this was one of the reasons why Orwell landed up on my list.

I think there was another reason which was very powerful in Orwell's mind. Throughout his life Orwell never liked being associated with anything that was too powerful or too successful. Well I was clearly unsuccessful in those days. The list no doubt had a great deal of distinction. But it didn't have much else. It didn't have sales for instance. Not to any extent. And of course we were loathed by the Communists who hit our books hard all the time. So the fact that we were unsuccessful must have been a sort of qualifying category which suited Orwell very well. After all when he went to Spain, of course, he didn't become a Communist, but nor did he fight for the Anarchists who were very powerful in Catalonia. He joined a miserable anarcho-Marxist group who were obviously going to get it in the neck, and did, called the POUM.

You think his going to Spain set his political opinions?

I do think that, very definitely, because there's nothing for setting your opinion about a certain category of person, such as Communists, than being shot at by them in the street.

When you took these people on, did you think you had someone extraordinary in Orwell?

Well, Orwell had a reputation among a limited circle of people as an interesting new novelist with four or five books behind him. I don't know that any of the others, except possibly Ethel Mannin, had much of a reputation. And I therefore probably thought that he was well above the average, and no doubt I must have read *The Road to Wigan Pier* at the time and thought highly of it. But you see, the real thing was, political publishing was very much my line at that time. The whole of that frightful period, the second half of the thirties, was dominated by Fascism, Communism and the others, and Orwell was clearly a political writer who took the sort of line that my firm was taking, and in a sense I recognised him as absolutely a must author for me to publish even if he were much less good than in fact he was.

Are you surprised by his fame?

Well of course after the publication of *Homage to Catalonia*, his fame didn't rise at all. This book was almost universally panned by all the critics. And we didn't sell the 1250 copies we printed until after his death twelve years later. This didn't increase his reputation. The next book he wrote [for me] was a little book called *The Lion and the Unicorn*, which appeared in a series of cheap paperback books which we published in 1941 and 1942. And this was quite a successful book in the sense that it sold 5000 or 6000 or 7000 copies. This contains a positive account of Orwell's political views, what a Labour government should do if and when it came to power after the war. This didn't increase his reputation very much because it was minor, it wasn't a literary work, it was a political pamphlet.

Outline what happened to Orwell from the time you met him to his death.

Well, I would say that it was the most obviously creative period of his life in which he brought out his two most important works, *Animal Farm* and *Nineteen Eighty-Four*. After he came back from Spain, he wrote, of course, *Homage to Catalonia* fairly quickly, and I think he lived in the country until the war broke out. Then he came back to London because he must have hoped to be involved in being bombed; this would be something that he would obviously enjoy. I was out of London for a year or so at the beginning of the war, we had a house in the country then, and when I came back, the porter of my block of flats was a sergeant-major of the St John's Wood Home Guard battalion and Orwell was a sergeant. So they persuaded me to join the Home Guard instead of doing something silly like fire-watching. And I was rapidly promoted from volunteer or Private Warburg to Corporal. And I therefore became Sergeant Orwell's corporal. He was Sergeant Blair of course. And we were regarded as dangerous Reds and we were put in charge of all the French, German and Polish Jews who were obviously regarded as dangerous Reds. He was very good – a very keen Home Guard sergeant. Always looked very jaunty, though dirty, on parade. And he took it very seriously. At the same time, of course, he was broadcasting to India in the interests of the war effort for the BBC.

Well, during this time he must have been writing *Animal Farm*. It probably took him two or three years. And I first saw it in 1944. I didn't see an awful lot of him except on parade. We had drinks at the pub and he used to tell me what was going to happen in the war, but he was a very bad prophet. And then of course, *Animal Farm* came out in 1945 and was an immediate success. Immediate. We printed as many copies as we had paper for, that is, 5000 copies, and they were sold within a month or two. And then we scrounged around and got more paper and we printed and printed and printed. And it's never stopped selling since. Well then, this was his first major success and it was the first time that he really had very considerable sums of money. This he liked. This he really liked and he said, 'Well for the first time, Fred, I can take you out to lunch at my expense.' Which he did.

And then I only saw him, of course, from one side, but he had this island holding on the west coast of Scotland, and he spent a lot of time there. And of course, he developed at some stage between 1945 and 1950 the further onslaught of TB. He was more or less cured of this in 1946, because David Astor had one of the new antibiotics, streptomycin, flown over from America, and he took it in a sanatorium outside Glasgow, and it more or less cleared him up. But then, of course, being what he was, he went back to a damp and unsuitable climate; and he had a very tiring journey to the mainland, to Glasgow, to see a specialist once a month, and this, I think, was fairly disastrous. Another thing, and this I have very much on my conscience, which was disastrous, was that all this time he was writing *Nineteen Eighty-Four* which at one time, by the way, was called *The Last Man In Europe*. And it obviously existed in a very mixed-up form and he wrote and asked me to find him a secretary to go up to Jura, where you had to cross two lots of sea, then you had to go on a mule for five miles, and the last five miles you walked. So it was not a very attractive job for a London typist. And I tried quite a few, but they wouldn't go. Had one of them gone, he might have been able to finish *Nineteen Eighty-Four* without breaking his neck over it. But I couldn't find him one and he typed it all himself – very well – and it came in, as all his books did come in to us, in a virtually perfect condition, with hardly a comma wrong. Well, as a result of this he broke down and had to leave. And he took himself or was taken to a sanatorium in Somerset. I visited him there with my wife, and we thought that it looked more like a sort of Arctic concentration camp than a place where people would get well from TB. And we sent down – after some objections from George – a very well-known London specialist in TB who said, 'Well I think we might be able to do something for this man if we got him to my hospital in London, University College Hospital.' Which is why eventually, but too late as it turned out, he went to the University College Hospital.

But before this he had finished *Nineteen Eighty-Four*. I read it, I was the first man in Europe, I think, to read it, and it made a tremendous impression on me. I thought it was an awe-inspiring book, a horrifying book, as it is, and it came out six months before he died. It was a sensation, more in Europe than in England; it was very much a seller in England but in Europe it was a political act of enormous importance. Because you must remember that after the war Russia, which had done so much to win it, was enormously powerful and in some ways admired, and this was – like *Animal Farm* but in a different way – the most powerful anti-Soviet Communism tract that you could find anywhere. And the Europeans treated it as such. The British never really worried much one way or the other about Communism at that time; it didn't have the same effect; it was judged more from a literary point of view over here.

How would you say Orwell's work came to you?

In absolutely perfect mint condition, so that it was a pleasure to look at, a pleasure to read even if it had been drivel. Nothing had to be done. Really nothing. Orwell as a writer was less trouble I should think than anybody I've ever met. The only trouble was that his agent was stone deaf and I had to negotiate terms with him. And Orwell wouldn't discuss terms; if you mentioned money to him he ran straight out of the room. Instantly. 'I can't talk about money, Fred.' You know, another thing about his relationship to his publisher. He didn't believe in telling anybody what he was doing next. I think the only man that he discussed his work with was Arthur Koestler. So when he was writing *Animal Farm*, all he said to me was, 'I'm writing about a farm where the animals revolt against the farmer and it's very anti-Russian, you won't like it, Fred.' This is what he said. And when he was writing *Nineteen Eighty-Four*, he said, 'It's all about the future.' That's all he told me. And I had a very inaccurate impression of what I was going to get.

What's your final opinion of him as a writer?

Well I would say without hesitation that, with Lawrence, he was the best and most influential writer between 1930 and 1950, possibly 1960; that his work is gathering strength if you can judge by sales. More and more people seem to buy him every year; hardcover, paperback, and all the rest of it. I can't assess how

Orwell helps people, but I know how he helped me while he was alive, and how much I regret his death, because he had a way of seeing through the appearance, of penetrating to the kernel of the argument, the nub of the thing, and putting it down.

From *Animal Farm* to *Nineteen Eighty-Four*

George Woodcock (b. 1912), Canadian writer and scholar, met Orwell during the war while Orwell was at the BBC and when Woodcock was active in the peace movement, working with British Anarchists and libertarians. They soon became good friends. His *The Crystal Spirit: A Study of George Orwell* (Jonathan Cape, London 1967) is perhaps the best account of Orwell's politics yet written.

This is the full text of his 'Recollections of George Orwell', *Northern Review*, August–September 1953.

Imagine Don Quixote without his horse and his drooping whiskers, and you will get a fair idea of what George Orwell looked like. He was a tall and angular man, with a worn Gothic face that was elongated by vertical furrows at the corners of the mouth. His rather narrow upper lip was adorned by a thin line of moustache, and the general gauntness of his looks was accentuated by the deep sockets from which his eyes looked out sadly.

I first met Orwell during the early years of the last war, when he was working at the Indian Department of the BBC in London. He had sent me an invitation to take part in a discussion panel on poetry which he was organising, and, since we had recently indulged in a rather violent dispute in the *Partisan Review*, I was a little surprised at such an approach. But I agreed, mostly, I think, to show that I bore as few ill feelings as Orwell himself evidently did.

A few days later I went along to the improvised wartime studio in a former Oxford Street bargain basement. Orwell was there, as well as Mulk Raj Anand, Herbert Read and William Empson, whom I already knew, and Edmund Blunden, whom I had not met before. The programme turned out to be a made-up discussion which Orwell had prepared skilfully beforehand and which the rest of the participants were given a chance to amend before it went on the air. All of us objected to small points, as a matter of principle, but the only major change occurred when Orwell himself produced a volume of Byron and, smiling around at the rest of us, suggested that we should read 'The Isles of Greece'. At that time the British government was officially opposed to the Indian independence movement (Gandhi was still in prison), and as the ringing verses of revolt were read the programme assumed a mild flavour of defiance which we all enjoyed. Orwell, I noticed, had a very rough-and-ready idea of radio production, and his own level voice was not effective for broadcasting. Afterwards we went to a tavern in Great Portland Street frequented by broadcasting men, where Orwell discoursed cynically on the futility of the trouble we had taken over a programme to which he doubted if more than two hundred Anglophile Indians would bother to listen. He was already feeling the frustration of a job that was mostly concentrated on the dissemination of official propaganda. By the next time I saw him, during 1943, he had resigned from the BBC and become the literary editor of *Tribune*, a socialist review which upheld the Bevanite wing of the Labour Party and at that time was sharply critical of the Churchill Government.

On this occasion I encountered Orwell on the top of a bus at Hampstead Heath. He immediately began to talk about the journalistic disagreements which had preceded our actual meeting. 'There's no reason to let that kind of argument on paper breed personal ill feeling,' he said. This disarming remark was typical of Orwell's attitude towards opponents with whom he found some common ground of liberal humanity or intellectual scrupulousness. He was ready to fight out debatable ideas in a bold and slashing manner that was reminiscent of the nineteenth-century polemicists, but this did not prevent him from remaining on the friendliest personal terms with his opponents, provided they were willing, which was not always the case. The only exception he seemed to make was towards the totalitarians. His battle with them was whole-hearted, and I remember his indignation when he once told me about a Communist poet who had published a bitter personal attack on him and later tried to be affable when they met in a public house. To Orwell this seemed the grossest hypocrisy, because he knew that the Stalinists detested him as one of their most dangerous enemies.

Not long after my second meeting with Orwell, he told me that he had just written a political fairy tale, for which he was then trying vainly to find a publisher. I was connected with a small press, and he wondered whether we might consider it. I mentioned the book to my associates, but none of them was particularly interested, and the suggestion was allowed to lapse. This was unfortunate, for the fairy tale was *Animal Farm;* Orwell's difficulty in placing it was due more than anything else to the widespread feeling at the time that it was undiplomatic and even a little unpatriotic to say very much in criticism of Communist Russia. One publisher, who has since become prominent in his anti-Communism, put about a report that the book was 'extreme and hysterical', and it was only after much peddling, and after he had thought of private publication, that Orwell eventually persuaded Secker and Warburg to bring out *Animal Farm*. He and his publishers were equally surprised when it turned out to be an international best seller.

I began to see more of Orwell while he was working at *Tribune*, where, despite the paper's rather narrow political dogmatism, he opened its literary pages to writers of all the left-of-centre viewpoints. But his generosity too often submerged his discernment for him to be a really effective editor, and usually the most interesting page of the *Tribune* was his own weekly piece, 'As I Please', in which he discoursed on any facet of life or letters that happened to strike his fancy. It was the best short essay-writing of the forties. Orwell's versatility was astounding; he could always find a subject on which there was something fresh to say in a prose that, for all its ease and apparent casualness, was penetrating and direct.

My acquaintance with Orwell developed into friendship in the latter part of 1944, mainly through a common concern for civil liberties. As always happens in time of war, the more intransigent minorities of opinion were sometimes rather harshly treated, and their members imprisoned or otherwise discriminated against. There was a great deal of discussion on this point among the English intellectuals. Some claimed that freedom of criticism and protest should be temporarily relinquished in safeguarding what they regarded as greater freedoms. Others, including Orwell and most of his friends, held with varying degrees of emphasis that the liberties of speech and writing could only be abandoned with danger to the general climate of intellectual life.

The issue was given added importance through the attitude of the National Council for Civil Liberties, which had become largely infiltrated by Communists and fellow travellers and was almost completely inactive in protecting non-Communists. The matter came to a head when three editors of a minority paper were sent to gaol for publishing anti-war views. A committee which had been formed to defend them was perpetuated to deal with other similar issues and, under the name of the Freedom Defence Committee, led a precarious but active existence from 1944 until 1949. Its leading members were a mixed group of intellectuals, artists and political workers drawn from every group between the Liberals and the Anarchists; only Conservatives and Communists were absent. Bertrand Russell, H. J. Laski, E. M. Forster, Herbert Read, Cyril Connolly, Benjamin Britten, Henry Moore, Osbert Sitwell and Augustus John were among its supporters, and Orwell became vice-chairman. I recollect that when I transmitted the committee's invitation to him he was at first hesitant about accepting. 'I don't want to get back on the treadmill of administrative work,' he said. When I assured him that no great demands would be made on his time, he agreed, and became, while his health allowed, much more helpful, both materially and morally, than his initial hesitation had led us to suppose. He wrote, advised and gave freely, occasionally he would buttonhole some influential person we wished to interest, and on rare occasions he would be persuaded to speak in public. A throat wound during the Spanish Civil War had robbed his voice of resonance, but he spoke with such unpretentious conviction that I never remember an audience treating him other than with attention and respect. It was through our constant contact with Orwell over such matters that my wife and I became friendly with him, and our business conversations developed into more informal and personal meetings.

What made Orwell such an excellent journalist and also gave his novels a reality that was much more than mere verisimilitude was his intense interest in the concrete aspects of living, in 'the surface of life', as he would say, and also the way in which his writing seemed to extend and amplify his daily life and conversation. Now, when I re-read his books, I am perpetually reminded of the talk on evenings we spent together, at our respective homes, or sometimes dining in Soho and going on to the Café Royal or some literary public house.

Orwell's own flat, where he lived with a small adopted son to whom he was extravagantly devoted, was in Islington, perched high up under the roof of a tall Georgian house in a square on the edge of a working-class district. It was a dark and almost dingy place, with a curious Englishness of atmosphere. There was a great screen plastered with cut-outs from magazines in the living room, on the walls hung Victorian portraits murky with bituminous shadow, and a collection of china mugs, celebrating various popular nineteenth-century festivals, crowded on top of the crammed bookshelves. By the fireplace stood a high-backed wicker arm-chair, of an angularly austere shape I have seen nowhere else, and here Orwell himself would sit. His study looked like a workshop; he was very fond of manual work, and when he was in London would often do some joinery as a relaxation from writing.

I do not think Orwell was entirely indifferent to comfort, but he certainly set no great store by appearances, and his times of hardship had given him an easy contempt for the trappings of the bourgeois life. His way of dressing, even when he was earning well, remained that of the poorer English intellectuals, and I never saw him clad otherwise than in baggy, grubby corduroys, a worn tweed jacket with leather patches on the elbows, and shoes which were never very well polished. John Morris, who disliked Orwell, wrote in *Penguin New Writing* an essay which suggested that this sartorial carelessness was an aspect of a childish and self-conscious rebellion against the standards of polite behaviour. It always seemed to me that, having once escaped from middle-class manners, Orwell just did not find them worth the trouble of resuming. Certainly he practised no self-conscious Spartanism, and on the few occasions when we visited fairly expensive restaurants together, I noticed that he enjoyed the food as well as anybody else. He seemed to have naturally modest physical needs, though he never rejected anything good when it came his way.

Whenever one arrived at Orwell's flat, or when he came wheezing up the stairs to one's own, there was at first a period of relative silence, for Orwell, though gregarious, was also a reserved man. Then, after a while, the conversation would start, over a meal, or sitting before a coal or peat fire, with Orwell rolling cigarettes of the strongest black shag he could find and drinking tea almost as thick as treacle. Sometimes the talk would develop into a monologue on his part. He had lived a very varied life, had been a policeman in Burma, a dishwasher in Paris, a bum and a grocer in England, had fought in Spain against Franco and lived for a while in Morocco. And he would tell of his experiences in such an entertaining way that one rarely had the least desire to interrupt him. His voice was rather flat, with the slight vestige of an Eton accent, but it had a monotonous kind of fascination and seemed to throw into relief the vividness of his descriptions. At other times we would converse on the strangest variety of subjects, and, however banal our text, Orwell would usually discuss it with such humour and thoroughness that he managed to lift it right out of its pristine dullness. For instance, we would talk about tea, and ways of making it, or about comic postcards, and he would bring in such a wealth of illustration and reminiscence and odd tags of information that one was stimulated to enter into the subject with as much zest as he. And then, a week or two later, one would find that this conversation had become a part of his writing and formed the basis of a leisurely, fascinating essay in some newspaper or magazine.

At yet other times, the conversation would range over deeper matters, and Orwell would expound his fears of the future of society, and dilate on the way in which the concern for freedom and truth had grown weak in popular consciousness, as well as in literature and politics. In this way he told us all the basic ideas of his masterpiece, *Nineteen Eighty-Four*, though, with a characteristic modesty, he talked little of the book itself, and until I saw it finally in print I had only the slightest idea of the plot. When he talked on such themes he could paint a really horrifying picture of the fate that might befall us. After such a session Herbert Read, who himself is not exactly a light-hearted man, once said to me: 'My God, Orwell is a gloomy bird!' And often, indeed, it did seem as though one had been listening to the voice of Jeremiah.

Apart from his accent, the only characteristic of the public school background that Orwell seemed to have retained was his emotional stoicism of behaviour. Even his anger was demonstrative only on paper, and, while his generosity and consideration for other people indicated the presence of deep feelings, he showed them rarely. He was certainly interested in women, but he never displayed the fact, and one unusually beautiful girl remarked to me that Orwell was the only one among her male acquaintances who never made her feel that he was aware of her as a woman.

During 1946 Orwell rented a house on the Isle of Jura in the Hebrides, to which he would retire for months on end. From this time onward we saw little of him, but letters frequently arrived in which he gave vivid little pictures of his life there and kept us posted on his activities. In August, 1946, for instance, he told me that he had just started a new novel, which he hoped to finish during the following year. It became *Nineteen Eighty-Four* and was destined to be his final book. A month later he sent a lengthy description of life on the island; the following passage shows the intense interest he always took in the concrete aspects of the life that went on around him and also in its social undertones:

> We have been helping the crofter who is our only neighbour with his hay and corn, at least when rain hasn't made it impossible to work. Everything is done here in an incredibly primitive way. Even when the field is ploughed with a tractor the seed is still sown broadcast, then scythed and bound up into sheaves by hand. They seem to broadcast corn, i.e. oats, all over Scotland, and I must say they seem to get it almost as even as can be done by a machine. Owing to the wet they don't get the hay in till about the end of September, or even later, sometimes as late as November, and they can't leave it in the open but have to store it all in lofts. A lot of the corn doesn't quite ripen and is fed to the cattle in sheaves like hay. The crofters have to work very hard, but in many ways they are better off and more independent than a town labourer, and they would be quite comfortable if they could get a bit of help in the way of machinery, electrical power and roads, and could get the landlords off their backs and get rid of the deer. These animals are so common on this particular island that they are an absolute curse. They eat up the pastures where there ought to be sheep, and they make fencing immensely more expensive than it need be. The crofters aren't allowed to shoot them, and are constantly having to waste their time dragging carcases of deer down from the hills during the stalking season. Everything is sacrificed to the brutes because they are an easy source of meat and therefore profitable to the people who own them. I suppose sooner or later these islands will be taken in hand, and then they could either be turned into a first-rate area for dairy produce and meat, or else they would support a large population of small peasants living off cattle and fishing. In the eighteenth century the population here was 10,000 – now less than 300.

Towards the end of 1946 the only large independent left-wing bookstore in London was bought out by the Communists. Orwell was appalled when I wrote him the news and immediately replied with a scheme for setting up a rival concern to maintain an outlet for individual publications. In a period of poverty, he had worked as salesman in a Hampstead bookshop, and now he was full of ideas as to how a new store might be run efficiently and independently. Nothing came of the project, and I think the letter he wrote on this occasion was intrinsically more interesting for some comments on his own works which illustrate the rigorously self-critical standards he set himself. I was then studying his books, and I had asked whether he could lend me a copy of a relatively little known novel he had written in the 1930s, *Keep the Aspidistra Flying*. 'I haven't a copy. . . .' he answered. 'I picked up a copy in a secondhand shop some months back, but I gave it away. There are two or three books which I am ashamed of and have not allowed to be reprinted or translated, and that is one of them. There is an even worse one called *A Clergyman's Daughter*. This was written simply as an exercise, and I oughtn't to have published it, but I was desperate for money, ditto when I wrote *Keep The A*. At that time I simply hadn't a book in me, but I was half starved and had to turn out something to bring in a hundred pounds or so.'

Actually, both books would have satisfied any ordinary journeyman writer, and Orwell's remarks show the seriousness with which he took his literary craftsmanship. His writing seemed effortless, but it was only so because of the exacting discipline he imposed on structure and verbal texture alike.

Orwell spent the winter of 1946–7 in London, but in the following spring he left once more for the Hebrides, and we never saw him again. Letters followed each other during the summer. Looking through them, I find Orwell approving my own intention to write a book on Wilde. 'I've always been very pro-Wilde,' he commented. 'I particularly like *Dorian Gray*, absurd as it is in a way.' I suspect that Orwell's liking for Wilde was based mostly on his natural sympathy for the defeated, since there is certainly little in common between the close discipline of his own work and the lushness of Wilde's, except perhaps a shared liking for surface colour.

During these months, Orwell was working with difficulty on *Nineteen Eighty-Four*, which he did not expect to finish before the following spring. 'It always takes me a hell of a time to write a book even if I am doing nothing else, and I can't help doing an occasional article, usually for some American magazine, because one must earn some money occasionally.'

It was at this time that Orwell took a decision which many of his friends regarded with disquiet. He announced that, apart from a trip to London in November, he intended to stay in the Hebrides over the winter. With his precarious health and his previous attacks of tuberculosis, it seemed rash indeed for him to remain in the damp [autumn] and winter climate of the Isles, but he was the kind of man with whom, one knew beforehand, it would be useless to argue once he had made up his mind. Moreover, he seemed already to have thought of plenty of reasons for staying, and he detailed them to me in a letter which made me feel his real motive was that infatuation with the semi-idyllic life of remote and fairly primitive communities which at times seizes demandingly on city-tired intellectuals.

'I can work here with fewer interruptions,' he told me, 'and I think we shall be less cold here. The climate, although wet, is not quite so cold as England, and it is much easier to get fuel. . . . Part of the winter may be pretty bleak, and one is sometimes cut off from the mainland for a week or two, but it doesn't matter as long as you have flour in hand to make scones. Latterly the weather has been quite incredible, and I am afraid we shall be paying for it soon. Last week we went round in a boat and spent a couple of days on the completely uninhabited Atlantic side of the island in an empty shepherd's hut – no beds, but otherwise quite comfortable. There are beautiful white beaches round that side, and if you do about an hour's climb into the hills you come to lochs which are full of trout but never fished because too unget-atable.'

In the event, Orwell did not get away from Scotland at all that winter. His health had been poor all summer, and in October it was probably made worse by a fishing accident in which his boat capsized and he and his small son were almost drowned. A little while after this it became evident that he was seriously ill with tuberculosis in the left lung. He was bedridden at home for two months, and when he next wrote me in January, 1948, it was from a hospital in Lanarkshire to which he had been removed a fortnight previously. 'I have felt a bit less like death since being here,' he remarked stoically, and he was hopeful of being about again by the summer and of getting a correspondent's job in a warm climate during the winter.

Sickness did not diminish Orwell's interest in what went on around him, and he was still much concerned about civil liberties. A purge of Communists in the British civil service began early in 1948, and, in spite of his hostility to Communism, Orwell thought that the methods of the government, which did not allow suspects to confront their accusers, formed a dangerous precedent. I think his words speak for themselves on this important issue.

'It is not easy to have a clear position,' he said, 'because, if one admits the right of governments to govern, one must admit their right to choose suitable agents, and I think any organisation, e.g. a political party, has a right to protect itself against infiltration. But at the same time, the *way* in which the government seems to be going to work is vaguely disquieting, and the whole phenomenon seems to me part of the general breakdown of the democratic outlook. Only a week or two ago the Communists themselves were shouting for unconstitutional methods to be used against the Fascists, now the same methods are to be used against themselves, and in another year or two a pro-Communist government might be using them against us. Meanwhile the general apathy about freedom of speech etc., constantly grows, and that matters more than what may be on the statute books.'

During the spring and early summer of 1948 Orwell seemed to be recovering, and in July he told us that he was going back to Jura. 'They seem to think I am pretty well cured and will end up perfectly OK so long as I don't relapse during the next few months.' As soon as he returned to the Isles he resumed work on *Nineteen Eighty-Four*. By September his condition had begun to worsen, but, though he was in what he called 'a ghastly state', he did not leave the island for treatment until December; he insisted on finishing his novel beforehand. 'The effort of doing so didn't make me any better,' he said. He certainly seemed moved by an obstinate sense of compulsion, and I have since felt that he knew he was unlikely to recover and wished to present in a complete form the book that was to be his testament.

I heard from him for the last time early in 1949. He had now gone to a sanatorium in Gloucestershire. He seemed contented there, and something of the grim old Orwellian humour came back when he discussed his treatment. 'They are giving me something called PAS which I suspect of being a high-sounding name for aspirins, but they say it is the latest thing and gives good results. If necessary I can have another go of streptomycin, which certainly seemed to improve me last time, but the secondary effects are so unpleasant that it's a bit like sinking the ship to drown the rats.' He was still interested in the affairs of the Freedom Defence Committee, which was waning fast from the sheer lack of enough supporters who at that time realised the need for a civil liberties organisation untrammelled by party ties.

In the spring of 1949 my wife and I left England for Canada

('The sort of country that could be fun for a bit, especially if you like fishing,' Orwell had commented when he heard of our plans), and we never seemed able to find the time for a trip to Gloucestershire before we went. It was one of those omissions one regrets after it cannot be rectified. After we reached Canada I wrote a couple of times to Orwell, but he was too sick to reply. We heard that he was getting worse and had gone into a London hospital, and then, at a Vancouver party one snowy evening in the first days of 1950, one of the guests came in and told me that Orwell was dead.

Since that time an image seems to have grown up in the popular mind, particularly in countries where his earlier books have been comparatively little read, of Orwell as a writer whose main message was one of anti-Communism. In fact, he had little in common with those frightened mediocrities who have nothing to offer but a negative operation to the totalitarians. It is true that from many reviews of *Nineteen Eighty-Four* one might gain the impression that it was devoted entirely to an attack on Communism, or even to an exposure of left-wing politics in general. Neither impression would be true.

Orwell did, indeed, detest the methods of the Communists, because he regarded them as both tyrannical and dishonest, and he saw in Russia an extreme example of the suppression of those humanist virtues which seemed to him essential for healthy social life. But it was only the most extreme, and not the only example, for he observed everywhere in contemporary politics the fatal tendency to displace in favour of expediency the necessary virtues of honesty and fair play. He gave a rather nominal support to the British Labour Government, but he realised that there also the dangers outlined in *Nineteen Eighty-Four* existed, and his warning should be regarded as applying to any society where the cult of the state becomes more important than the welfare of individual man. Everywhere he saw, in varying degrees, that steady erosion of the personality whose final stage is, after all, the subject of his last novel.

Orwell, more than most of his contemporaries, represented in our time Matthew Arnold's conception of the man who is:

Wandering between two worlds, one dead,
The other powerless to be born.

In many respects he was a survivor of the free-fighting liberals of the nineteenth century, a partisan of the values which men like

Emerson, Thoreau and Dickens strove to maintain. But he also looked to a future in which he hoped men might outlive the night of tyranny and falsehood, of ignorance and mediocrity, into which we so often seem to be passing. None, indeed, knew better than he how heavy the odds were against such a hope, but he still thought it was worth fighting for with all the indignation and humanity of his nature.

A Philosopher in Paris

Sir Alfred (A. J.) Ayer (b. 1910), philosopher, met Orwell by chance in Paris in 1945. He told me that they first started talking about a common admiration for Dickens. One of the many themes of *Nineteen Eighty-Four* is a defence of empiricism and a sense-data theory of knowledge: Winston Smith in *Nineteen Eighty-Four* tried desperately to hang on to a belief that there is an objective external world knowable to our senses, against the Party's view which Smith learned through O'Brien that our concepts (his concepts) are the real world: thinking (or power in O'Brien's case) makes it so. It would be nice, and wholly plausible, to think that Orwell took this from Ayer's *Language, Truth and Logic* (1936, new ed. 1946), but Ayer says that they never discussed philosophy and it is not amongst Orwell's known collection of books.

This passage is from Ayer's autobiography, *Part of My Life* (Collins, London, 1977).

Paris in 1945 attracted many English visitors on one pretext or another. Mr Attlee came to the Embassy, some time before the General Election brought him to power, but had little to say to the Duff Coopers or indeed to anyone else. Laurence Olivier, who came with a theatrical company and enjoyed a great success with his Parisian audience, showed a similar modesty at the party which was given for him. . . . Another new friend that I made at this time in Paris was George Orwell, who was then a foreign correspondent for *The Observer*. He had been in College at Eton in the same election as Cyril Connolly, but had left before I came there. I first heard of him in 1937 when he published *The Road to Wigan Pier* for Gollancz's Left Book Club. By the time that I met him in Paris, I had also read two of his other autobiographical books, *Homage to Catalonia* and *Down and Out in Paris and London*, and greatly admired them both. Though I came to know him well enough for him to describe me as a great friend of his in a letter written to one of our former Eton masters in April 1946, he was not very communicative to me about himself. For instance, he never spoke to me about his wife, Eileen O'Shaughnessy, whose death in March 1945 left him in charge of their adopted son, who was still under a year old. I had assumed that it was simply through poverty that he had acquired the material for his book *Down and Out in Paris and London* by working as a dish-washer in Paris restaurants and living as a tramp in England, before he escaped into private tutoring, but I came to understand that it was also an act of expiation for his having served the cause of British colonialism by spending five years in Burma as an officer of the Imperial Police. Not that he was wholly without respect for the tradition of the British Empire. In the revealing and perceptive essay on Rudyard Kipling, which is reproduced in his book of *Collected Essays*, he criticises Kipling for his failure to see 'that the map is painted red chiefly in order that the coolie may be exploited,' but he goes on to make the point that 'the nineteenth-century Anglo-Indians . . . were at any rate people who did things,' and from his talk as well as his writings I gained the impression that for all their philistinism he preferred the administrators and soldiers whom Kipling idealised to the ineffectual hypocrites of what he sometimes called 'the pansy left'.

Though he held no religious belief, there was something of a religious element in George's socialism. It owed nothing to Marxist theory and much to the tradition of English Nonconformity. He saw it primarily as an instrument of justice. What he hated in contemporary politics, almost as much as the abuse of power, was the dishonesty and cynicism which allowed its evils to be veiled. When I first got to know him, he had written but not yet published *Animal Farm*, and while he believed that the book was good he did not foresee its great success. He was to be rather dismayed by the pleasure that it gave to the enemies of any form of socialism, but with the defeat of Fascism in Germany and Italy he saw the Russian model of dictatorship as the most serious threat to the realisation of his hopes for a better world. He was not yet so pessimistic as he had become by the time of his writing *Nineteen Eighty-Four*. His moral integrity made him hard upon himself and sometimes harsh in his judgement of other people, but he was no enemy to pleasure. He appreciated good food and drink, enjoyed gossip, and when not oppressed by ill-health was very good company. He was another of those whose liking for me made me think better of myself.

Orwell at *Tribune*

T. R. (Tosco) Fyvel (b. 1907), writer, journalist and broadcaster, was introduced to Orwell by Fredric Warburg in 1940 and together they edited 'Searchlight Books', in which Orwell's *Lion and the Unicorn* appeared. Fyvel and Orwell became and remained good friends. Fyvel's recent biographical and critical study *George Orwell: A Personal Memoir* (Weidenfeld & Nicolson, London 1982) has been well received, but we print here simply the more detailed account of Orwell as literary editor of *Tribune* which Fyvel wrote for Miriam Gross's *The World of George Orwell* (Weidenfeld & Nicolson, London 1971).

The special relationship between Orwell and *Tribune*, which lasted roughly from 1943 to 1949, was clearly of profit to both sides. To *Tribune*, Orwell gave the cachet of his highly individual outlook. Conversely, the pressure of weekly journalism must have drawn from him many penetrating shorter pieces which otherwise would have remained unwritten. Orwell and I had seen a good deal of each other in the early days of the war and then been separated. When we met again it was in the spring of 1945, in his final weeks as literary editor of *Tribune*; I myself had just returned from two years in what was then called the 'Mediterranean Theatre' and found London at the end of the war a battered, grey and tired-looking place, at first sight hard to re-adjust to. On my arrival, my publisher Fred Warburg had given me the typescript of *Animal Farm* to read, adding that certain people in London, like Victor Gollancz, actually opposed its publication for fear that it might harm the Anglo-Soviet alliance. Back from the wars (if at several removes) I shook my head at this self-centred literary notion of the level at which Stalin operated. Reading George's strangely moving fable, I was impressed how enormously he had gained in literary technique – but also how pessimistic he had become since the heyday of the optimistic socialist beliefs which we had shared in 1940–1.

George himself, tall, gaunt, with lines of suffering etched more deeply in his face, also seemed to me tired, and looking more than just two years older, when I called on him in the little literary office of *Tribune* where he sat sadly eyeing a pile of new books for review like a set of enemies. He asked whether I would be interested in taking over his job. I said that I would rather like it, but could only do so in the autumn. He declared that he would soon leave in any case – he was desperate to be free. I was sure he had performed the job of literary editor meticulously because he could simply not tackle a job of work in any other way; but he had sat in this little office since November 1943, the war was now nearing its weary end and he felt tired and constrained.

A word about *Tribune*. Like many a successful left-wing journal, it was a fluke that came off. As a small socialist weekly, it was started (and owned) in 1937 by Sir Stafford Cripps – a wealthy and briefly violently left-wing Labour Party leader – to support his ideas for a popular 'United Front' of the British Labour, Liberal and Communist Parties. These ideas of a 'United Front' with Communists proved short-lived (Labour stalwarts like Ernest Bevin soon saw to that!), and when in 1940 Churchill, as War Premier, appointed Cripps British Ambassador to Moscow, Cripps wanted to close *Tribune* down. But at the last minute it was taken over by Victor Gollancz, London's famous and enthusiastic left-wing publisher. This arrangement also proved temporary as under the impact of war, Gollancz's enthusiasms shifted from politics towards Christianity; and so he was pleased when in 1943, in a second last-minute rescue, *Tribune* and its financial burden were taken over jointly by George Strauss, a well-to-do Labour MP, and Israel Sieff, a noted intellectual Jewish businessman and philanthropist, mainly to provide a platform for their friend Aneurin Bevan – that rising, fiery Labour Party star from the Welsh mining valleys.

Now, like Bevan's political career, *Tribune* in the latter part of the war suddenly came to life. Bevan stood on the Labour left less because his views were extreme than because his socialism was vibrant and confident. Under his direction *Tribune* was pro-Russian but at the same time libertarian and anti-Communist, calling persistently for a socialist government to take over from Churchill after the war. Indeed, with both Labour and Conservative ministers included in Churchill's Coalition Government, *Tribune* was often the only Fleet Street voice which dared directly to attack Churchill's war policies. As his editor, Bevan had brought in Jon Kimche, a prominent wartime journalist; to serve as literary editor, Kimche chose his old friend George Orwell – they had known each other as far back as 1934 when they had both been employed in a bookshop in Hampstead where Kimche, as he recalls, sold books with enjoyment in the mornings while Orwell did the same in moody anger during the afternoons.

I had come across a few copies of the magazine while in Italy. Flipping the pages, I had wondered how Nye Bevan with his Welsh rhetoric and his itch for office and his wish to reform British health, housing and (as he had told me in an interview) the popular press, got on with Orwell, who, amidst the euphoria of a world war being won, held fast to his incorruptible pessimism about the future. Evelyn Anderson, then assistant-editor, told me that there was really no conflict: in their casts of mind Bevan and Orwell moved on parallel lines which would never meet. In Jon Kimche's recollection, the weekly editorial meetings were rather like a stage play by Pinter: the participants spoke only in monologues. For instance, Nye Bevan might give a fervent lecture on nationalising the coal industry, his editorial for the week. After this, George ('dressed like a typical left-wing intellectual which he was not') would observe how depressing it was getting rid of Hitler only to be left with a world dominated by Stalin, American millionaires and some tinpot dictator like De Gaulle – this would be *his* theme for his weekly 'As I Please' column. Yet the result of this non-dialogue was an exciting wartime weekly journal.

While Orwell tried hard to be a reasonable literary editor, dealing with other people's work was not his strong side. But his 'As I Please' column gave the same distinction to the paper's literary end that Aneurin Bevan's socialist line gave to the front half. It was written in that style of personal reportage which had produced some of the most vivid literature of the period, the style of a writer turned reporter who has participated in the events he describes and so gives them an extra dimension – Hemingway at Caporetto and in the Caribbean, Orwell in Burma and Barcelona, Isherwood in Berlin, Koestler in jail, Vincent Sheean in various places. This literary style, special to its age, can probably not be repeated (Norman Mailer describing a march on the Pentagon is, by comparison, writing a deliberately mannered account about a 'Happening') and Orwell's 'As I Please' stands out as perhaps the only example of its being used for sustained routine journalism.

What surprised me when we met again in 1945 was how he had turned himself from a rather agonised writer who claimed he rewrote each page four or five times into an efficient and indeed prolific journalist. In addition to his *Tribune* job, and while completing *Animal Farm*, he had, for two years, managed to write regular book reviews for the *Manchester Evening News* and *The Observer* and a regular London Letter for *Partisan Review*, a surprising output amidst the endless time-wasting of war. But by the spring of 1945 he had reached exhaustion point as wartime journalist. I found that his personal life was also in tragic dislocation. His wife Eileen had died under a minor operation, leaving him with a baby son whom they had just adopted. Above all he wanted to shed the pressures of being *Tribune*'s literary editor. He felt he was not suited to an office job.

There he was right. During his own solitary years of writing he had lost the editorial toughness to shape and cut other people's work. The book reviews in *Tribune* were very ordinary. Perhaps one forgets how hard it was to function as literary editor during the war, with so many writers away, with barren publishers' lists, postal uncertainty and, of course, the flying bombs. At any rate, it seems Orwell rarely *sent* books out for review. Instead, news of a possible soft touch soon got round and there was a steady stream of callers to George's little office in the Strand, eager to get a book for review or leave an article or poem. As I noted when I succeeded him, apart from personal friends of George's like Stevie Smith, Alex Comfort and Julian Symons, the literary standard of these *Tribune* regulars was not very high.

But what could he do? To Evelyn Anderson, who worked on the political section in the next room, he seemed constantly burdened by the dilemma of what should have priority – his own high standards of English language and style or the desire to help a struggling, impecunious fellow-writer for whom *Tribune*'s fee of a guinea for a review plus the sale of the book might mean the difference, as George saw it, between eating or not eating. He was also worried over misprints in *Tribune*, inevitable under the sketchy wartime proof-reading. Mrs Anderson remembers him being upset for days because she herself, through fatigue, had allowed 'verbiosity' to appear in one of his own paragraphs. Yet his basic problem, however fiercely he might flay intellectuals in general, was that he had not the heart to tell a would-be contributor that the piece on which he had slaved was fit only for rejection. At the same time he would not print anything that was downright bad. In face of this dilemma, Orwell's famous honesty sometimes deserted him: he failed to answer letters, or he pretended he had not yet got round to reading the thing; and so the drawers of his desk became gradually filled with a whole mass of unrejected literary rejects which I found when I took over, and which he was only too glad to hand on. . . . To Orwell as journalist, even after he had left his office, *Tribune* was still his first love. He remained a close friend of Evelyn Anderson and Michael Foot who now edited the paper. He would often drop into the office and ask one of the secretaries to share a sandwich and glass of beer at the next-door pub. The arrangement when I started as literary editor was that he would write occasional non-political pieces, but the first one he proposed almost started us off on the wrong foot. In his first contribution as an outsider, he intended to say that the new Labour Government must make it its first socialist task to abolish all titles, the House of Lords and the public schools, and that Aneurin Bevan with such purely bureaucratic reforms as the National Health Service and council house estates was quite on the wrong track. I protested that I could not start off my job with such a direct attack on Nye Bevan and laughed George out of the idea. This essay was never written. Rather a pity, I now think.

Against this, I was able several times to tempt him to write essays by pushing special themes his way. One of the best originated when we discovered how, as children, we had both enjoyed that one-time fabulous American bestseller, *Helen's Babies* by John Habberton. From this starting point, he wrote that moving little essay 'Riding Down to Bangor'. Indeed, in 1947, before he departed for the Isle of Jura and before his final illness, he contributed another short series of 'As I Please' pieces which included some of the gayest and wittiest of his essays, classics like 'The Sporting Spirit'. As I knew, Orwell could rewrite even such slight pieces three or four times, paring them of each unnecessary phrase. They represent the lighter, warmer aspect of his mind while he was writing *Nineteen Eighty-Four*: there was always spring, there were flowers and the common toad, children's books and nonsense rhymes, there was his own, prejudiced self to laugh at. It is worth noting, in fact, how *Tribune* journalism continued to bring out this other side of Orwell's nature.

Canonbury Square and Jura

Susan Watson (née Henderson) (b. 1918), took a job as house-keeper in 1945 to look after George and his adopted son, Richard. She had been married to a Cambridge mathematician and her divorce was going through at the time. She was interviewed by me in 1974 and by the BBC in 1983, but has written this fuller memoir especially for Orwell Remembered.

I went to work for George Orwell in the summer of 1945. Walking down a hill in Hampstead one day I met Rayner Heppenstall who asked me if I would be free to take on a job as nurse/housekeeper to George Orwell and his adopted son Richard. He explained that George's wife had recently died. I was free, having just completed a job in an international nursery. I had not heard of George Orwell, but Rayner said we had friends in common – Hetta and William Empson. Hetta fixed a meeting at her house one evening. When I arrived, George was already there. I liked him immediately and thought he looked very lonely. He showed me some photographs of Richard and asked me when I could start work. I said I should like to meet Richard and see the flat before deciding, so it was arranged that I should go to Canonbury, where he lived, the following Saturday; then we should go together to see Richard who was staying with his aunt Gwen O'Shaughnessy in Greenwich.

When I reached Canonbury Square, I could not find the flat because the entrance is at the back, so I rang from a phone box in the square. George said he could see me from his window, told me not to move, and came down to fetch me. From the outside the flats were bleak, rather like a tenement dwelling, and we climbed flight after flight of steep stone stairs to his top floor flat.

We sat down and he asked me if I could cook. 'Not well,' I said, 'when I was married we had a cook general.' 'Never mind, we can always have fish and chips.' I didn't much like that idea and determined to learn to cook.

We went over to Greenwich where George asked me if I would like to help him bath Richard. While I was washing him, George said, 'You will let him play with his thingummy, won't you?' I answered, 'Yes, of course.'

When Richard was tucked up in bed, George asked me out to dinner. He took me to Canuto's, a beautifully old-fashioned plush restaurant in Baker Street with gilded marble pillars and middle-aged waiters. George said he had to leave me for a minute, would I order two drinks. Then he went to stand behind a pillar. I ordered the drinks, and as soon as the waiter had brought them, he emerged. Later he told me that he considered waiters to be very good judges of character, so because I had been served quickly, I had earned the waiter's seal of approval. It seemed to me an unusual way to engage a nurse. During dinner, he asked me how much I would like to be paid. I asked for a pound a week more than I had been earning and he agreed immediately. It was a very generous payment for those times.

I went back to Hampstead delighted. The job would suit me down to the ground because I had worked with babies before, and also, being in the throes of a divorce, would have a comfortable home for my daughter Sarah when she came to me in her holidays. I packed my trunk, including a cookery book which I still have, and joined George and Richard on the following Saturday.

I did not know then that George was suffering from TB or I would not have let him carry my trunk up all those stairs. I was to learn later that he took no care of his health.

A natural routine developed. George worked from eight-thirty or nine in the morning, going out to lunch at the local pub or to meet friends. He was always back for high tea which was the main point of the day. He liked northern English cooking. Kippers were a prime favourite or black pudding boiled first, then fried with onions and served on a bed of creamy mashed potatoes. Then there would be Gentleman's Relish on toast, or brown bread and butter or home-made scones with jam. We had cake twice a week. All this was accompanied by tea from a huge brown enamel pot. It was so strong that, when rationing allowed, it took eleven spoonfuls to brew (or rather stew it, since George liked it to stand for a while). This has driven me to prefer China tea.

He also loved home-made jam. One day he invited his friend Geoffrey Gorer, an anthropologist, who at that time was studying chimpanzees. It was partly to find out if Richard was developing as well as the chimps. Geoffrey Gorer watched him in the bath and said that he had got beyond the monkey stage, so George was quite satisfied. He went home with him after tea and returned with a terracotta urn full of damsons laid on cabbage leaves which he dumped on the kitchen table for me to make jam with the next day.

George had an aged aunt, I think her name was Nellie Limouzin. She was invited to high tea one day and arrived wrapped in black satin decorated with jet bugle beads. George got out his large collection of McGill postcards to show her and asked me not to bring in tea until he had put them away as she would be embarrassed if I saw her enjoying them.

He always returned to work after tea and often continued typing until three in the morning. I got so used to the sound of the typewriter that I woke up when it stopped.

At ten o'clock I used to take him his hot chocolate in a pink mug with a picture of the elderly Queen Victoria on it. He preferred Cadbury's chocolate. Fry's was very much a second-best. Ever since his prep-school days, he had been fond of chocolate, and had a bar of Bournville plain beside his bed.

He sometimes took a break from work to do some carpentry, using Richard as his 'mate' to hand him the nails. In London he made a toy boat for Richard and a fire-screen to put in front of the very smoky sitting room fire. One day, when I was frying onions, I went to answer the phone or to see to Richard, and the handle of the carving knife caught fire. I took it to George, feeling upset and afraid he would be angry, but he simply said, 'Never mind, now's my chance to give it a new deerhorn handle. You won't recognise it by the evening.'

He really enjoyed doing practical and creative things.

For Sunday lunch he liked underdone roast beef with Yorkshire pudding, the potatoes roasted under the joint so that the meat juices seeped into them. A steamed pudding followed. When there was no time to make them, I used tinned ones I had discovered. They were called Mrs Peaks. I opened the tins very carefully at both ends to preserve the shape and covered them with lemon sauce or golden syrup. George once asked me how I made the shape so perfect and I replied as I thought cooks should that it was my secret. I don't know whether he ever guessed.

It was during Sunday lunch and sometimes at high tea that he told me about the books and authors he most enjoyed – Joseph Conrad whose precise use of language he admired; Jack London who had disguised himself to enter the East End and write *People of the Abyss*; Arthur Morrison whose *Hole in the Wall* and *Child of the Jago* described a similar world; Dickens, of course, and P. G. Wodehouse. George had written an essay in defence of him and was quite certain he was not pro-Nazi. He always spoke out when he suspected an injustice was being done. He lent me some of these books to read while saying that it was bad for the mind to read too many novels. He was also reading Victor Serge and James Burnham at that time.

Animal Farm was published while I was at Canonbury. On the publication day, George came home and said he had been slogging round the bookshops moving it from the children's shelves to the adult ones. The booksellers had assumed from the title that it was a children's story. He then gave a copy to my eight-year-old daughter.

There was a lot to do in the flat so George engaged Mrs Harrison to help with the cleaning. She came for a couple of hours in the mornings, bringing her small son, Kenny. He and Richard used to run up and down the passage. Mrs Harrison silenced Kenny with great doorsteps of bread and jam, so that his face was always jammy. He used to call her 'mum' and Richard, copying, started to call me 'mum'. One day, after tea, George stood up with his back to me and said, 'I can't have Richard calling you "mum".' 'He only does it because he hears Kenny do it. He'll soon stop,' I replied. 'He must call you "Nana".' This made me laugh and say, 'I'm not a typical nurse in a bombazine dress, so may we settle for "Susan"?'

That's what we did. Except that Richard couldn't pronounce his s's and so it came out 'Toozie'.

Tuesday was my day off with one exception: George asked me if I would mind changing to another day so that he would be free to go out and meet 'The Old Earl' as he called Bertrand Russell. On my day off George insisted that I should leave the house at 9.30 and that I could return as late as I liked without missing the last bus or tube. If I should do so, he said, I was to go to the nearest police station and get them to phone him; then he would come and bail me out. I didn't look forward to this prospect and determined it should not happen, but I think George would have enjoyed it.

George was devoted to Richard and looked forward to Tuesdays because he so much enjoyed their time together. He was a wonderful father and could do everything for the baby if need be. He told me that during the bombing he was looking after Richard on his own and was proud that he had only missed one bottle because of the greater necessity of going down to the air raid shelter. Some people thought that after Eileen's death he would give Richard up, but he never once thought of this.

On Tuesdays George sometimes took Richard out into the square or to visit friends. Celia Kirwan (now Celia Goodman) or

Inez Holden came to visit him fairly often. They were both good friends to George. I only remember Sonia Brownell calling on two occasions.

One Monday night I heard a commotion in the passage. I went out to find George having a haemorrhage. He was walking towards the kitchen and I asked if I could help him. He said yes, I could get some ice and cold water to put on his head. I made him go back to bed immediately then wrung a teacloth out in cold water, wrapped some ice in it and put it on his head. He had never mentioned to me that he had TB or any chest complaint, but then, he was a very concealing person. He used to cough frequently with a short bark of a cough, but I thought that was the result of the bullet which had hit his vocal chord in Spain.

Next day was my day off and I had arranged to go to a Shakespeare play with a friend. I had mentioned it to George. He came into my room, ill as he was, and said, 'You *must* take your day off.' 'B----r my day off,' I said and sent him back to bed, where I managed to make him stay until he was better. He refused to see a doctor, having no faith in them, so I thought of a ruse. I phoned the doctor and told him that Richard had a cold, although he was a very healthy little boy and never had colds. When the doctor came, I told him that I was worried about George. I did not tell him that George was tubercular, because I thought he should tell him that himself, but he did not, and the doctor failed to diagnose it.

A fortnight later, George was quite well and he got up. At tea one evening soon after, he told me that he hoped to live until Richard was about thirteen and asked if I would stay with him, looking after Richard, until then. I said yes. Then he said he would show me where his papers were and that I could deal with them. He also told me that after his death he did not want any biography or anything else written about him. He said that if anything was to be written, he was the person to do it, but he did not intend to, because in an autobiography you had to tell absolutely the whole truth. He used Mark Twain's autobiography as an example.

For many years, for this reason, I refused to talk to anyone who was researching about George, but now I feel that so much has been written about him that if there were to be biographies or programmes which were not very good, people would get incorrect information from them, so it is important to try and express the truth as George felt it to be about things. To have misinformation about him would partly make his own struggle less.

It was also about this time that he was saying he must buy himself some new clothes but that he had given his coupons to Eileen when she went into hospital, and they had been stolen there. There was a photograph of her on the mantelpiece, holding Richard, which always stirred me. He said to me that he had had a happy marriage and that they would never have separated, but that it was not completely happy as he had not always treated her very well. I just said I was sorry, and that was that. I think he didn't really notice what was happening to other people, and did not realise how ill she was. I found him a curious mixture of caring for people and being obtuse about their motivations and sensibilities. She probably concealed her illness from him too because of his own and because they were adopting Richard. I do know from my own experience that if you have to live with an organic complaint or chronic illness you just get used to it and carry on. It's just part of your life, and if you are not well sometimes, that's just too bad. I think he was like that because of his tuberculosis and probably did not realise how much Eileen was deteriorating.

As he was talking about Eileen he told me that he had almost completed the arrangements for renting a house in the Hebrides, on the Isle of Jura, and that he would like to get away from London, the continual telephone calls and all his commitments following the success of *Animal Farm*. As Richard was walking it would be good for him too. At this time he intended to use the Jura house only for holidays. He asked me if I would come. I think he was longing to get away from the confines of the flat. He showed me some beautiful fishing flies. Fishing had been a favourite hobby of his since boyhood.

Our preparations involved an exciting shopping spree for paraffin lamps, candles, oilskins, Wellingtons, snake bite serum and army surplus blankets. We bought enough flour to fill the zinc-lined tin trunk he had had in Burma since, he said, we would not be able to get any there. He was quite right.

At the fishmongers I spotted a sixteen-pound jar of pickled onions. George loved them and they would go well with the rabbits he intended to shoot and all the cheese we were taking so I decided then and there to buy it. I had to take Richard out of the pram to wheel the onions home, but George was delighted, and later the Pickfords van was to transfer them from Canonbury to the Hebrides.

George said I could have a fortnight's holiday, and I really needed it, so I took Richard to stay with a friend while I did various things in London and said goodbye to family and friends. Suddenly, only ten days later the doorbell rang, and there stood tall, cadaverous George. 'You're coming to Jura with me today,' he said.

I packed Richard's things, collected him and cancelled the dentist's appointment which I had left until last.

We set off for King's Cross and the long journey to Jura. Richard enjoyed it very much and at the end George said, 'Haven't you been a good boy?'

We travelled by train to Glasgow then by boat to Tarbert East, a bus took us across the Mull of Kintyre to Tarbert West and then another boat to Craighouse at the southern end of Jura. We were still twenty-six miles from the house at Barnhill, so we went by taxi to within three miles of it where the road became impassable to normal traffic. We walked from there, George carrying Richard on his shoulders.

When we arrived, I found George's sister Avril firmly ensconced. George hadn't told me she was there, though I learned later that she had just arrived one day. We had met earlier in London and from the start she disliked me and I disliked her. It was nothing that we did, we just disliked each other. After a lovely tea which she had prepared, she told me that she fought for what she wanted, which I took to mean my position in George's household. I replied that I did not fight, and as far as I was concerned if I had anything she wanted, she was welcome to it.

There were only two occasions when we had open disagreements. One day I was trying to put Richard's jersey on and he started to cry because it was tight. Avril was watching me and said, 'You should *smack* him.' I said that the only person who had the right to smack Richard was his father. I knew that George would never smack him because he always treated Richard as an equal.

She went on to say that I should not call George 'George' but 'Eric' and, 'call yourself a nurse when you can't darn socks?' She also said that the island was an unsuitable place for me because I was disabled. I decided to talk all this over with George. I took it to him one evening when she was out, and said that if she continued to interfere in this way it would be better if I left because after all she *was* his sister and I would respect her because of that. George said he did not want me to go and explained that she had had recent bereavements and had given up her flat in London. When we went back to London, he said, she would return and we would bring someone else out, so would I wait.

Our nearest neighbours on Jura were Donald and Katie Darroch. They had a croft nearly two miles from Barnhill and we took it in turns to go there for our daily supply of milk. They were both so kind and gentle. Katie churned butter and patted it into blocks decorated with thistles. Donald brought us the post every ten days from Ardlussa, eight miles away.

One day, Mr and Mrs Fletcher who lived at Ardlussa came to visit us and invited Richard and myself to a children's party they were giving. We had no transport so Donald suggested that if we would like to ride to the party, he would lead us on his cart-horse. I had to borrow a dress from Avril. It was a good, warm dress – brown with pink stripes and pink bobbles at the neck. Richard wore his most respectable corduroy trousers and best jersey, but somehow managed to look like a farmer's-boy among the Highland gentry. We had a beautiful tea with strawberries.

Having missed my dentist's appointment in London, I developed abscesses on my front teeth and was forced to go to Glasgow to have them extracted. I had to wait for my dentures to arrive and as soon as I put them in, Avril said 'Eric, what do you think of Susan's new teeth?' He said they looked very nice but thought it better not to mention that I had false teeth. It was while I was away in Glasgow that Avril talked to George. I don't know what was said, but on my return, George asked me up to his room. He said would I like to go straight away with sixty pounds or stay and work it out, returning to London when he did? I thought it would be best to leave straight away, and that is what I did, though with very great regret. I returned to London and under-went an operation which I hoped would improve my balance and ability to walk. Unfortunately it went wrong. I wrote to George from hospital saying how much I missed Richard and him. He sent me a photograph of them both. Later, when I was back home, he wrote inviting me to lunch and to collect a suitcase I had left at Canonbury.

When I arrived, George came to the door holding Richard who recognised me at once and started to giggle. Avril came along the passage and said, 'He's forgotten you.' Just at that moment I felt so fed up.

Richard went into the sitting room, hid behind the scrap screen and started to play peep-bo as he and I had often done. George followed me into the bedroom and asked whether I had received a parcel he had sent to the hospital. I hadn't as I had left before Christmas. It had either been lost in the post or stolen. I enquired at the hospital later but no one knew about it. He said,

'What a pity, there were such beautiful things in it.' Then he said, 'I'm very ill, Susan.' Because I was still feeling hurt by Avril's remark, I just said I was sorry, I was going to have lunch with Mrs Harrison. I took my suitcase and left.

That was the last time I saw him. Later I heard that he'd been taken ill and sent him some tobacco because even if he couldn't smoke it, to have it by him might have cheered him up. I also wrote to him when he was at University College Hospital to ask whether I could visit him, but he said that owing to the side effects of the strong drugs they had been giving him, his hair and his teeth were falling out, and he didn't want me to see him in such a condition.

At no time did I blame him for what happened. Our relationship was a good one, based on mutual respect. I miss him very much and think of him as a fine and completely irreplaceable person.

His Jura Laird

Mrs Margaret Nelson (b. 1917) came to Jura with her first husband, Robin Fletcher, an Eton housemaster, when he inherited the Ardlussa Estate, the north part of the island which includes Barnhill. As reforming landlords, not interested in the shooting, they tried to restore crofting and make the home farm profitable. They sought a tenant for Barnhill so that the crofters north of the house would not be so isolated. David Astor recommended the Orwells to them.

Mrs Nelson is interviewed by Nigel Williams for the 1984 BBC TV *Arena* programme, *Orwell Remembered*.

Mrs Nelson, when did you first meet George Orwell?
It was in 1947 he came, after having corresponded with us for a long time – about a year I think it was. But my husband had met him in London the winter before he came and had a discussion about Barnhill and the difficulties of living there.
Did he get the impression then that Orwell wanted to get away from things?
I think so, I think he had talked to David Astor when he was at

The Observer and I think that he then had in the back of his mind the idea of some very remote place that he wanted to go to to write over the years . . . and he thought that Jura was probably the place that he would like to come to.

Your role then was that you were trying to improve the north end of the island?

Yes, we were living here as a family. My husband had come back from the war and we were trying to build up the community and the farming and the estate generally, and he arrived in April 1947. I remember very vividly Orwell coming in and how ill, how terribly ill, he looked – and drawn: a sad face he had. Of course, he had recently lost his wife and he had his little boy Richard to look after whom he'd adopted and he looked very, very sad and drawn and ill.

It's an extraordinary place for a man in that condition to come to, isn't it? Was life much harder than it is now?

Much harder, because there was no telephone nearer than Craighouse, which was twenty-seven miles away, petrol was rationed, the only shop was down in Craighouse and our only communication was by the post van which came three times a week, and that only came to here. And then the post would go on either by somebody with a bicycle up to Barnhill or later on by car or something once a week.

Did you see much of him?

Yes, we saw a lot of him. He was always coming down either to the post or to meet his friends who were coming to stay, or to collect his rations from the shop. When he first came it was to buy a bicycle; the motor bicycle was always breaking down and he was always sitting beside the road tinkling with it. Then he would come for help. In those days several of the men on the place had come back from the war and two of them were extremely good with engines and making do and they were always having to go up and help him and rescue him and get the motor bicycle going again. He wasn't a terribly practical person I don't think, but he enjoyed the time when he was doing something practical.

His coming to live here fulfilled a dream, don't you think?

Yes, I think that he had an idea for a book and it was, I think, quite a long time in his mind and he wanted to get away from all pressures and contacts with other people and get away on his own to write it, to get it out of his system.

He did actually stay in your house down here?

Yes, he stayed twice. He stayed the first time that he came –

before we took him up to Barnhill to see it. And he stayed when he was ill. He was brought down by Richard Rees when he was ill, and the doctor down in Craighouse got a specialist from Glasgow to come and see him here and he stayed up in his room above here for four or five days. So we did see quite a lot of him – he was always coming in.

He was very ill on that occasion wasn't he?

He was very ill on that occasion and the specialist said to us, 'Don't let him go back up that road again because he might have a severe haemorrhage any moment which would finish him', and then the specialist went away next morning back to Glasgow. But Eric wouldn't stay; he got his friend Richard Rees to come down from Barnhill to fetch him and they went back up the road, luckily without any bad consequences. . . . He didn't stay because he felt that it was unfair on us; we had four small children and he didn't think that, as he had rampant TB, it would be fair on us to stay in the house any longer. I said to him that we kept all his things separate and would obviously burn his pillow and bedding and stuff like that afterwards, because it was very, very infectious, but he still said it wasn't very fair on us and he went back up the road to wait till he could get to hospital. . .

Was he a happy man do you think?

No . . . he was a sad man. I think he very much missed his wife – and I think I always felt that he was sad in himself probably because we were a family and a happy family working away here and that probably brought home to him a bit, you know, what he had lost. He was devoted to Richard. And I think that was one of the reasons that he came here – because of Richard. I think that there were two reasons: one was that he could get away so that he could write his last book and write this message that he felt he had to get across, and the other was to give Richard a country upbringing.

He'd come down and perhaps the flour was short in the shop and, you know, had we got any flour to spare – those sort of mundane conversations I had with him all the time. So I just really remember him being extremely ill and extremely ill-looking and very concerned about Richard all the time. He would show more concern to me, probably, because I had small children myself.

Do you think he thought that he was going to die?

Yes, I'm sure he did because when he was ill up here, when we were waiting for the specialist, he had several long conversations with my husband then and he said that he hoped that he would finish his book before he died. He certainly did that, he certainly did.

Can we just move on to talk about Orwell as a political writer because he was a committed socialist coming to a part of Scotland which remained unchanged, in terms of its social structure, for hundreds of years. Did he react in the way that you would expect a person of those political views to react to this very tight community?

Yes. One of his first things was that he did think that the whole island should be divided up into smallholdings and that there should be dairy farms everywhere. After he had been here for a bit and lived here and also done a bit of farming with Richard Rees and Bill Dunn (see page 231), he realised the impracticability of that. He realised that dairy farming was impossible here, and where would you sell the milk and all that kind of thing.

It is very hard land to farm isn't it?

Very, very hard land to farm and our communications are very difficult too. You cannot grow enough winter feed here for big farms.

Can we just talk about when his sister came to live with him? When was that?

She came in '47. I think that she came on holiday first of all and then saw the situation there and decided to stay and look after Richard and house-keep for Eric. She was the mainstay of everything, she was really. Without her I don't think it would have been possible for them to stay up there – she was very practical, extremely nice, with a great sense of humour – always ready to laugh when things went wrong and able to see the funny side of it.

He was devoted to his adopted son.

I very clearly remember when Richard fell off the back of a chair at Barnhill and cut his forehead open and he had a really bad gash and Eric wrapped him up in a sheet and brought him down here for us to get the doctor. Well, in those days the doctor was umpteen miles away in Craighouse and we had no telephone, so we kept Richard here and somebody went with a car down to Craighouse, got Dr Sanderman who was a very old man, and he and I had to stitch up Richard's forehead in the bathroom.

Quite a few of Orwell's friends came up to visit him, didn't they?

Yes, they did and it was quite tricky really because there was no telephone; if anyone sent a telegram, very often the telegram would arrive with the post and very often it would arrive after the people had actually arrived themselves. So they would get to here and wonder what to do next and whether anybody was going to come down to meet them; sometimes somebody came down in a boat with an outboard and sometimes, when they had a car, somebody would come down in a car. Well, they would come and wait around and we would give them a meal. Sometimes we would help them on their way up, sometimes we would all just wait around until somebody came down from Barnhill to fetch them.

So you did get to know his circle as it were?

Well we did, there were quite a lot of people came and, you know how easy it is to muddle people up, but we did get to know quite a lot of them, yes. We had quite long conversations with various people and a lot of them arrived here after a very difficult journey from London – by boat and two different trains and two different buses and then perhaps they came up on the post van from Craighouse which would have taken them a long time; they were sometimes quite resentful that we should live in a place like this. Then, after a week at Barnhill they got to realise what isolation was like and they would be down here. . . .

Didn't he and Richard Rees have a scheme for setting up a farm together?

Yes they did. Richard Rees we did get to know very well, because he was often the one sent down to meet people who were coming, and he was sent down to get the post; he was a very kindly person – very fond of Eric and very helpful to everybody. He had a bit of money and he suggested to Eric that they do a bit of farming in a very small way and it was then that they asked Bill Dunn to come.

Did you ever get any mad Bohemians stalking down?

Well they didn't come stalking, but they did come, yes. There were quite a few who, I suppose, fancied themselves rather in the literary world or something. Obviously when Avril came she managed to dislodge them fairly quickly I think. . . .

When you read the book were you surprised that the man you knew had written those things?

Well I was, yes. *Coming Up for Air* and *The Road to Wigan Pier* and those ones, they were very gloomy and I was rather surprised that he had written them. *Nineteen Eighty-Four* is a very horrific book. I didn't read it for quite a long time afterwards and, you know, I was amazed that he could have sat up there at Barnhill in that isolation, writing that book. But he'd had the ideas crystallising in his head before he came and he just needed the place to get away from people to write it.

Wrecked in the Corryvreckan

Henry Dakin (b. 1927), son of Orwell's older sister, Marjorie, came to Jura on leave from the army in August 1947, and was involved in a disaster in which Orwell misread tide tables, failed to lash on the outboard motor securely, and nearly drowned with his nephew, niece and his son. They had been on a camping expedition to the other side of the island. Corryvreckan is one of the most famous, indeed legendary, whirlpools in the Western Isles.

This account was written up from notes I made after interviewing Henry Dakin in 1976, which he later corrected and enlarged. Lucy was his younger and Jane his older sister.

He decided to camp on the other side of the island and four of us went round in a boat, Eric, Lucy, Ricky [Richard was now three years old] and me, with the camping gear and tent. We had a couple of days there. Eric liked fishing, we stayed in fact in a kind of hut there. On the way back, there was much looking up of dates and tides, but he must have misread them. Jane and Avril had walked back, but when we turned round the point there was already a fair swell, the boat was rising and falling a lot, but we were not worried because Eric seemed to know what he was doing and he did spend a lot of time mending and caulking the boat, and we had an outboard motor. But as we came round the point obviously the whirlpool had not receded. The Corryvreckan is not just the famous one big whirlpool, but a lot of smaller whirlpools around the edges. Before we had a chance to turn, we went straight into the minor whirlpools and lost control. Eric was at the tiller, the boat went all over the place, pitching and tossing, very frightening being thrown from one small whirlpool to another, pitching and tossing so much that the outboard motor jerked right off from its fixing. Eric said, 'The motor's gone, better get the oars out, Hen. Can't help much, I'm afraid'. So I unshipped the oars and partly with the current and partly with the oars, but mostly with the current, tried to steady her and we made our way to a little island. Even though that bit of it was very frightening, nobody panicked. Eric didn't panic, but nobody else did either. Indeed, when he said he couldn't help you very much, he said it very calmly and flatly. He was sitting at the back of the boat, he wasn't particularly strong; I was younger and stronger and sitting near the oars.

We got close to a little rock island and as the boat rose we saw that it was rising and falling about twelve feet. I had taken my boots off in case I had to swim for it, but as the boat rose level with the island, I jumped round with the painter in my hand all right, though the sharp rocks were painful on the feet, turned but saw the boat had fallen down. I still had my hand on the painter but the boat had turned upside down. First Lucy appeared, Eric appeared next and cried out, 'I've got Ricky all right.' Eric had grabbed him as the boat turned and pulled him out from under the boat. He had to swim from the end of the boat to the side of the island, still hanging on to Ricky. He seemed to keep his normal 'Uncle Eric' face the whole time, no panic from him or from anyone. And they were all able to clamber up on to the island. . . . So we were left on this island about a hundred yards long and I could not see all of it because the rocks rose in folds – we were left with the boat, one oar, a fishing rod and our clothes. Eric got his cigarette lighter out, never went anywhere without it, and put it out on a rock to dry. We had not been there three minutes when he said he would go off and find some food. A slightly ridiculous thing, it struck me afterwards, because we had had breakfast only two hours before and the last thing that any of us was thinking of was eating or of hunger. When he came back, the first thing he said was, 'Puffins are curious birds, they live in burrows. I saw some baby seagulls, but I haven't the heart to kill them. I thought we were goners,' he concluded. He almost seemed to enjoy it. We waved a shirt on the fishing rod about, and after about one and a half hours a lobster boat spotted us and picked us up. Picked us up with some difficulty, because he could not come up close to the island because of the swell and had to throw a rope across and we clambered along the rope one by one, Eric taking Ricky on his back.

The lobsterman landed us at the north of the island and we just walked about a quarter of an hour or twenty minutes and came across Avril and Jane working hard hoeing in a field. They said to us, 'What took you so long?'

Working at and on Jura

William ('Bill') Dunn (b. 1921) was an ex-Army officer who came to Jura in 1947 to farm. After five months he moved down from his farm above Barnhill and joined Orwell and his sister Avril where he tried to farm Barnhill itself. He married Avril shortly after Orwell's death and together they brought up Richard ('Ricky'), Orwell's adopted son.

Here he is interviewed by Nigel Williams for the 1984 BBC TV *Arena* programme, *Orwell Remembered*.

Bill, where are we standing now?
This is the garden at Barnhill. It was really a complete wilderness when the Blairs – that's Eric and Avril – came out to take residence here. It's not all that different now, though Avril put down flower beds and fruit trees, and things like that. They all seem to have disappeared – there have been several people here since then.
How did you come to be here in the first place? How did you come to be living with Avril?
Well I didn't start here. I actually came to Jura. I put an advertisement in the *Oban Times* because I wanted to get away from Glasgow and I really wanted to start farming. Obviously you didn't need so very much money to get some small patch here and that's what I did, eventually. Robin Fletcher answered my advertisement and so I came to see him and he suggested a scheme which was that if I liked it here – I stayed for the summer – we could work something out on a profit sharing basis. But in the meantime, that summer of '47, Richard Rees was here and he suggested he might put up a thousand pounds. He wouldn't do any farm work but he would be a sort of sleeping partner and I would do the work. And then it was suggested – because he was a great friend of Eric's – that I would come and live here with the Blairs, Avril and Eric, which I did; I stayed there until he [Rees] finally left after Eric died. . . . Eric liked to take an interest in agriculture, but he didn't really know very much about it . . . he never did any agricultural work at all, he said that he wasn't really fit anyway. He was very fond of young Richard and he was keen on the garden and, in fact, too keen, because after he came back from Hairmyres Hospital the first year that I was here, he was told not to do anything and Avril was always taking the wheelbarrow out of his hands. He was always trying to do something or digging or that sort of thing, which was obviously not supposed to be very good for him. . . . *Nineteen Eighty-Four* was the only book that he wrote when he was here. As far as I know. I don't know of any other but I'm sure he wrote letters and correspond-

ence for various magazines.

Where did he work?

Well I seem to recall at first that he worked in that end room downstairs but latterly he seldom seemed to come out of his bedroom. And he did everything there.

Bill, was it a difficult situation? Was he a difficult man?

No not a bit, no, he was very easy to get on with. . . . We didn't see very much of him really. He'd come down for meals and chat about the news and one thing and another, and then he'd just say, 'Well, I must go and do some work', and disappear.

And how about the sea? Did he have much to do with that?

Yes – I think that he was quite keen. He had this boat that he got the first year that I was here. It was a twelve-foot dinghy with an outboard engine. I know that he did go . . . for bread or something – and the thing is, the time that he did that he was very late back and there was a slight sort of mist and, of course, Avril was very upset . . . she said something to him when he came back and he said, 'Oh well in this part of the world you don't worry about people being late for meals – you have got to just accept that people misjudge things.' Then the same year, about September time, there was some lovely weather. It was '47, we had about six weeks of brilliant weather: flat calm. And he took the family, Jane, his niece, and his nephew, Henry, and another niece Lucy, and Avril and young Rick and they went round the back through the gulf round to a bay where there is a small house and they picnicked there for a little while. Then when they were due to come back again he more or less did guess the tide pretty reasonably, because it was in his favour, but still there were wee whirlpools whizzing around and Avril and Jane decided that they didn't want to be in this wee boat again and so they just walked over the hill. I remember that I was making hay with the chap who was there, Donald Darroch. There was no sign of this small boat coming back . . . and Avril and Jane joined in the haymaking and we were there for hours and then Eric, in bare feet and obviously shipwrecked, appeared and he was furious that no one had sent a rescue party. Avril got her own back by saying, 'Well you told us that you never bothered if people came late.' He said, 'That's right, that's quite right', but he had actually got shipwrecked, literally. . . . The outboard engine wasn't tied with a piece of rope, which is a must, and it just came loose or something and the whole thing had got pulled off the stern.

Were he and his sister close? Was it a close relationship, because you later married Avril didn't you?

I did, yes. Well I would have said slightly impersonal . . . there was absolutely no sign of affection. I would have said a bit of a cold fish . . . I wouldn't say that they were a very affectionate family.

Did Avril like his books?

Yes she did, and she read them all. Avril was an avid reader, she read anything. I think that she was most impressed with *Nineteen Eighty-Four*.

One of the things in Orwell's work is that he is often talking about life in the pub, ordinary life, ordinary people. That's the thing that he lays great stress on. Do you think that he knew that life?

I honestly wouldn't think so, you know. I mean, he was a staunch socialist as we all know, but if he had to live with working-class people, I don't think he would have got on. I don't think that he would have liked that at all. In my opinion I don't honestly think that he had anything in common with the British working class. In fact, I heard that, on some show, I think it was on television some years ago, where some miners were talking about him; they said that he was a delightful fellow, but he just wasn't one of them at all. He wasn't on the same wavelength.

Farming this land was a difficult experience, wasn't it? You think that it is possible to make a go of it?

No, I don't honestly think so. The only thing is, the arable land is very limited and you can grow a certain amount of some things just to feed cattle; but generally speaking it's inferior grazing.

What happened the last time he left the island?

Yes, well, the very last time – the last time that I ever saw him – we had a bit of an experience. He was due to go away and we had this old Austin, a 1934 or 1936. Avril was driving it and Eric and young Richard were in the back and I was in the front with Avril. You have probably seen this road, it was a damn sight worse then – and the thing just sank into the road and I can't remember now whether it was in the ditch. I think it probably was – if you get anywhere near the side of the road you just slide in – and at that time we had a great big lorry; it was an idea of Richard Rees's that we should have a lorry and, of course, I mentioned the figure of a thousand pounds for our capital and Richard Rees went and got this thing for about half the capital. . . . It was a sort of white elephant. However, it possibly did something to keep Eric going a wee bit longer – because this was in January, at night, and very cold when we sunk into the bog or whatever it was. Avril and I walked back here and got this big lorry – hoping that we might be able to pull the car out of the hole. And, of course, we couldn't, because it was jammed somehow. It just so happened that it was about the one place in the whole of the road from here to Ardlussa where something could get past, and that was very lucky, we got past and we took them down in the lorry.

And that was the last time you saw him?

It was the last time I saw him. He had to stay in the village in Ardlussa with Angus McKechnie . . . he was going to take him down next day.

What did you like most about him?

Well, he was imperturbable, he was terribly calm, and he was always very pleasant. He was really a nice person, very nice, but as I say, I never ever had a very long conversation with him.

A Memoir by Anthony Powell

Anthony Powell (b. 1905), novelist and memoirist, was two years behind Orwell at Eton and though he began to take an interest in his work from 1936, they did not meet until 1940. Towards the end of the war, they began to meet regularly, lunching once a week with mutual friends and visiting each other's homes. Powell seems to have resisted the temptation to paint a portrait of Orwell in his great series of novels *A Dance to the Music of Time*.

This piece appeared as 'George Orwell: A Memoir' in *Atlantic Monthly*, October 1967. The same material appears in his *Infants of the Spring* (Heinemann, London, 1976), the first volume of his autobiography.

George Orwell was about two and a half years older than myself. He once complained that I was too fond of drawing attention to a difference in age that put him, he felt, at a disadvantage. A school list recalls with almost uncomfortable clarity the features of most of those of his seniority. For some reason Orwell's face eludes me. Even one of those *carte de visite* photographs taken at the age of sixteen or seventeen did not suggest a boy I knew by sight. I have absolutely no recollection of him at Eton. This is strange because we were, I think, in the same company of the Officers' Training Corps, and must often have seen each other hurrying across Cannon Yard on the way to Monday morning parades. In those days Orwell was, of course, called Eric Blair – 'Blair K.S.' in the list, since he was a King's Scholar.

He wrote under the name of 'Orwell', partly because he pre-ferred separate identity as an author, partly because he disliked the idea of family origins in Scotland. Later, he had a house in Jura, where I think he would have settled had he lived, but in his early days he was irritated by what he regarded as overemphasis on kilts, tartan, bagpipes, and so forth, above all by the compara-tively recent innovation in popular journalism of writing 'Scot-tish' for 'Scotch'. The Orwell is a river in Suffolk; 'George', the most characteristically English Christian name. I once asked if he had ever thought of legally adopting his *nom de guerre*. 'Well, I have,' he said slowly, 'but then, of course, I'd have to *write* under another name if I did.'

When *Down and Out in Paris and London* appeared in 1933, someone recommended it, adding: 'You'll never again enjoy sauté potatoes after learning how they're cooked in restaurants.' I read the book, and was impressed by its savagery and gloom. At the same time, I cannot claim to have immediately marked down Orwell as a writer of whom one would obviously hear more. However, a year or two later, when I saw a copy of *Keep the Aspidistra Flying* in a secondhand bookshop, I bought it. Again, I liked the novel for its violent feelings and presentation of a young man at the end of his tether, rather than for its form or style, which seemed strangely old-fashioned in treatment, as in a sense did much of the author's point of view. I spoke of this book one night dining with Cyril Connolly. Connolly then told me Orwell was one of his oldest friends, acquaintance dating back to their private school (described in 'Such, Such Were the Joys') and con-tinued in College at Eton. They had, as it happened, just recently re-met. Connolly gave a sobering account of Orwell, his rigid asceticism, political intransigence, utter horror of social life, at the same time emphasising, in his physical appearance, the heavy lines of suffering and privation marked deep in Orwell's hollow cheeks. The portrait was a disturbing one. How-ever, Connolly, in his own special way, was enthusiastic about Orwell. He urged me to write him a fan letter. This I did, thereby making my first Orwell contact, in 1936.

Connolly's picture of a severe, unapproachable, infinitely dis-approving personage was to some extent borne out by the reply I received. Orwell was at the time running, with his first wife, Eileen O'Shaughnessy, a small general shop near Baldock in Hertfordshire. His letter, perfectly polite and friendly, had also something about it that cast a faint chill, making me feel, especially in the light of Connolly's words, that Orwell was not for me. I was so sure of this that when opportunity arose of meeting him in the flesh, I was at first unwilling to involve myself in so much hard living and high thinking – more especially in wartime, when existence was uncomfortable enough anyway. That was in 1941. I was on leave, and my wife and I were dining at the Café Royal. An old friend, Inez Holden, a writer at that time working in an aircraft factory, came across to us from a table at the far side of the room. She said that the man and woman with her were George and Eileen Orwell, and suggested we should join them after we had finished dinner.

To make it slightly more of an occasion, as one did not 'go out' much in those days, I had changed into 'blues', patrol uniform, an outfit with brass buttons and high collar. I felt certain Orwell would not approve of that. It was no doubt bad enough in his eyes to be an officer at all; to have dressed up in these pretentious regimentals, at once militaristic and relatively ornate, would aggravate the offence of belonging to a stupid and brutal caste. However, in spite of such apprehension – made light of, I admit, by my wife – we moved over in due course to Orwell's table. I sat down with some trepidation. Orwell's first words, spoken with considerable tenseness, were at the same time reassuring:

'Do your trousers strap under the foot?'

'Yes.'

'That's the really important thing.'

'Of course.'

'You agree?'

'Naturally.'

'I used to wear ones that strapped under the foot too,' he said, not without nostalgia.

'In Burma?'

'You knew I was in the police there? Those straps under the boot give you a feeling like nothing else in life.'

His voice had a curious rasp. Evidently it was consciously designed to avoid striking a note that could possibly be regarded as 'public school'; at the same time, its tone made no concession whatever to any other known form of 'accent' or dialect. This was a manner of speaking absolutely in keeping with the rest of Orwell's carefully controlled approach to life, though when, after the Independence, returned Indian Civilians (Orwell's father had been in the Indian Civil Service) were more often met with in England than formerly, I was once or twice reminded of Orwell's tone. Nevertheless, it would be true to say that he had, as it were, resigned from the world in which he had been brought up, or anything like it, while never really contriving to join any other.

Tall – as has more than once been remarked, closely resembling the Gustave Doré conception of Don Quixote – he also looked remarkably like Cézanne's portrait of the painter's friend Monsieur Choquet, a Customs House official. The grooves in the cheeks of which Connolly had spoken were at once apparent on either side of Orwell's mouth. He wore a narrow moustache, neatly clipped, along only the lower level of his upper lip. This moustache, as long as I knew him, was always a bit of a mystery to me. I never quite had the courage to ask about it. It was perhaps Orwell's only remaining concession to dandyism that undoubtedly lurked beneath the surface of his self-imposed austerity, momentarily revealed, for example, by the strapped trousers. Indeed, contemporaries at school even speak of a tendency in those early days towards the mannerisms of a P. G. Wodehouse hero. Perhaps the moustache, although in itself essentially un-Wodehousian, partook to some extent of this rigorously suppressed side of Orwell's nature. Perhaps, on the other hand, it had something to do with the French blood inherited through his mother, which also made him look like the Cézanne portrait, or those fiercely melancholy French workmen in blue overalls, pondering the philosophy of life at the zinc counters of a thousand *estaminets*. Certainly this last image was the nearest Orwell ever achieved in the direction of an even faintly proletarian appearance. It was the moustache, the moustache alone, that provoked thoughts of France, because nothing could have been more English than his consciously old tweed coat and corduroy trousers, which always maintained exactly the same degree of shabbiness, no worse, no better.

'Does it matter, my coming in these clothes?' he once asked, before entering the room at a party we were giving.

The question is an example of the extraordinary unreality of much of Orwell's approach to life. By that time he and I knew each other well. The clothes were the clothes he always wore. Why should I have invited him if I thought them inadequate? It was hardly to be expected that he would turn up in a brand-new suit. Did he half hope for an unfavourable answer?

'Yes. George, it does matter. They won't do. You can't come in. We will meet another time.'

In justice to him, some of his suppositions regarding social behaviour were so strange that he might not have been surprised by a reply in those terms. I am certain that denial of entry on such grounds would have made little or no difference on his side to our friendship. It would merely have confirmed his worst suspicions, perhaps even pleased him a little to find his views on conventional tyranny so well justified.

After the first meeting at the Café Royal, we arranged to lunch together, a year or two later, when I was stationed in London. For some reason we failed to make contact at the small but very crowded Greek restaurant in Percy Street he had suggested, each thinking the other had not arrived and eating his meal there alone at a table. I saw Orwell on the way out.

'Come and sit for a moment,' he said; 'I ordered a bottle of wine. I'm afraid I've drunk most of it, as I thought you weren't going to turn up, but there's still a drop left, as I couldn't get through it all.'

Wine, at that period of the war, was hard to get and expensive. It was characteristically generous of him to have provided it. At this time he was, I think, employed on some broadcasting service, not in want, but certainly not particularly well off, as none of his books had yet begun to sell to any extent, though his name was becoming known. With all his willingness to face hard times – almost welcoming them – Orwell was by no means a confirmed enemy of good living, as the bottle of wine shows, though tortured by guilt when he felt indulgence was overstepping the mark. This sense of guilt is, of course, generally attributed to Orwell's 'social conscience'. He himself would, at least by implication, ascribe such feelings to that cause. My own impression is that the guilt lay far deeper than anything having its roots in mere politico-social convictions acquired by reading and observation. Guilt had, I think, been deeply implanted in him at an early age; no doubt inflamed to some extent by experiences as a schoolboy about which he wrote, possibly contrasting these, like Kipling, with a happy childhood; for although he was inclined to let it be thought his home had been Victorianly severe, his sister's memories suggest that he was, in fact, rather 'spoilt'. Guilt, so it seems to me, always pursued him, perhaps because of that, for one suspects that an emotion so deeply engrained must have had very precocious origins.

If you went for a country walk with Orwell (he came down for the day to Shoreham, in Kent, where my wife and elder son lived during the latter part of the war), he would draw attention, almost with anxiety, to this shrub budding early for the time of year, that plant growing rarely in the south of England. He was, it is true, very fond of flowers, but there was something about this determined, almost scientific, concentration on natural history or agricultural method that seemed an effort to excuse the frivolity of our ramblings.

'Interesting to note the regional variation in latching the field gates,' he remarked. 'Different even in the same county.'

Guilt, naturally enough, harassed him in matters of sex.

'Have you ever had a woman in the park?' he asked me once.

'No – never.'

'I have.'

'How did you find it?'

'I was forced to.'

'Why?'

'Nowhere else to go.'

He spoke defensively, as if he feared I might blame him for this urban pastoral. It was a Victorian guilt, and in many ways Orwell was a Victorian figure, for, like most people 'in rebellion', he was more than half in love with what he was rebelling against. What exactly that was, I was never quite sure. Its name was certainly legion, extending from inequities of government to the irritating personal habits of certain individuals. For example, he complains (in the essay 'How the Poor Die') that English hospital nurses wear Union Jack buttons. This used to puzzle me, because, even at the period of which he wrote, if you wanted, in an excess of chauvinistic fervour, to sport a Union Jack button, I do not believe you would have been able to procure one for love or money. Then one day it occurred to me that the button in question probably indicated the hospital at which the nurse had qualified, some such insignia possibly resembling design of the flag. To see such an emblem as a piece of flaunting jingoism was, in its way, a mild form of persecution mania.

Many of Orwell's prejudices seemed equally to belong to this world of fantasy. I may be unjust. Our mental surroundings are, after all, always subjective enough. It is largely the way you look at things. At least no one would deny the nightmare world envisaged by Orwell, if a true one, was in drastic need of reform.

'Take juries now,' he would say. 'They're mostly drawn from the middle classes. Some fellow comes up for trial on charge of stealing. He's not wearing a collar. The jury take against him at once. "Suspicious-looking chap." Unanimous verdict of guilty.'

Orwell himself was not at all unaware of the manner in which his own imagination strayed back into the Victorian Age, or, for that matter, of the paradoxes in which some of his enthusiasms involved him. Indeed, he liked to draw attention to the contradictions of his own point of view. He was fond of repeating that if some sort of agreement could be reached by the nations, 'world economics could be put right on the back of an envelope', but never revealed how this was to be done. To his Victorianism he constantly returned, both in conversation, and so far as possible, in life, the latter represented by the places he inhabited. He was delighted, for example, with the period flavour, certainly immense, of the basement and ground floor he took during the war in a small house in Kilburn, North London. The terrace had been built about 1850. It conjured up those middle-to-lower-middle-class nineteenth-century households on which his mind loved to dwell, particularly enthroned in the works of his favourite novelist, Gissing.

'They would probably have kept a "Buttons" here,' he said, enchanted by the thought.

We dined with the Orwells at this house one night, prior arrangements being made for sleeping there too, owing to the exigencies of wartime transport. The sitting room, with a general background of furniture dating from more prosperous generations of bygone Blairs, had two or three eighteenth-century family portraits hanging on the walls.

'When George went to the Spanish War,' said Eileen Orwell, 'we panicked at the last moment that he hadn't enough money with him, so we pawned all the Blair spoons and forks. Then, some weeks later, his mother and sister came to see me. They asked why the silver was missing. I had to think of something on the spur of the moment, so I said it seemed a good opportunity, George being away, to have the crest engraved on it. That was accepted.'

I never knew Eileen well. My impression is that she did a very good job, in what were often difficult circumstances. At the same time, it was, I think, an exception for her to tell a story like that. She was in general not much given to making light of things, always appearing a little overwhelmed by the strain of keeping the household going, which could never have been easy. Possibly she was by temperament a shade serious for Orwell, falling in too easily with his own tendency to gloom, when he may have required a wife to shake him out of that natural state occasionally. It is at least permissible to wonder whether that were not so.

Orwell's egotism, which was, as he himself was always pointing out, considerable, took a deeply melancholic form, which may well have needed some counter-irritant in a constant companion.

'If I have a dog, I always think my dog is the best dog in the world,' he used to say, 'or if I make anything carpentering, I always think it's the best possible carpentry. Don't you ever feel the need to do something with your hands? I'm surprised you don't. I like even rolling my own cigarettes. I've installed a lathe down in the basement. I don't think I could live here without my lathe.'

The night we dined there, I slept in a camp bed beside the lathe. It was an unusual, though not entirely comfortless, apartment, and anyway, by that stage of the war, one had become used to sleeping anywhere. At about 4.0 a.m. there was an air raid. The local anti-aircraft battery sounded as if it were based next door, because the noise of the guns was absolutely deafening, far louder than usual. Orwell came blundering downstairs in the dark.

'I'm rather glad to have been woken up,' he said. 'It means we shall get some hot water in the morning. If you don't restoke the boiler about this time, it runs cold. I'm always too lazy to leave my bed in the middle of the night, unless, like tonight, there's really much too much noise to sleep anyway.'

There can be no doubt that the bad health that prevented him from taking an active part in the war was a terrible blow to Orwell. He saw himself as a man of action and felt passionately about the things for which the country was fighting. When he heard Evelyn Waugh was serving with a Commando unit, he said: 'Why can't someone on the Left ever do something like that?' He himself was a sergeant in the Home Guard, always speaking with enjoyment of the grotesque do-it-yourself weapons issued to that force, ramshackle and calculated to explode at any moment. Goodness knows what he would have been like in the army. I have no doubt whatever that he would have been brave, but bravery in the army is, on the whole, an ultimate, rather than immediate, requirement, demanded only at the end of a long and tedious novitiate. It is even possible Orwell might have found some of army routine sympathetic. He was not without a love of detail. Nevertheless, his picture of the army, as of the rest of life, was based on an earlier period.

'Did you ever handle screw guns?' he asked me.

Admittedly pikes were issued – and strongly recommended –

at the beginning of the war, when invasion seemed about to take place at once; even so, the term 'screw gun' can scarcely have survived into the twentieth century. I once enquired how discipline had been maintained in the International Brigade during the Spanish Civil War.

'You appealed to a man's better side,' Orwell said. 'There was really not much else you could do. I took a chap's arm once when he was being tiresome, and was told afterwards I might easily have been knifed.'

Orwell was in his way quite ambitious, I think, and had a decided taste for power; but his ambition did not run along conventional lines, while he liked his power to be of the *éminence grise* variety. This taste was no doubt partly due to his sense of being in some manner cut off from the rest of the world; not allowed by an irresistible exterior force to enjoy, more than very occasionally, such few amenities as human existence provides. That did not prevent his strong will and natural shrewdness from making him an effective negotiator. Indeed, his genuine unworldliness, in the popular sense, was used by him with considerable effect when handling those who were rich or in authority. He would somehow unload on them the whole burden of his own guilt, until they groaned beneath the weight. He was not at all afraid of making himself disagreeable to persons whom he found in their dealings disagreeable to himself.

'If editors, or people of that sort, tell you to alter things, or put you to a lot of trouble,' he used to say, 'always put them to trouble in return. It discourages them from making themselves awkward in the future.'

It is interesting to speculate how Orwell's life would have developed had he survived as a very successful writer. The retirement to Jura, even at the preliminary warning signs of financial improvement, was probably symptomatic. Orwell could, I think, only thrive in comparative adversity. All the same, one can never foresee the effect of utterly changed circumstances. Prosperity might have produced unguessable changes in him and his work. It would inevitably have invested him with still more complications of living; complications which, according to his system, would each have to be rationalised to himself and weighed in the balance. His gift was curiously poised between politics and books. The former both attracted and repelled him; the latter, close to his heart, were at the same time tainted with the opium of ease and escape. So far as day-to-day politics are concerned, Orwell could never have become integrated into any

243

normal party machine. His reputation for integrity might be invoked, his capacity for martyrdom relied on, his talent for pamphleteering made use of, but he could never be trusted not to let some devastatingly unwelcome cat out of the political bag. With books, on the other hand, in spite of an innate 'feeling' for writing and criticism, he always had to seek the means of attacking some abuse or injustice to excuse his attention to them. This did not prevent them, in my opinion, from being his true love.

In his own works, he returns more than once to the theme that, had he lived at another period of history, he would have written in a different manner. I do not believe this to be a correct judgement. I find this talent far removed from that objective sort of writing which he saw as an alternative to what he actually produced. His interest in individuals – in books or in life – was never great. Apart from the projections of himself, the characters of his novels do not live as persons, though they are sometimes effective puppets in expressing his thesis of the moment. Orwell had a thoroughly professional approach to writing and a finished style, though his literary judgements were sometimes eccentric. As mentioned above, he would canvass Gissing, quite seriously, as the greatest English novelist.

Orwell liked to keep his friends in watertight compartments, pursuing various interests with various groups. He was fond of saying that it was a pity writers quarrelled amongst themselves so much, because, in the last resort, they were much more like each other than like other people. Towards the end of the war, I suggested introducing Malcolm Muggeridge to him. 'I shall probably sock him on the jaw,' Orwell said, but they got on well, and there was a time when the three of us used to lunch together once a week. Orwell always had a weakness for the presence of a disciple or two of his own in attendance, changing these from time to time. The first to be initiated at these luncheons was the writer Julian Symons, who has amusingly described his introduction there as a 'left-wing understrapper'. Under the impact of additional Orwell henchmen, less acceptable or merely too numerous, the meetings lost their personal character and gradually faded away. Again, one suspects, Orwell found the earlier luncheons 'frivolous', insufficiently directed towards a practical aim like placing articles or founding a magazine.

He was easily bored. If a subject did not appeal to him, he would make no effort to take it in, falling into dejected silence, or jerking aside his head like a horse refusing an apple it suspects of sourness. On the other hand, when his imagination had been caught, especially by some literary question, he would discuss it endlessly. He was one of the most enjoyable people I have ever met with whom to mull over such things, full of quotations, though far from verbal accuracy in these.

The adoption of a child, the sudden death of Eileen, the world-wide success of *Animal Farm*, the serious worsening of his own health all combined within the space of a few months to revolutionise Orwell's life. The loss of his wife just after the much meditated acquisition of the boy especially created a situation that would have caused many men to throw in the sponge. No doubt some arrangement for readoption could have been made. It would have been reasonable enough. No such thought ever crossed Orwell's mind. He had enormously desired a child of his own. Now that the child had become part of the household, he was not going to relinquish him, no matter what the difficulties. In fact, one side of Orwell – the romantic side that played such a part – rather enjoyed the picture of himself coping unaided with a baby. Let this point be made clear: Orwell *did* cope with the baby. It may have been romanticism, but, if so, it was romanticism that found practical expression. This was characteristic of him in all he did. His idiosyncrasies were based in guts.

He would still go out at night to address protest meetings – 'probably a blackguard, but it was unjust to lock him up' – and the baby would be left to sleep for an hour or two at our house while Orwell was haranguing his audience.

'What was the meeting like?' one would ask on his return.

'Oh, the usual people.'

'Always the same?'

'There must be about two hundred of them altogether. They go round to everything of this sort. About forty or fifty turned up tonight, which is quite good.'

This down-to-earth scepticism, seasoned with a dash of self-dramatisation, supplied a contradictory element in Orwell's character. With all his honesty and ability to face disagreeable facts, there was always about him, too, the air of acting a part. He came to see me one day when our younger son was lying, quiet but not asleep, in a cot by the window. I went upstairs to fetch a book. When I returned, Orwell was assiduously studying a picture on the wall at the far side of the room. The child made some sign of wanting attention, and I went over to the cot. Straightening the coverlet, which had become disarranged, my hand touched a hard object. This turned out to be an enormous clasp knife. I took it out and examined it.

'How on earth did that get there?'

For the moment the mystery of the knife's provenance seemed absolute. Orwell looked away, as if greatly embarrassed,

'Oh, I gave it him to play with,' he said. 'I forgot I'd left it there.'

The incident, infinitely trivial, seems worth preserving because it illustrates sides of Orwell not easy to express in direct description; his attitude to children; his shyness, part genuine, part assumed; his schoolboy leanings; above all, his taste for sentimental vignettes. Why, in the first place, should he wish to burden himself in London with a knife that looked like an item of a fur trapper's equipment? Why take such pains to avoid being found playing with a child, a perfectly natural impulse, flattering to a parent? If some authentic masculine sheepishness made him hesitate to be caught in such an act, why leave the knife as evidence? It was much too big to be forgotten.

I think the answer to these questions is that the whole incident was arranged to create a genre picture in the Victorian manner of a kind which, even though he might smile at the sentimentality, made a huge appeal to Orwell's imagination and way of looking at things. He was, so to speak, playing the part of a strong, rough man, touched by the sight of a baby, but unwilling to confess, even to himself, this inner weakness. At the same time, he had to be discovered for the incident to achieve graphic significance.

Orwell would not, I think, deny that sentimental situations had a charm for him. I can imagine him discussing them in relation to another favourite theme of his, 'good bad poetry'. It should, of course, be added that in his own books Orwell is too practised a writer to be betrayed into presenting sentimentalities in their cruder form, though he is fond of showing them, so to speak, brutally in reverse; for example, his taste for such episodes as lovers' assignations ruined by forgotten contraceptives or 'the curse'.

In due course the trouble with Orwell's lung became so bad that he had to take to his bed. It was fairly clear that he was not going to recover. Only the length of time that remained to him was in doubt.

'I don't think one dies,' he said to me, 'so long as one has another book to write – and I have.'

During these last months he married Sonia Brownell, first met some years before when she was on the staff of Connolly's magazine, *Horizon*. In spite of the tragic circumstances of Orwell's failing condition, marriage immensely cheered him. I saw a good deal of him when he was in hospital. In some respects he was in better form than I had ever known. There was a flicker now to be seen of the old alleged Wodehousian side.

'I really might get some sort of a smoking jacket to wear in bed,' he said. 'A dressing gown looks rather sordid when lots of people are dropping in. Could you look about and report to me what there is in that line?'

War shortages still persisted where clothes were concerned. Nothing very glamorous in male styles was to be found in the shops. Decision had to be taken ultimately between a Jaeger coat with a tying belt, or a crimson jacket in corduroy. We agreed the latter was preferable. It was a small concession to an aspect of human existence that Orwell had for years strenuously denied himself. Sitting up in bed now, he had an unaccustomedly epicurean air – only, unhappily, his conviction that having an unwritten book in you preserved life proved untrustworthy. I have often wondered whether he was buried in that coat.

The Orwell legend, now substantially launched in a shape scarcely capable of modification, presents on the whole a tortured saint by El Greco (for whom Orwell would certainly have made an admirable model), a figure from whom all human qualities have been removed. From time to time angry arguments rage as to where precisely Orwell stood politically. I am not here concerned with that side of him, although I think it worth remarking that it took courage in that now largely forgotten, but then rather nauseating, political climate of the immediately post-war period (where the things attacked in the book were concerned) to fire the broadside of *Animal Farm* – especially on the part of a writer of left-wing principles, liable to be smeared in a manner that could do him real professional harm. I want to put on record not so much that – his courage – but what I remember of him as a friend, one for whom you felt a curiously protective affection, with whom, in spite of differing opinions on almost every subject, I seem so often to have had such oddly enjoyable times.

Quixote on a Bicycle

Paul Potts (b. 1911), a Canadian poet and author, knew Orwell from about 1944, and was a steady friend and admirer. He sold his poems in broadsheets and was a well-known figure in the old Bloomsbury and Fitzrovian literary world of the pubs and cafés, though not the Bloomsbury of private houses. His affection, indeed his devotion, towards Orwell is obvious, but his account of how he nearly published *Animal Farm* is accurate. Later Orwell invited him to visit Jura.

'Don Quixote on a Bicycle' is the name of this chapter from his book *Dante Called You Beatrice* (Eyre and Spottiswoode, London 1960).

The great thing about Orwell was Orwell. He was ultimately better than anything he wrote. That makes him very good indeed. To me he was a greater poet than Dylan Thomas. This of course is private language and needs some explaining. Dylan Thomas would have both allowed and understood this kind of remark. Orwell never wrote any poetry. In a certain sense he wasn't an artist at all. He was a journalist, but only if Swift and Hazlitt were journalists.

The only two modern poets he really liked were Yeats and Eliot. But there was something about him, the proud man apart, the Don Quixote on a bicycle (and if Saint Thomas More was the first Englishman, as one historian called him, then Orwell was perhaps the last) that caught one's imagination right away. That made one think of a knight errant and of social justice as the Holy Grail. One felt safe with him; he was so intellectually honest. His mind was a court where the judge was the lawyer for the defence. One fact that has never been mentioned about Orwell, despite all that has been published on him since his death, is that his mother was a Frenchwoman.

From this Latin distaff side he got his love of living and of life. But being Orwell he did not try to ape the French as so many intellectuals do. He used the French taste he had inherited to live an English life well. Nothing could be more pleasant than the sight of his living-room in Canonbury Square early on a winter's evening at high-tea-time. A huge fire, the table crowded with marvellous things, Gentleman's Relish and various jams, kippers, crumpets and toast. And always the Gentleman's Relish with its peculiar unique flat jar and the Latin inscription on the label. Next to it usually stood the Coopers Oxford marmalade pot. He thought in terms of vintage tea and had the same attitude to bubble and squeak as a Frenchman has to Camembert. I'll swear he valued tea and roast beef above the OM and the Nobel Prize.

Then there was the conversation and the company; his wife, some members of his family or hers, a refugee radical or an English writer. There was something very innocent and terribly simple about him. He wasn't a very good judge of character. He was of roast beef, however. He loved being a host, as only civilised men can who have been very poor. There was nothing Bohemian about him at all. However poor he had been it did not make him precarious. But he tolerated in others faults he did not possess himself. I don't think there was a man in all England who could say Orwell had ever borrowed half-a-crown from him. And I know – I am absolutely certain – that there was not a man anywhere in Europe who could say that he had borrowed one without returning it.

He carried independence to such lengths that it became sheer poetry. One day up on the Isle of Jura in the Hebrides we had to move some furniture from the nearest village to his house. A distance of some seven miles over a road that made that famous one, leading to the Irish capital, look like an autostrada crossing the Plains of Lombardy. Some very rich people, friends of Orwell's, who had a hunting lodge on the other side of the island, had a whole garage full of brakes and station wagons and jeeps – five I believe. Yet he refused to borrow the use of one for a few hours. We had to pack those chairs and that table on our backs across seven miles of some of the most beautiful scenery in Europe. This by a man who was a chronic invalid. He could have borrowed the use of one of those cars almost as easily as he could have been told the time had his watch stopped.

He was proud and his pride got him into the literature of the world; he was chivalrous and his chivalry put him among the great radicals of England.

He combined the honesty of his class with his own vision and made an art out of it. The class he came from was that of the poorest of the poor gentry. The class that produced both Shakespeare and Nelson. Writing about him like this brings back the atmosphere he created and makes me happy again for a moment, in the particular way that one was happy in his company.

It wasn't really until after his death that I knew how much he liked me. He was very reticent, other people told me. I used to think my temperament might embarrass him a bit, but I am a great stickler for equality and so was he. I never once asked for, received or accepted a literary favour from him all the years I knew him. On balance I don't really regret this. Although at least a couple of editors told me that they would publish my verse if I got him to write for their magazines. I never got published in any paper he edited because I was a friend of his. On the contrary, I first got to know him personally because I was writing for a paper he edited. I never asked him to review my various books of verse although there were two poems of mine he did like immensely, yet he often volunteered to get me out of trouble.

Once while I was visiting in the home of a comfortably-off Catholic woman my hostess started in on a vile attack against the Jews. I quietly walked over to a statue of Our Lady, standing on a niche against the wall, broke it against her mantelpiece and put the broken pieces into the fire, saying that as these were her opinions she would hardly want the portrait of a Jewish woman in her home. It turned out that her statue was an antique and worth much more than an advance on a book of verse. I never heard the last of it. Orwell offered to do the paying. I soon put a stop to that. I never did manage to afford to pay for it myself. I don't think that Our Lady would have minded very much.

He was very masculine; not necessarily a bad thing in a man, but in the sense that he was every inch a man, and not in the sense that he was a penny-halfpenny trying to be tuppence. He had a dry intelligent wit. He never appeared to know when he was being funny. He was much nicer looking than any photograph I have seen. He walked beautifully and had marvellous hands. He was kind looking but it was a masculine kindness – most kindness isn't. When talking about something he was really interested in, when exposing a fraud or defending a victim of tyranny, ignorance or prejudice, then he looked positively beautiful. Wherever he lived, even if it was only in a block of flats in St John's Wood, he turned one room into a workshop. He enjoyed playing at carpentering. He loved horses and otters and hares. Hated rabbits, didn't like cats very much. Loved the country, especially the highlands. Never thought of himself as a Londoner. The only time he really enjoyed living there was during the blitz. The War Office had more trouble in keeping him out of the army than it did in getting hundreds of others to join.

His first wife was a lovely, generous and humorous Anglo-Irish woman, who willingly shared his early hardships and then died just as the tide was turning, a few weeks before the publication of *Animal Farm*. Her heart failed while she was under the anaesthetic when she was undergoing a very minor operation. It was so minor that she did not tell him when she was actually having it performed. He was in Germany at the time for *The Observer*. When he got back there was only half a letter waiting for him, in the last sentence of which she had written: 'I'll finish this, this afternoon, when I come out of the operation'.

The day he got back from Germany, the day after she died, I had an appointment with him, by previous arrangement, in the afternoon. When I got to the office and was told the news I wanted to leave. However there were very definite messages in several places along Fleet Street asking me to stay put. I spent the next few days with him, at his never stated, but constantly implied request – it was more of a suggestion than an invitation. A few months previously he and his wife had adopted a baby boy. It was a real marriage, not perfect. But nothing except her death, that came so suddenly and too early, would have broken it up. I heard him call another woman by her name, on two occasions, after her death. I make a point of this because some very nasty and equally untrue remarks have been made in print by a journalist, in the popular Sunday paper sense of the word, about Orwell's attitude to his wife's death. The suffering of a silent man is harder to have to witness than that of a talkative one. His attitude to women as a whole was not unlike that of a decent army officer in a rifle regiment.

His mind was limited, but he knew his own limitations. Inside those wide limits it was a first-rate mind. It had more kindness than love, but more anger than contempt. It was like a breath of fresh air to hear him talk about literature, politics, history or Victoriana. He was a storehouse of odd information about weird subjects. Yet I would have trembled to think what would have been the result had he written a book about Ireland. He wrote beautiful English prose. The kind of English that people usually embarrassed by beauty could appreciate. As you can sometimes get the feeling of a city through the memory of one street, to me all Paris is contained in any of those thin little streets running down to the Seine from the church of St Germain-des-Prés. So too one can get at the atmosphere of a writer's work by the temperature of one of his sentences. In Orwell this is the sentence:

No wall in the world is well built enough to be allowed to remain standing, if it surrounds a concentration camp.

When I first read that, in his essay on Salvador Dali, I felt a movement down my back, as I had done the first time I read the great love poems of William Butler Yeats or walked for the first time into the presence of a Van Gogh. This is what I call physical criticism. It can't make a mistake.

He had an awful job getting *Animal Farm*, the first book that really made him famous, published at all. It was right at the height of the Anglo-Stalin friendship. Many publishers turned it down on the grounds that it was not an auspicious moment to bring out such a book. In the end it was translated into about fourteen languages, including Russian, and published in perhaps twenty-two countries. He actually paid considerably more in income tax on his royalties from it than he had earned altogether during the previous ten years. He made about forty pounds out of the book before *Animal Farm* – a book of three essays entitled *Inside the Whale*.

At one point I became the publisher of *Animal Farm* – which only means that we were going to bring it out ourselves. Orwell was going to pay the printer, using the paper quota to which the Whitman Press was entitled because of the broadsheets and pamphlets I had published before the war. We had actually started to do so. I had been down to Bedford with the manuscript to see the printer twice. The birthplace of John Bunyan seemed a happy omen. Orwell had never spoken about the contents. I had not liked to ask as any questions might appear to have an editorial accent. He had, however, talked about adding a preface to it on the freedom of the press. I first read *Animal Farm* in the train on the way down to see the printer in Bedford. As I got half-way through it I found myself looking at my fellow-passengers and feeling myself tempted to have a peep under the seat to see if there was any more dynamite about. The printer was an old-fashioned working-man radical. A real craftsman and a spiritual descendant of the printers who were willing to go to prison rather than refuse to print the 'Rights of Man'. That essay on the freedom of the press was not needed as Secker & Warburg, at the last minute, accepted the book.

Incidentally there must be an unpublished essay of Orwell's on Conrad, I believe, but I am not at all certain of the subject, lying around somewhere. He had sent it, by request, to the editor of a magazine that had had to stop publication before he could use it. He once actually asked if I would try and get hold of it for him. I did try. We often wondered when looking at reviews of *Animal Farm* pouring in from Spanish, Danish and Czech papers what would have been its fate in the world if it had first appeared in pamphlet form under the imprint of the Whitman Press. Very often the only words we could understand in some of the reviews in the foreign press were 'Swift' and '*Gulliver's Travels*'. However, when we came across them we knew it was a good review!

The two books, *Animal Farm* and *Nineteen Eighty-Four* on which the wideness of his fame is built, are by no means his best work. But they are better than his early novels. He wasn't of course a novelist at all, but critics who concern themselves with him as such are merely trying to dismiss, obscure or ignore his more serious work. The canon of his writings consists of *Down and Out in Paris and London*, *The Road to Wigan Pier*, *Homage to Catalonia*, possibly his best work. And the essays, always the essays, all of the essays, but especially the one on Dickens and the second section of *Inside the Whale* which is concerned not with Henry Miller himself, to whom the essay as a whole is devoted, but with English writing at that period. Orwell played a role in the literature of his time not unlike that played by Parnell in the politics of his day. Given just a few more writers of equal calibre with his burning passionate integrity we might have enjoyed a new Augustan age, for he had the independence of Swift mixed up with the humility of Oliver Goldsmith.

While he was attacking the bullies on the right he nearly starved to death. Once he turned to the bullies on the left, the right having been temporarily beaten, he made his fortune. This was due to no lack of integrity on his part. For he never fell for Communism for a moment although he was more deeply concerned with social justice than most men, and more unselfishly so than some. It had cost him plenty in the thirties and on the left to be so uncompromisingly anti-Communist, yet he liked reading Trotsky and even more reading Rosa Luxemburg. For all his masculineness the fact that it was a woman who had such a good mind, a better one than Lenin's, did attract him.

As for the British anarchists and near-anarchists, vegetarians and sex reformers, he found them the most disappointing of all. As they never had the slightest chance of getting into power anyway he thought that they might as well have stuck to their principles, whereas all they seemed to do was get bogged down in the mess of their doctrines. About their principles, they chopped and changed, like a Christian Brother on a debating platform with a lot of non-conformists. He loved Bartolomeo Vanzetti, however, as much as I do; whose hands were smelly with the smell of the fish he peddled, but to whom all the poor of the whole world were what Beatrice was to that great Florentine Sir, his countryman. Because of him, Piedmont can stand un-ashamed in front of Tuscany. At the trial of the anarchists during the war, the British judge, Sir Norman Birkett, as he then was, behaved better in his role than did the prisoners in the dock in theirs, which of course was a better role.

He was by temperament a Tory radical. Had more in common with William Cobbett than he did with Tom Paine. He was not especially a republican though he hated the idea of titles, thought that the Labour Party should have put John Ball's head on a postage stamp, and done away with the House of Lords during their first week in office. Although he wrote a lot for *Tribune* he was very pro-Ernest Bevin. But the Tories were quite impossible in the thirties – ask Winston Churchill. So he had to make a place for himself – on the left. But he never joined a committee. He was once tempted to do so, he said, just so that he could resign. When his front wheel got a puncture he had to mend it himself. He used words in fact to puncture the greed he did not share, and to call attention to a beauty he did not make. Freedom was a verb to him, equality a necessity. He was very English, as English as the grass that grows along the Thames at Runnymede.

Almost the first thing he said to me as I walked into his hospital chalet, high up in the Cotswolds, after I had got back from Jerusalem, was, 'I see we have lost Haifa.'

I had an awful job not to bend down and begin looking for it under his bed. On another occasion in the kitchen at Barnhill, on Jura, he told me quite seriously that he much preferred the Church of England to Our Lord. Yet he wasn't all that mascu-line, he liked Italians better than Spaniards, and Chinese rather than Indians. His readers will remember the excellent descrip-tion in *Homage to Catalonia* of an Italian soldier fighting for the Spanish Republic against Mussolini; yet the only character he added to the huge family of English fiction to join Falstaff and Little Nell, was Boxer, the horse in *Animal Farm*. He hated Catholicism, Communism and the whole caboodle of 'filthy little doctrines striving for our souls'.

The happiest years of my life were those during which I was a friend of his. Nobody who ever knew him at all well will ever forget the shy excited warmth of his welcome, if one dropped in on him unexpectedly. He worked regularly but never made a fetish of it. No editor could ever complain that he was late with a manuscript. Even after he was world famous he could never refuse a request for an article from the editor of a small magazine that could not afford to pay. I twice caught him, while he was literary editor of *Tribune*, shoving a banknote into an envelope with the manuscript of a poem that was too hopelessly bad even for him to be able to print. (Other literary editors please copy.) He looked as guilty when I caught him doing this as he must have when as a small boy he was caught helping himself to the jam. Anyone who reads this will gather that I knew Orwell a great deal more intimately than I knew Dylan. Yet I continually use the sur-name of one and the Christian name of the other. That is due to the difference in the character of the two men. It was hard to be familiar with Orwell; it was equally impossible not to be with Dylan.

There is a passage somewhere in *Homage to Catalonia* which might be taken to be a true portrait of the kind of man he was. He was describing how, during a lull in the fighting one day on the Aragon Front, he had been detailed to go out into a fox-hole in the no-man's-land between the opposing lines of trenches, and try a spot of sniping at the enemy. Whenever Orwell was about to write or say anything at all romantic he always prefaced it, as if to excuse himself, by making some very ordinary down-to-earth statement. In this case he starts off:

Perhaps it was because I was cold and hungry and very bored and I wanted to get back into my own lines as soon as possible, as I had been waiting for hours and had not seen anybody. When suddenly, quite unexpected by me, a man appeared above the enemy lines running in a great hurry, holding up his trousers – he had neither belt nor braces – rushing along to the lavatory.

Orwell continues:

Well, I came here to shoot Fascists and a man caught short like that is not a Fascist. So I returned to behind my own lines without firing at him.

I wonder what his political commissar thought of that bit of Englishness. I quote him from memory.

The enormous courtesy of the man; the shy, almost awkward respect for life and the desire to give a fair field to an opponent. In this man's presence, there have been kings who would have looked parvenus.

He loved Eliot's poems, hoped their author thought well of him. Disliked Pound and his work, but allowed me to come to his defence in the columns of a left-wing journal. Would be hard on a friend's work, in print, in case his praise would be thought of as nepotism. There indeed may be a Red Indian language somewhere on the northern borders of Manitoba and Saskatchewan in which the word for independence is George Orwell. When he helped a lame dog over a stile, he had the good sense and the respect, not for the lameness, but for the dog, to make certain that it was that particular stile that that particular dog wanted to cross.

He wasn't very conscious of the kind of writers whose work in literature was like his. He loved nineteenth-century America. Mark Twain could easily have been his favourite author. In many small things he was more like a New Englander then than an Englishman now. Loved good bad poets, Vachel Lindsay, Kipling and Chesterton. I would have rather known him than have won the Nobel Prize; when one asked him out to dinner, in one's turn, he always had the generosity to let one pay the bill. Although I'm sure he always had the extra money in his pocket just in case. He rolled his own cigarettes with the strongest tobacco he could find; would have liked to have been able to brew his own beer. Hated staying in other people's houses, loved having friends in his own. He never thought as much of Ignazio Silone as I did, nor of Sean O'Casey. Knew nothing about painting, but knew that he knew nothing. Didn't think having talent was all that important; said that talent by itself was like a tart, would go anywhere the money was. Smoked more than he drank. Listened as much as he talked. Loved appreciation from his peers, never troubled what the others thought. Knew who his peers were. Was incapable of playing to the gallery. Had as much moral courage as a whole Command full of Irishmen had of the other kind. Loved England, about the only left-wing middle-class intellectual of the time to do so. This made him a good traveller. Loved Bertrand Russell, hated the *New Statesman* – they often tried in vain to get him to write for them. Could tell a joke against himself. One morning Beaverbrook phoned up and asked him to dinner; he was writing a weekly article in the *Evening Standard* at the time. Not political or literary but about 'How to make a cup of tea, etc.' Not wanting to go, he answered, 'I haven't got a dinner jacket.' Back came the answer immediately. 'Come to lunch then.' He did go and enjoyed it. But he never would do serious political reporting for the Beaverbrook Press. On another occasion when he got back to Paris, from a visit to the part of Germany reached by the now advancing allies, dressed in uniform (he was a War Correspondent for *The Observer*) and was staying at the Hôtel Scribe, which was the Paris HQ for Allied War Correspondents, he looked in the register to see if there was anyone interesting to talk to. War Correspondents as such were, he said, terrible bores. To his delight he found Hemingway's name. He had never met him. He went up to his room and knocked. When told to come in, he opened the door, stood on the threshold and said, 'I'm Eric Blair.' Hemingway, who was standing on the other side of the bed, on which there were two suitcases, was packing, and what he saw was another War Correspondent and a British one at that, so he bellowed, 'Well what the –*y*ing hell do you want?' Orwell shyly replied, 'I'm George Orwell.' Hemingway pushed the suitcases to the end of the bed, bent down and brought a bottle of Scotch from underneath it and still bellowing said, 'Why the –*y*ing hell didn't you say so. Have a drink. Have a double. Straight or with water, there's no soda.'

He died on the eve of going to Switzerland. I, like a lot of his friends, called to say good-bye. Cut into the door of his hospital room was a small window. One could look through it, and see him before knocking. That afternoon I saw he had fallen off to sleep. He needed sleep badly, found it hard to come by. I left without waking him, leaving a packet of tea outside the door. After all, he'd be back in a couple of months and up again. Ever since I had known him he'd been given up as hopeless. During that time he'd lived a fuller life than a whole company of A.1 recruits. Under his influence all his friends stopped taking the doctors seriously.

Later that same evening someone brought me the *Evening Standard* in which it said that he was dead. It also said that he had been a great English writer. No death had affected me so much since my father's. Yet I had been through two wars. I didn't go to his funeral, it was a literary affair. I was a bit too shabby again. There never seems much use going to a funeral unless, of course, there is no one else to do so.

Once before a good bad poet from the Pacific coast of North America paid his own tribute to another great English radical writer. Now it is only those people who really do believe that Mr Micawber was a bad lot and that Uriah Heep was actually sorry, who will think it too presumptuous a folly, for me to place this other spray of Western Pine, among the English Oak and Holly, that form a perpetual wreath, placed because of a whole generation's regard, on the memory of a man.

I suppose what made Orwell so permanently attractive as a person, and so readable as a writer, was that he was so ordinary really, normal if not average. He had none of the extravagances of an artist, none of the irresponsibilities of a Bohemian and none of the selfishness of an intellectual. He was Britishly balanced and Saxonly sane. Some people used to say that he was a much more complicated character than I realised or allowed. Yet to me, he was, on the whole, a very simple person. Simple in the original and non-sentimental meaning of the word, single; he was all of one piece. I have heard it said, both before and since his death, that he had a very cruel streak in his nature. This I never actually noticed. Having been told about it, I had the feeling that they were not altogether mistaken. But given Orwell's whole temperament, it would only be directed, if it did exist, against people in power, at those stronger or senior to him. Orwell was once introduced to a refugee woman writer who had recently published a book about delinquent children in war-time London – an excellent book it was too – who is reported to have said, 'I never want to meet that man again, he is so cruel.' Most people who have written about him since his death don't seem to have had a clue as to what he was all about. Stephen Spender and John Wain are marked exceptions. To understand Orwell, you had to know something of the world he came out of, not necessarily to have come out of it oneself. Not only was he personally somewhat like my father, but he came from the same England, actually the same county, Norfolk. It was a world of poor gentlemen, whose sons in their generations had to go to what were then the colonies. There was nothing Bohemian or even metropolitan about him, although he had often sat in the Café Royal or The Dôme. Just because he was sent to Eton didn't mean that he was rich. In fact, his parents were much poorer than, on being told about Eton, most people from non-public-school-going families could realise.

He was attacked by some doctrinarians for having served as a policeman in Burma. Now European policemen, under the British administration, discharged duties more closely approximating to those of a magistrate in England, so anyone who knew Orwell at all well, will guess that quite a number of poor people in Burma did not go to jail, simply because George Orwell was a policeman. He was, on several occasions, even attacked for broadcasting to India during the war. The programmes he arranged consisted of talks about D. H. Lawrence, Eliot and Forster.

To revert to his alleged cruelty for a paragraph. He once had it in his power to be very cruel to me. I had gone out, it was on Jura, to bring back some firewood. When I came into the house with a huge armful of it, it transpired that I had chopped down the only nut tree on the place. Seeing how upset I was, that night at dinner, he burst into a huge smile and said, 'Paul, cheer up. Have some more beef.' I've already mentioned how highly he valued beef.

Orwell wasn't a creative writer of the first range. He did, however, write some very fine English prose, as good as Lincoln, Tom Paine and Jefferson.

Speaking for a moment as a British Columbian, there was more in him and in his work to make one feel proud of the English connection than all the Guards officers that ever swaggered out of Wellington Barracks. Indeed there is something very lovely about England, to have produced a policeman like this.

For myself I shall always remember a man with a cough, mending a kitchen table with a piece of wood he had cut from a dying tree. I shall never forget the widowed husband looking after the twice orphaned son. This always sick man made his typewriter take on the suggestion of a white steed. In his hand the Biro he used for corrections could never quite help looking a bit like a drawn sword. His doctors thought him a bad patient. They should have heard, they probably did, what he thought about them. In his company a walk down the street became an adventure into the unknown. Indeed there will always be an England, as long as there is, from time to time, an occasional Englishman like this. In short his life was a duel fought against lies; the weapon he chose, the English language.

On thinking of him, a certain Don Quixote de la Mancha rides into mind on his horse Rosinante. Yet he was so local he made England look English. This world has seen his kind before all right, before yesterday, not recently, but long ago. Perhaps Sir Thomas More was a relation or did he go to school with Walter Landor? On him a tweed jacket wore the air of knightly armour. A cup of tea was wine before a battle. He carried no shield, used for a weapon plain facts loaded into simple English prose. His kind has walked this way before all right. You'll find them in the Bible. Amos might have been a cousin once removed. His name, already an adjective to use against a bully, men will remember for kindness and courage. He has left a feeling that he was something more than just another writer justly famous. It was as though each one of all his readers had found the family crest – a crest to tell of something very simple and that thing beautiful.

Telling the Russians

Gleb Struve (dates unknown) an American scholar and specialist on Soviet literature, was at the School of Slavonic Studies, London University, in 1944. He wrote to Orwell and congratulated him on his piece in the *Tribune* column about Soviet falsification of history. They met and corresponded. It was Struve who introduced Orwell to Zamyatin's futurist novel *We*, which is one of the many sources of *Nineteen Eighty-Four*. Struve is far more clear than many literary critics that *Nineteen Eighty-Four* is primarily a satire – he believed the people in Eastern Europe and Russia would find it amusing.

Struve wrote this tribute to Orwell for a Russian language journal, *New Russian Wind*, 19 February 1950. It is here translated by our colleague at Birkbeck, Susan Saunders Vosper.

The death of the English writer, George Orwell, three weeks ago, deserves a mention in the Russian Press. His fame comes from writing a satire on the evolution of the Soviet Union [*Animal Farm*, printed in a Russian translation in the paper *Posev*] and his novel *Nineteen Eighty-Four* which was printed last year and which I wrote about in *New Russian Wind* (10 July 1949). . . .

I had the occasion to meet him soon after the end of the war, when he returned from a tour of the Western zone of Germany on commission from *The Observer* newspaper. It was even then not necessary to open his eyes to the evil of Stalinist totalitarianism, but a visit to the Displaced Persons camps gave him valuable information. Our meeting was due to the interest which Orwell, having read my book on Soviet literature, showed in E. I. Zamyatin's novel *We*, which up to that time had not been printed in Russia. Right up to his death, Orwell helped me petition for a new English edition of this novel, which had come out in America in 1925. I managed to find a publisher and the novel was given a new translation, but, unfortunately, the publisher went bankrupt before having managed to issue the already-printed book. Already ill with tuberculosis, Orwell, from the sanatorium where he stayed during the last years of his life, continued to petition about this publication. Zamyatin exerted an undoubted influence on Orwell's own last novel. But the essential difference between Zamyatin's *We* and *Nineteen Eighty-Four* rests in the fact that the former, written in 1920, was a genuine prophecy, whereas Orwell, in writing his satire, drew his material from contemporary, and especially Soviet, reality. This was not felt by many American critics, who only saw in the novel an imaginary anti-utopia, and even suggested that Orwell had in mind the evolution of the English system under a workers' state (Orwell decidedly rejected these conjectures). Meanwhile, it occurs to me that even the date chosen by Orwell for the title is not accidental, why '1984' and why not '2000' or '1998' (i.e. fifty years after our time)? You see, 84 is 48 in reverse, the novel was written in 1948, and by his somewhat veiled date it seems to me that Orwell wanted to hint that he was not writing about the future, nor about what awaits us, but about what is already staring us in the face in the Soviet Union and in the subjected parts of Europe, where recent history is wiped out, what is, appears not to be, and, conversely, incessant mythological happenings occur, the cult of the Leader is set up etc. It is not accidental that unlike Zamyatin and Aldous Huxley, Orwell put no stress in his own satire on elements of technical progress. He wrote, not a utopia, but a satire, and this many people have not understood and have not caught the meaning of.

Russian readers should remember with gratitude that, in giving permission for a Russian translation of *Animal Farm*, Orwell refused in advance all royalties, not only on the publication of the *Posev* translation, but also on a separate publication which he had in view. Incidentally, an even earlier translation had been produced in Germany in Ukrainian. Orwell wrote to tell me a strange story about this translation: the American wartime authorities confiscated a large part of the publication and handed it over to the Soviet repatriation commission!

Orwell was only forty-six years old when he died.

Stephen Spender Recalls

Stephen Spender (b. 1909), poet and critic, met Orwell in 1938 and despite having been attacked by Orwell as typical of the 'nancy left' and political dilettantism generally, they became good friends, Spender visiting Orwell in a sanatorium in Kent in 1938 and regularly during his last illness in University College Hospital in 1949.

There are interesting references to Orwell in Spender's book of essays and reminiscences *The Thirties and After* (Fontana, London, 1978), but this is taken from a BBC interview recorded on 7 May 1963.

Mr Spender, I want to ask you for an assessment of George Orwell as a man and as a writer.

I think that obviously the first thing that anyone would say about George Orwell is that he was honest. When I say that he was honest I don't mean just that he was truthful as a writer, I mean that the qualities of truth which showed in his writing he also practised in his life and in his existence. He had a kind of quality about him that reminded one of plain living, bread and cheese, English beer and so on. He had really rather a working man's kind of attitude; he occasionally said very obviously true things. Occasionally he had points of view that struck one as being eccentric and rather cranky and peculiar to him. I was told, for instance, that he kept a diary during the war in which he prophesied what was going to happen on any given day in the next few days, and in this diary he was always wrong; and I believe it's never been published for this reason. And this, I think, illustrated his crankiness. He was traditional in a way which goes back to a very old tradition in English life, before industrialism, to the English village. He believed essentially in small communities of neighbours who knew one another very well and therefore he had a great deal of sympathy with the anarchists. He judged everything, every movement, every chord, by the standards of what it ought to be in terms of living. Therefore you might say that the basic reason why he wasn't a Communist was because the Communists weren't Communists and George Orwell was one. What he noticed about the Communists was that they weren't Communists, they were power-mongers. For the same reasons he wasn't a Conservative. If the Conservatives were people who really loved their country and were prepared to pattern their lives on the best qualities of England he would have been a Conservative. I think one might say that he was a Christian, a Christian of a rather primitive kind, almost a Tolstoyian Christian. Of course, he had the virtues of all these attitudes which he showed in his work. His writing shows the honesty of his life – it shines all through his writings. But he also perhaps had some bad qualities which went with this. Perhaps he was really rather envious of his fellow Etonians – one forgets easily that he was an Etonian and I think maybe he disliked the idea of other Etonians for some reason. Maybe there was a kind of unhappiness in his life which also influenced his work.

Would you say that he was a rebel? From what did his rebelliousness spring?

Well, that really rises from the last question. I think his rebelliousness was based on his practising what he preached. He wanted people to practise what they preached. If you were a socialist, for instance, he wanted you to live like a socialist. He wanted you to share everything with everyone, and therefore he rebelled against what is called the 'Establishment' of England. He particularly disliked the intellectuals I think, and he particularly disliked the intellectuals of the left more than he disliked the intellectuals of the right. And I'm afraid I'm included in this as one of the people whom he disliked as an intellectual because he felt that we didn't practise what we preached. We lived one kind of life while we talked about another kind of life. For instance, one is an intellectual socialist but one sends one's son, let us to say, to Eton. George Orwell wouldn't have done this. He would have sent his son to a grammar school or to a working-class school.

I think he had a certain lack of sympathy with poets and with the highest forms of the imagination, and with asceticism, and art altogether. I think this is where his own puritanism played him a bit false; he didn't really understand poetry – he disliked for instance the poetry of T. S. Eliot very much and he didn't really understand intellectual life, unless intellectual life was connected with a puritan kind of living. He disliked the rich – he disliked the idea of people being rich. He criticised the Labour Party at the end of the war because they didn't take enough money from the rich. He didn't care about whether it was good economics to do this: he just thought they ought to soak the rich anyway. He liked the workers and, of course, liking the workers in a sense made him a rebel, although it didn't make him a revolutionary. On the whole he liked the idea of poverty and low life. I don't think he would have been very happy in a society in which socialism worked and everyone became rich. He liked public houses and he liked, when he was in a public house, ordering a pint of bitter or a pint of dark and not talking about beer or lager. He liked working-class accents and we are now going to come to one of his weaknesses. I think that he didn't really like to be with people who were his equals intellectually or culturally speaking. I think he was jealous, perhaps, of other writers and I think that on the whole he tended to associate with people who didn't criticise him very much.

What has been his impact on the post-war generation?

I should say very little, I suspect, though I don't really know that the young don't read him. I think perhaps that they read *Nineteen Eighty-Four* because *Nineteen Eighty-Four* is one of the works that are now almost included in science fiction, but they probably don't think it's good science fiction. I think a good many people would like his essay on his preparatory school and I think that anyone who cares about writing – and the young, of course, do care about writing – would be interested in his literary criticism and in particular his essays in which he talks with great authority on how to write good English.

What is still valid in his books and in his approach to life?

I think essentially what is valid is of course his honesty, his truth which commands respect and I don't think anyone can really dismiss or sneer at George Orwell. What remains valid in his life and remains valid in his work is undoubtedly his very good writing. He wrote in extremely good and pure English and I think this remains valid and I think that anyone who wants to read good English should study George Orwell.

It has been said that Orwell has now become a classic. What do you have to say to that?

I doubt whether this is really true. I think that if he's become a classic he's probably become a rather minor classic. I mean, I daresay one could associate *Animal Farm* with *Gulliver's Travels* which, after all, was not the most important work of Swift. *Animal Farm* like *Gulliver's Travels* was a political pamphlet which has become a book children love reading or which one can read with pleasure for the prose. I should think his position as a classic would be rather close, say, to that of Samuel Butler – author of *The Way of All Flesh*.

Going back to the Spanish experiences, what would you say was the effect of that period on Orwell's life and books?

Well, I think that, of course, Spain had a very great influence on Orwell. One of its direct effects on his life which should be mentioned is that it made him ill. He was shot in the Spanish Civil War and he never quite recovered his voice, and I think that probably one might say that in the long run he was killed by being in the Spanish Civil War. The Spanish Civil War, of course, confirmed his dislike of Communism and of authority altogether. He didn't like a war which was conducted by some central authority. What appealed to him in the Spanish Civil War was the fact that there were sort of irregular troops, the POUM, the anarchists, and so on, fighting on the side of the Spanish Republic. Having joined the irregulars he didn't really much like the idea of the Spanish Republic itself, which he regarded as a kind of central authority, rather Communist dominated, trying to impose its rule on the irregulars. In the rising in Barcelona, for instance, which took place in the middle of the Spanish war in which the anarchists fought against the Government troops, he strongly took the side of the POUM, the anarchists.

Would you say that the success of Orwell's last two books was partly due to the cold war atmosphere? And if so what should we think of them today?

The success of *Nineteen Eighty-Four* yes, and which other one? Animal Farm.

Animal Farm, yes, was perhaps a bit due to the cold war, but I should say at once that this idea wouldn't have pleased Orwell. Orwell didn't write his books to give comfort to anti-Communists even though he was an anti-Communist. He tested everyone by measuring what they preached against what they were supposed to be practising. With the Communists, as *Animal Farm* shows, if you measure what they preach against what they're supposed to be practising, there's great occasion for humour to be derived from this. I remember talking to him about this when he was dying – and pointing out to him that *Life* magazine had taken up *Animal Farm* and were using it as anti-Communist propaganda, and this distressed him a good deal. He said that this was the last thing he wanted to do. He had no desire to be on the side of *Life* magazine against the Communists.

But preaching as he did against politics and politicians and the machine of politics, wouldn't you say that he was breeding apathy or cynicism or detachment from the social life?

Well, I think perhaps he was at the end of his life. I mean you might say that *Nineteen Eighty-Four* really preaches a complete indifference and shows that the proletariats – the proles as not interested in the political issues. But after all, in the first place this was written when Orwell was a sick man, and in the second place he's not writing it exactly in order to say to the reader that the reader should be a prole. What he's really saying is that these are the values of personal living which the reader should support. And in order to support these values the reader is bound to become involved in some sort of social action, I should think.

So you can say that he was a pessimist?

I think that the side of Orwell which was pessimistic was a sick side and, after all, was revealed when he was a sick and dying man so I would not like to say that Orwell was a pessimist. I think that Orwell really was a socialist who wanted people both to live socialist lives and to live socialist lives in a kind of socialist, anarchist society.

In Muggeridge's Diaries

Malcolm Muggeridge (b. 1903), writer and broadcaster, met Orwell through Anthony Powell in 1944. During the next year, the three of them lunched together regularly until Orwell went to Jura.

Muggeridge wrote a general appraisal of Orwell in Miriam Gross's *The World of George Orwell* (Weidenfeld and Nicolson, London, 1971), hinting that Orwell at heart really shared Muggeridge's own changing views towards Christianity. But we prefer to print, as less known, the entries relating to Orwell's last days, when Muggeridge visited him regularly in hospital, from his diary, *Like It Was* (Collins, London, 1981). The editor, John Bright Holmes, says that 'I have not worked from the author's original diaries but from a typed copy'. Diaries are marginally more reliable as evidence than memory, but they are, of course, a created literary form, not an intercepted communication to God. Few other visitors were so sure that Orwell was dying, and no one else remembers so many Jews at the funeral or suspected that 'he was at heart strongly anti-Semitic'. However Muggeridge puts his name to these as diary entries made at the time.

his new novel, *A Question of Upbringing*. Extremely taken with it as a piece of writing, and some of it very funny.

In the evening went to see George Orwell who is now in the University College Hospital. He looks inconceivably wasted, and has, I should say, the appearance of someone who hasn't very long to live – a queer sort of clarity in his expression and elongation of his features. We chatted about Hughie and other things, and then Sonia Brownell, who is supposed to be going to marry him, came in – large, bouncing girl, quite pleasant, I thought. Somewhat disconcerted because before entering she looked for a long time through the glass at the top of the door. George full of reminiscences about his relations with H. G. Wells and the quarrel they had, but I couldn't really make head or tail of what it was all about. Sonia goes to see him every day, which is very nice for him. George more peaceful than he was, but his mind still grinding over the same political questions. Always feel affectionately towards him. . . .

4 October 1949

Tony looked in and I told him about the letter I'd had from Sonia Brownell saying that she and George would be married on October 12 and that, to George's great delight, as they were to be married in hospital they would have to have a clergyman. I said that, in a sense, George had developed TB in order to be married by a clergyman which otherwise he'd never have had the face to do.

6 October 1949

Stayed with George Orwell for an hour or so talking about politics. He said that he wanted to buy a bed-jacket for his marriage. I thought of something from Jaeger's, but Tony took the matter up and said he was going to get him an elaborate velvet smoking jacket. I decided to let it go at that. George in quite good form, obviously pleased about getting married, told me about special licence, etc., said that there was a clergyman on the premises and that he would officiate, but that, surprisingly enough, as George put it, 'deathbed marriages' were not very common.

25 October 1949

George Orwell really does seem better. He was sitting up in bed in his cerise coloured velvet jacket bought for his wedding, and seemed remarkably cheerful. George said that he thought that and beauty' were essential to the good life. I fell on him pretty heavily for this, which is a silly derivative from Gissing, Samuel Butler, E. M. Forster, etc. George would not have it. He pointed to an advertisement for men's underwear in the evening paper which showed the god Mercury wearing a new brand of under-pants, and said that such blasphemy hurt his feelings much more than mockery of the Christian religion. I said I registered my dis-agreement and would take up the point at a later date. Sonia, now his wife, came in and seemed rather tired, I thought. She has immediately developed the trait which Tony and I consider characteristic of most matrimonial relationships – i.e. envy, rather than jealousy, of her husband. When George's supper was brought in, she said that, after all, he had a wonderful life, waited on hand and foot compared with her struggles with Connolly's bad temper at the office of *Horizon*.

26 October 1949
Finished off revising *Comrade Caliban*.

Bought two volumes of Surtees at Hatchards as a wedding present for George. Very pleasant books with coloured prints, which I would have liked to have kept for myself. . . .

20–21 December 1949
Looked in to see George Orwell, who is really very poorly. He looks quite shrunken now and somehow waxen. Said ruefully that he was having penicillin injections and they found difficulty in finding any meat into which to stick the needle. Can well believe it. He still talks about going to Switzerland, doing some fishing there, and mentioned that he'd decided to get a blue serge suit because he thought he was too old now to appear in corduroy trousers, etc. More than usually touched by him. Fancy that he's got an idea he's had it, and isn't altogether sorry. Very fond of his adopted kid, and would like to write another book or two. We talked about Eliot, and he agreed with me. Also agreed that Conrad's *Under Western Eyes* is one of the best novels of recent times. Said that he'd absolutely no appetite now, and that he was having insulin to try to ginger him up.

25 December 1949
. . . Having heard the King's speech, Tony and I strolled to-gether to see George, who looked very deathly and wretched, alone, with Christmas decorations all round. His face looks

picture I once saw of Nietzsche on his death-bed. There was also a kind of rage in his expression, as though the approach of death made him furious – as it did Mrs Dobbs, of whom he somehow made me think. Poor George – he went on about the Home Guard, and the Spanish Civil War, and how he would go to Switzerland soon, and all the while the stench of death was in the air, like autumn in a garden.

12 January 1950

Looked in to see George Orwell, who seems more deathly than ever, very miserable, says he's losing ½ lb a week in weight and has a high temperature every day. Typical of him that he said the doctors won't allow him to take aspirin because it upsets his temperature chart. George said he'd been reading accounts of the proceedings of the enquiry into capital punishment, and that he was quite convinced that judges like Lord Goddard want to keep hanging because they derive erotic satisfaction from it. Tried politely to indicate that I thought this utter rubbish. Also mentioned that Monckton Milnes, whose biography I have been reading, had wanted to marry Florence Nightingale. George remarked that Milnes's tastes were derived from the Marquis de Sade, and I said that if Florence Nightingale had married him, she might have become known as the lady of the whip. . . .

21 January 1950

Heard in the morning that George Orwell had died in the early hours (about 2.30 a.m.) of a haemorrhage, which didn't really surprise me. Thought that in a way his death was sadder than Hughie's because he passionately wanted to go on living, and thus there was no sense of peace or relinquishment in him. Thought much about his curious character, the complete un-reality of so much of his attitude, his combination of intense romanticism with a dry interest in some of the dreariest aspects of life – e.g. Gissing. Remembered Hughie's phrase about him – that he was like a gate swinging on rusty hinges, and that he only wrote sympathetically about human beings when he regarded them as animals – e.g. *Animal Farm.* All the same, there was something very loveable and sweet about him, and without any question, an element of authentic prophecy in his terrible vision of the future. His particular contribution to this sort of literature was his sense that a completely collectivised State would be pro-duced not as Wells had envisaged in terms of scientific heartless but vivid eroticism, but to the accompaniment of all the dreary debris and shabbiness of the past – mystique of material-ist Puritanism, the dreariest and saddest of all human attitudes which have ever existed.

Wrote two paragraphs on George for Peterborough and declined various requests for magazine articles. Thought of him, as of Graham, that popular writers always express in an intense form some romantic longing. . . .

22–23 January 1950

. . . Question of George's funeral presenting complications which inevitably reflect those of his life – namely, whether he should be buried in an English village under a yew tree or cremated with his Jewish revolutionary friends in Golders Green. Probably Finchley will be settled for – a compromise.

Rather interested to find when I spoke to the undertaker and mentioned that the clergyman concerned was our vicar here, Mr Rose, that he at once said that he knew him well and had many dealings with him. 'In fact,' he said, 'I'm lunching with him today.' It appeared that they lunch regularly to talk over present and future business. Hope that all has been satisfactorily arranged and that nothing will go wrong.

NB George died on Lenin's birthday, and is being buried by the Astors, which seems to me to cover the full range of his life.

25 January 1950

Tony and Violet with Sonia Orwell came in after supper. Sonia was obviously in a very poor way. We talked about *Horizon* and Connolly. Felt sorry for her but not sympathetic. She remem-bered Kitty's mother one day appearing at the office with a manuscript, scene easily imagined. We wondered what Sonia would now do with herself. Tony said that she was 'a painter's girl'. I saw what he meant. She said that really *Horizon* had gone on existing because of the war, it having provided Cyril Connolly with a means of evading military service, among other things.

26 January 1950

In the morning George's funeral, a rather melancholy, chilly affair, the congregation largely Jewish and almost entirely un-believers; Mr Rose, who conducted the service, excessively parsonical, the church unheated. In the front row, the Fred Warburgs. Then a row of shabby-looking relatives of George's element in the whole affair. The bearers who carried in the coffin seemed to me remarkably like Molotov's bodyguard. Tony had chosen the lesson from the last chapter of the Book of Ecclesiastes, which was very wonderful, I thought, particularly the verse: 'Then shall the dust return to the earth as it was: and the spirit shall return unto God who gave it.' Also the verse ending: '. . . man goeth to his long home, and the mourners go about the streets.'

Interesting, I thought, that George should have so attracted Jews because he was at heart strongly anti-Semitic. Felt a pang as the coffin was removed, particularly because of its length, somehow this circumstance, reflecting George's tallness, was poignant.

Read through various obituary articles on George by Koestler, Pritchett, Julian Symons, etc., and saw in them how the legend of a human being is created, because although they were ostensibly correct and I might have written the same sort of stuff myself, they were yet inherently false – e.g. everyone saying George was not given to self-pity, whereas it was of course his dominant emotion.

Tribune's Obituary

Julian Symons (b. 1912), writer and critic, wrote this obituary of his friend in the journal which Orwell had most cared for. Symons had met Orwell in 1942 after having been unfairly attacked by him as the joint author of a peace pamphlet that Orwell thought 'showed the overlap between Fascism and pacifism'. Orwell apologised and Symons grew to admire him greatly. He wrote an extraordinarily perceptive review of *Nineteen Eighty-Four* in the *Times Literary Supplement:* he was one of the few people to stress its character as a contemporary satire rather than a projection of a possible future. And he wrote a fine critical 'Appreciation' as a postscript to a bookclub edition of *Nineteen Eighty-Four* (Heron Books, London, 1970).

In person he was quite remarkably tall and thin; and his clothes, engraved on his narrow face; his dark hair, untouched with grey, bristled upwards untidily; his shoes were size twelve. His voice was curious: it remained through the longest speech pitched on one deep, classless, almost uninflected note. The effect was monotonous, and yet not without charm.

In this deep voice he was always ready to discourse on the most varied subjects: the best way of making tea, working-class domestic habits, the origins of popular songs, the psychological bases of Communism and pacifism, the merits of Rudyard Kipling, the future of the Labour party. Upon all these, and many other, subjects he talked with what at first appeared the plain man dogmatism of a super-typical man in the street: but behind the dogmatic commonsense, one became gradually aware, was a rich fund of eccentricity. His elaboration of the ten essential points to remember when making tea showed splendid practical mastery of his subject: and yet there was beyond doubt something odd in the fervour with which he expounded them. Similarly, his view that by ceasing to exploit directly a large part of the Empire British socialists ensured a lower standard of living in their own country was the kind of uncomfortable remark that is rarely made in left-wing circles: but it was a little eccentric to maintain, as he did frequently, that a positive moral obligation rested upon intellectuals of the left to point out this truth as often as possible.

Such an eccentricity – such a richly over-realistic realism – marked his attitude to many forms of experience. At one time I joined him regularly for lunch one day a week in a restaurant of his choosing, where the food in its tastelessness resembled the meals described in *Nineteen Eighty-Four*. Out of the various unattractive dishes on the menu he would choose, upon the whole, the least pleasant; and then he would eat it with every appearance of appreciation. I suggested one day that we might change to another restaurant, and he was positively distressed. Shaking his head gravely he looked down at the revolting mess served up to us, and said with almost convincing assurance, 'You won't get anything better than this anywhere.'

Equally typical was the course of reasoning that led him to stay in London during the war, when he could have lived in the country. 'I hate life here,' he said, 'I shall leave London as soon as the war is over. But you can't leave when people are being bombed to hell.' Such a spirit is rare in our time; it is not the less

Jura. For the last three years of his life he bore the terrible routine of hospital life with remarkable stoicism.

The particular time of his death was, one feels, especially tragic; he was at last to leave hospital and go with his wife to Switzerland. When I saw him on the Thursday before he died he was worrying, with fine Johnsonian insularity, about the problem of tea. 'I don't know if I shall get proper tea in Switzerland,' he said. 'They have that filthy China stuff, you know. I like Ceylon tea, very strong.' He was pleased because for some time he had not been allowed to write, and he thought that in Switzerland this ban might be raised. He spoke of a short novel that was in his mind, and a study of Joseph Conrad's political books, *The Secret Agent* and *Under Western Eyes*. He also elaborated a thesis that the Communist Party's object in putting up a hundred election candidates was to help defeat the Labour Party. 'I shall go to Switzerland next Wednesday,' he said, and laughed, 'if I don't catch cold.'

Thirty-six hours later he was dead.

His talent as a writer reflected, more directly than is usually the case, the contradictions of his character. What can have led him, one wonders, to join the Burma Police? And yet the curious innocence of his nature, combined with an almost schoolboyish respect for tradition, made such a move less unlikely than it appears at first sight. It was natural, also, that he should react violently from an experience which must have been, for a man of his sensibilities and sympathies, most unpleasant. The rest of his life might be summed up in terms of such actions and reactions: from left-wing intellectualism, from Communism, to some degree from the Labour Party. It was political innocence, again, that led him to join the POUM in Spain, and earned him a quite unfounded reputation as an anarchist or Trotskyist; his dis-illusionment, not only with the Communist party which sup-pressed the POUM, but also with so-called libertarian parties themselves, was deep.

The particular quality that shines in his books was the ability to profit by such painful experiences, to put down aspects of his personal life, viewed with this peculiarly innocent eye, in direct and powerful prose. In his first book, *Down and Out in Paris and London*, and in his first novel, *Burmese Days*, his full power as a writer is already shown. His descriptions of objects and scenery have a wonderful exactness and power, he can draw and hold our interest whether he is describing the technique and practice of dish-washing in Paris or a tiger-hunt in Burma. His ability to present both sides of a case, each in its own ethical terms, is already apparent. His defects as a writer are evident too: he catches only the outward aspect of human beings, though he does that marvellously well. His directness of approach has its limitations in an over-simple treatment of human character.

Limitations, one says: but they are limitations only if one considers George Orwell primarily as a novelist. He did not consider himself in that light; he was in fact a strangely individual artist who for economic reasons wrote novels. He was inclined to deplore the hasty writing and mechanical nature of some of the books he wrote during the thirties – books which were written, quite simply, for money. And yet his power as a writer remained untouched by the lesser, and ephemeral, work he produced; he was one of the few considerable writers of our time who have emerged with talents triumphantly unscathed from an abyss of day-to-day journalism.

Just how fully George Orwell had preserved his talent was shown by the publication in 1945 of *Animal Farm*. It is typical of him, again, that he wrote this anti-Stalinist satire in 1942, at the time when the Soviet Union probably reached its highest point of popularity in this country. The book was refused by very many publishers; one marvels equally at their prudence and at their inability to recognise fine writing. For this sad little fairy-story of a Utopian experiment that failed was infused with all its author's tenderness and disenchantment. Writing a satire that was nominally a fairy tale, George Orwell exploited fully his knowledge of and sympathy for children. The story is a revelation of the childishness (in the best sense) of his own nature: the recollection of events in childhood – like the wonderful passage about fishing in *Coming Up for Air* – always held particular appeal for him; and he saw Utopia very easily in terms of the simple touching fable of animals, traditionally subject to humanity, taking charge of their own lives. *Animal Farm* has been much praised, and yet perhaps the miraculous skill with which the book is balanced between fairy-tale literalness and symbolic satire has not been fully appreciated. At the first wrong word the fable would topple to bathos: but in fact it is perfectly maintained, so that Boxer is never ridiculous but truly pathetic, and the final scene in which the pigs carouse with the men on two legs instead of four has precisely the effect its author intended.

The colours have darkened in *Nineteen Eighty-Four*, a book which was finished while its author was already a sick man. The triumph of totalitarian Stalinism has finally been achieved; authoritarian control has passed from the bodies of men to their minds; tyranny is slowly being perfected, so that it shall be eternal. *Nineteen Eighty-Four*, in spite of its great popular success, is a book marked by George Orwell's faults; and yet even in its passages of crude sensationalism the clean hard style holds the book together, even in his most extreme pessimism, hope in libertarian socialism is never quite lost. 'If there is hope at all,' Winston Smith reflects when he finds himself betrayed in his effort to join a revolutionary organisation, 'it is in the proles.' And it is to this faith in the revolutionary power of the proletariat that the author of *Animal Farm* adhered to the end of his life.

The faith is old-fashioned in this day of a socialism which some of us think is altogether too scientific, but in certain respects George Orwell was an Edwardian, even a Victorian, figure. He will be remembered as a writer particularly by *Animal Farm*: but he should be remembered equally as a man whose unorthodoxy was valuable in an age of power worship, who brought to the literature of our age the rare assets of a courageous spirit and a generous mind.

The New Statesman & Nation's Obituary

Sir Victor Pritchett, whom we have already quoted (see p. 166) wrote this obituary in the magazine which was Orwell's old antagonist, *The New Statesman and Nation*, a tribute that would seem to make amends for Kingsley Martin's notorious refusal to print anything by Orwell which was critical of the Communist Party in Spain. We print this obituary because not only is it a noble piece of writing, but because its critical judgements are informed by a genuine, reminiscent knowledge of the person.

George Orwell was the wintry conscience of a generation which in the thirties had heard the call to the rasher assumptions of political faith. He was a kind of saint and, in that character, more likely in politics to chasten his own side than the enemy. His instinctive choice of spiritual and physical discomfort, his habit of going his own way, looked like the crankishness which has often cropped up in the British character; if this were so, it was vagrant rather than puritan. He prided himself on seeing through the rackets, and on conveying the impression of living without the solace or even the need of a single illusion.

There can hardly have been a more belligerent and yet more pessimistic socialist; indeed his socialism became anarchism. In corrupt and ever worsening years, he always woke up one miserable hour earlier than anyone else and, suspecting something fishy in the site, broke camp and advanced alone to some tougher position in a bleaker place; and it had often happened that he had been the first to detect an unpleasant truth or to refuse a tempting hypocrisy.

Conscience took the Anglo-Indian out of the Burma Police, conscience sent the old Etonian among the down-and-outs in London and Paris, and the degraded victims of the Means Test or slum incompetence in Wigan; it drove him into the Spanish Civil War and, inevitably, into one of its unpopular sects, and there Don Quixote saw the poker face of Communism.

His was the guilty conscience of the educated and privileged man, one of that regular supply of brilliant recalcitrants which Eton has given us since the days of Fielding; and this conscience could be allayed only by taking upon itself the pain, the misery, the dinginess and the pathetic but hard vulgarities of a stale and hopeless period.

But all this makes only the severe half of George Orwell's character. There were two George Orwells even in name. I see a tall emaciated man with a face scored by the marks of physical suffering. There is the ironic grin of pain at the ends of kind lips, and an expression in the fine eyes that had something of the exalted and obstructive farsightedness one sees in the blind; an expression that will suddenly become gentle, lazily kind and gleaming with workmanlike humour. He would be jogged into remembering mad, comical and often tender things which his indignation had written off; rather like some military man taking time off from a struggle with the War Office or society in general.

He was an expert in living on the bare necessities and a keen hand at making them barer. There was a sardonic suggestion that he could do this but you could not. He was a handyman. He liked the idea of a bench. I remember once being advised by him to go in for goat-keeping, partly I think because it was a sure road to trouble and semi-starvation; but as he set out the alluring disadvantages, it seemed to dawn on him that he was arguing for some country Arcadia, some Animal Farm, he had once known; goats began to look like escapism and, turning aside as we walked to buy some shag at a struggling Wellsian small trader's shop, he switched the subject sharply to the dangerous Fascist tendencies of the St John's Wood Home Guard who were marching to imaginary battle under the Old School Tie.

As an Old School Tie himself, Orwell had varied one of its traditions and had 'gone native' in his own country. It is often said that he knew nothing about the working classes, and indeed a certain self-righteousness in the respectable working class obviously repelled his independent mind. So many of his contemporaries had 'gone native' in France; he redressed a balance. But he did know that sour, truculent, worrying, vulgar lower class England of people half 'done down', commercially exploited, culturally degraded, lazy, feckless, mild and kind who had appeared in the novels of Dickens, were to show their heads again in Wells and now stood in danger of having the long Victorian decency knocked out of them by gangster politics.

By 'the people' he did not mean what the politicians mean; but he saw, at least in his socialist pamphlets, that it was they who would give English life of the future a raw, muddy but inescapable flavour. His masochism, indeed, extended to culture.

In a way, he deplored this. A classical education had given him a taste for the politician who can quote from Horace; and as was shown in the lovely passages of boyhood reminiscence in *Coming Up for Air*, his imagination was full only in the kind of world he had known before 1914. Growing up turned him not exactly into a misanthrope – he was too good-natured and spirited for that – but into one who felt too painfully the ugly pressure of society upon private virtue and happiness. His own literary tastes were fixed – with a discernible trailing of the coat – in that boyish period: Bret Harte, Jules Verne, pioneering stuff, Kipling and boys' books. He wrote the best English appreciation of Dickens of our time. *Animal Farm* has become a favourite book for children. His Burmese novels, though poor in character, turn Kipling upside down. As a reporting pamphleteer, his fast, clear, grey prose carries its hard and sweeping satire perfectly.

He has gone; but in one sense, he always made this impression of the passing traveller who meets one on the station, points out that one is waiting for the wrong train and vanishes. His popularity, after *Animal Farm*, must have disturbed such a lone hand. In *Nineteen Eighty-Four*, alas, one can see that deadly pain, which had long been his subject, had seized him completely and obliged him to project a nightmare, as Wells had done in his last days, upon the future.

Index

Acknowledgements

The publishers, and Audrey Coppard and Bernard Crick, wish to thank the many contributors listed here who have allowed us to use their material for this book. (In spite of all efforts we have been unable to trace Roger Beadon, May Deiner, Joe Kennan, Denys King-Farlow, Georges Kopp, Gleb Struve, or their executors.)

David Astor, Jacintha Buddicom, Lettice Cooper, Stafford Cottman, Henry Dakin, Jack Denny, Sarah Doria for Dennis Collings, William Dunn, Robert Edwards MP, Kay Ekevall, Mabel Fierz, Sally Magill for Jack Common, Mrs E. M. Marrison for L. W. Marrison; Jane Morgan for Humphrey Dakin, Jane Morgan, Margaret Nelson, Richard Peters, Ruth Pitter, Paul Potts, Reynolds Porter Chamberlain for Fredric Warburg; Steven Runciman, Brenda Salkeld, Mrs R. G. Sharp for R. G. Sharp, Sydney Smith, Susan Watson.

We also thank the following for giving permission to quote from published materials in copyright:

George Allen & Unwin (Publishers) Ltd., extract from *Inside the Left* by Fenner Brockway; reprinted by permission of The Bodley Head for Hollis & Carter, extract from *A Study of George Orwell* by Christopher Hollis; Melvyn Bragg, use of interviews from BBC *Omnibus* programme 1970; Chatto & Windus and A. D. Peters & Co. Ltd., extract from *Cab at the Door* and *Midnight Oil* by V. S. Pritchett; Collins Publishers, extracts from *Part of My Life* by Alfred Ayer, *My Life and Soft Times* by Henry Longhurst and *Like It Was* by Malcolm Muggeridge; Andre Deutsch and Deborah Rogers Ltd., extract from *Enemies of Promise* by Cyril Connolly; Heinemann (William) Ltd., extract from *Infants of the Spring* by Anthony Powell; David Higham Associates Ltd., extract from *Four Absentees* by Rayner Heppenstall published by Barrie & Rockcliffe, and *Like It Was* by Malcolm Muggeridge; *New Statesman*, V. S. Pritchett's obituary of Orwell; reprinted by

permission of Penguin Books Ltd., extract from 'Some Are
More Equal than Others' by John Morris from *Penguin New
Writing 40* (1950) ed. John Lehmann (Penguin Books 1950)
pp. 90–97; reprinted by permission of A. D. Peters & Co. Ltd.,
extract from interviews given by Sir Richard Rees, Arthur
Koestler, Stephen Spender, and extract from *George Orwell: A
Fugitive from the Camp of Victory* by Richard Rees; Paul Potts,
extract from *Dante Called You Beatrice*; Neville Spearman Ltd.,
extract from *My Friend Henry Miller* by Alfred Perlès; *Tribune*,
Julian Symon's obituary of Orwell; Weidenfeld & Nicolson Ltd.,
extracts from *The World of George Orwell* edited by Miriam Gross;
George Woodcock from 'Recollections of George Orwell',
Northern Review.